The Politics of Religion in Soviet-Occupied Germany

The Politics of Religion in Soviet-Occupied Germany

The Case of Berlin-Brandenburg 1945–1949

Sean Brennan

LEXINGTON BOOKS
Lanham • Boulder • New York • Toronto • Plymouth, UK

Published by Lexington Books
A wholly owned subsidiary of The Rowman & Littlefield Publishing Group, Inc.
4501 Forbes Boulevard, Suite 200, Lanham, Maryland 20706
www.lexingtonbooks.com

Estover Road, Plymouth PL6 7PY, United Kingdom

British Library Cataloguing in Publication Information Available

Library of Congress Cataloging-in-Publication Data

Brennan, Sean (Sean Philip), 1979–
    The politics of religion in Soviet-occupied Germany : the case of Berlin-Brandenburg,
1945-1949 / Sean Brennan.
        p. cm.
    Includes bibliographical references
    ISBN 978-0-7391-5125-9 (cloth : alk. paper) — ISBN 978-0-7391-5127-3 (electronic)
    1. Christianity and politics—Germany—Berlin—History—20th century.
2. Christianity and politics—Germany—Brandenburg—History—20th century.
3. Communism and Christianity—Germany—Berlin—History.   4. Communism and
Christianity—Germany—Brandenburg—History.   5. Berlin (Germany)—Church
history—1945–   6. Brandenburg (Germany)—Church history—1945–   I. Title.
    BR115.P7B685 2011
    322'.109431509044—dc23   2011030759

∞™ The paper used in this publication meets the minimum requirements of American
National Standard for Information Sciences—Permanence of Paper for Printed Library
Materials, ANSI/NISO Z39.48-1992.

Printed in the United States of America

Contents

v

Preface

My interest in the experience of the Catholic and Protestant churches in the Soviet occupation zone of Germany is related to my broader research interests in the history of religious institutions under Communism, an ideology and political system which called for the creation of atheistic societies where religious faith was a relic of a thankfully discarded past. In addition, the Soviet occupation of Germany is a fascinating period in modern European history, where a Communist dictatorship, the most important of the Soviet satellites in Central and Eastern Europe, was constructed on the ruins of a National Socialist regime, which had nearly destroyed the USSR. I hope this book helps to illuminate both vital stories.

I would like to thank numerous people and institutions without whom this book would not have been possible. First, I wish to express my gratitude to the Nanovic Institute for European Studies at the University of Notre Dame, particularly its head, Dr. James McAdams. Their dissertation fellowship allowed me to travel to Moscow and Berlin to conduct research in various archives in both countries over a ten-month period. I wish to thank the archivists and librarians at the various institutions I used during my research trips, especially the staffs of the State Archive of the Russian Federation in Moscow, and the Bundesarchiv and the Evangelischer Zentral Archiv in Berlin.

Numerous people from various institutions assisted me in this project, none more so than my dissertation advisor at Notre Dame, Semion Lyandres, who provided invaluable assistance over the past decade on this challenging project, and who demonstrated great patience and support over the past decade. Also of great assistance were the other members of my doctoral committee, James McAdams, Doris Bergen, and Bill Miscamble, all of whom read the manuscript and offered extremely helpful advice. A number of fellow graduate students and colleagues at Notre Dame greatly aided me on this project, especially Steven Brady, Andrew Orr, Tuan Hoang, Jonathan Den-Hartog, Maria Rogacheva and Mike Westrate. I also wish to thank my friends from our rotating panel at ASEEES over the past seven years, Jennifer Wynot Garza, Bob Goeckel, David Doellinger, T. David Curp, and James Felak, all of whom have provided importance advice on this project since its earliest stages. Norman Naimark, Hope Harrison, and Bernd Schaefer answered my various inquiries concerning the Soviet occupation of Germany in an efficient and detailed manner.

I am glad my colleagues in the History Department at the University of Scranton took a chance on a scholar with an interest in the complexities of Russian-German relations and have given me a wonderful academic home. I particularly wish to thank Mike DeMichele, Bob Shaffern and Roy Domenico, who spurred me on to the transformation of my dissertation into a suitable manuscript. Also of invaluable help were my editors at Lexington Books, Joseph Parry and Erin Walpole, whose guidance was essential in the completion of this book, as were the comments of the anonymous reviewer.

Finally, I wish to thank my family, especially my mother and father, who first stimulated my love of history by taking my siblings and I to various historic sites across the United States, and who always emphasized academic and personal success. I dedicate this, my first historical monograph, to my dear wife Lisa, without whose unwavering love and support I would have never completed this book. Her encouragement and patience during trips abroad and long days in the distant archives made it all possible.

Abbreviations

ACA   Allied Control Authority
ACC   Allied Control Commission
ARAC   Allied Religious Affairs Committee
CDU   Christian Democratic Union
CPSU   Communist Party of the Soviet Union
DIAC   Directorate of Internal Affairs and Communications
FDGB   Free German Trade Federation
FDJ   Free German Youth
GDR   German Democratic Republic
KPD   Communist Party of Germany
LPD   Liberal Democratic Party of Germany
LR   State Government (German organs of self-government)
OMGUS   Office of the Military Government for Germany, United States
PV   Provincial Administration (German organs of self-government)
SED   Socialist Unity Party of Germany
SBZ   Soviet Occupation Zone
SVAG   Soviet Military Administration in Germany

Introduction

The Politics of Religion in Soviet-Occupied Germany discusses the religious policies of the Soviet military authorities and their German allies in the Soviet zone, but more importantly, who devised them, how they did so, and how they attempted to implement them. In doing so, it illustrates how the Soviet authorities recreated the Soviet zone along Stalinist lines with regard to religious policy, a process which they implemented throughout all of Eastern Europe as well in East Germany. I examine how these policies were devised, but I have placed greater emphasis on their implementation in the central province of the Soviet zone, Berlin-Brandenburg. The SVAG (*Sovetskaia Voennaia Administratsiia v Germanii*, Soviet military administration in Germany) and the SED (*Sozialistische Einheitspartei Deutschlands*, Socialist Unity Party of Germany) policies towards the churches became more negative as the Stalinization of the Soviet zone accelerated, the foundations for later SVAG and SED attempts to minimize the public role of the churches had been laid during the early period of the occupation. The Soviet zone of Germany, the lynchpin of the Soviet empire in Eastern Europe, proved to be both the exception and the rule with regards to post-1945 Soviet religious policies. My book explains what this contradiction reveals about Soviet rule in Germany as well as the origins of the SED-regime's largely hostile but complex approach towards religious institutions.

Furthermore, this work demonstrates how the leadership of the churches responded to the policies of the SVAG and the SED, especially after they took an increasingly anti-religious tone during the late 1940s. The diverse responses of the church leadership in the Protestant Church during the Soviet occupation reveal the foundations of the eventual break within the leadership of the Protestant Church in the 1960s over the issue of how to deal with the atheist SED-regime. At the same time, the stances of Protestant and Catholic leaders Dibelius and Preysing as stalwart opponents of the creation of the "second German dictatorship" in the 1940s demonstrate how the churches became central actors in the East German dissident movement in the 1970s and 1980s. My research reinforces the traditional analysis of the Soviet occupation as establishing the foundations for the GDR, including its policies regarding religious life. The religious policies of the Soviet authorities excellently mirror the overall approach of the Soviet attitude towards the German question; in that their initial caution and limited nature was dictated by Moscow's goal of constructing a communist state in all of Germany. Once this possibility began to dissipate by the late 1940s, the Soviet zone of Germany was put on the "fast track" towards the Stalinist model, and this lead to a harsher anti-religious policy. This process did not end in 1949 but continued to resonate throughout the history of the two Germanys and the Soviet Empire in Eastern Europe.

HISTORICAL BACKGROUND

While the SVAG and the SED did not have a set of specific religious policies planned from the very beginning of the occupation in May 1945, their actions towards the Catholic and Protestant churches in Berlin-Brandenburg were guided by a general Marxist-Leninist hostility to religious faith and religious institutions, which viewed them as impediments to the creation of Soviet-style institutions in eastern Germany. The limits of the SVAG's and the SED's actual power at the ground level in the Soviet zone, during the early period of the occupation, as well as their preference to take a slower pace in creating a Soviet-style German state as compared to the rest of Eastern Europe, gave SVAG and SED religious policies an opportunistic and flexible quality. Nowhere is this more evident than the "religious freedom" propaganda campaign waged by both the SED and especially the SVAG during the occupation, where their leniency with regards to some religious issues and the social role played by the churches, especially their charitable activities, was used as clear evidence of Soviet tolerance for religious freedom in an SED-led Germany. Yet there should be no doubt the religious policies of the SVAG and the SED in Berlin-Brandenburg, with regards to church's relationship to CDU, religious education or youth and women's organizations, moved to marginalize any role the churches could play in the political, economic, and social life in the Soviet zone of Germany, a process which would be accelerated after the founding of the German Democratic Republic in October 1949.

I selected Berlin-Brandenburg as the geographic focus of my research not merely due to its extensive state and religious archival holdings, but because it was the political and religious hub of the Soviet zone. As the most populated and urbanized of the five provinces of the Soviet zone, the leadership organs of the SVAG, SED, CDU, and the Catholic and Protestant churches were all located in this province. Major policies in political, economic, cultural, and religious life were often implemented by the SVAG and the SED in Berlin-Brandenburg before they were applied to Sachsen, Sachsen-Anhalt, Thuringia, and Mecklenburg. In addition, only Thuringia had a similar number of Catholics to compare with the Catholic population of Berlin-Brandenburg, although in both cases Protestant Germans remained in the majority. Perhaps most importantly, it was in Berlin-Brandenburg, with the enclave of capitalism, liberal democracy, and religious freedom in the American, British, and French sectors of the former German capital of Berlin, that the pressures of the competition between the Soviets and the West were most keenly felt. This proved accurate for religious life in Soviet-occupied Germany as well, as both SVAG and SED authorities feared the influence of "reactionary" Catholic and Protestant clergy in the service of "Anglo-American imperialism" spreading from West Berlin to all of Berlin-Brandenburg, and from there to the entire Soviet zone.

This work is not, however, merely a story of Soviet and German Stalinists in Berlin-Brandenburg brutally crushing religious institutions while hapless clergy and laity watched on ineffectively. The leadership of the Protestant Church in the Soviet zone was divided about what approach to take to the new Soviet authorities, but they were determined to preserve the institutional independence of the church along with its special role in the fields of religious education, youth and women's work, and charitable relief. The Protestant leadership in Berlin-Brandenburg was no exception to this, as Bishop Otto Dibelius was zealously defended what he saw as the Protestant Church's central role in helping Germany to recover from the vestiges of Nazism and the Second World War.

The Catholic Bishop of Berlin, Konrad von Preysing, pursued a largely similar approach regarding the role of the Catholic Church in the province of Berlin-Brandenburg, although Preysing was in a stronger position to speak as the leading voice for the Catholic Church than Dibelius was for the Evangelical Church. Both leaders were initially willing to give the Soviet authorities and their German "friends" the benefit of the doubt regarding their promises to rebuild German democracy, even though most of the senior leadership of the churches politically sided with the CDU. Once SVAG and SED religious policies began to take a more openly hostile tone and the creation of a

Stalinist East German state began in earnest, both Dibelius and Preysing put themselves at the forefront of popular resistance to the imposition of Stalinist rule in the Soviet zone of Germany.

The Christian Democratic Union in the Soviet zone also played a vital role in this process, especially during the period of its political independence under its first two chairmen, Andreas Hermes and Jakob Kaiser, from 1945 to 1947. The party was formed by the Soviet authorities to represent the political interests of bourgeois religious Germans in the SED-dominated antifascist bloc. However, Hermes and especially Kaiser strove to direct the CDU as a genuine alternative to the Marxism-Leninism-Stalinism of the SED, with its own guiding ideology of Christian Socialism. The CDU was not formally aligned with either the Protestant or the Catholic Church, and all three institutions strove to discourage the appearance of the churches openly directing the political positions of the CDU, despite private statements by clerical leaders offering support to the CDU.

Hermes and Kaiser firmly agreed with Dibelius and Preysing concerning the special role of the churches in helping Germany recover from the effects of Nazi rule and defeat by the Allies. The guiding ideology of Christian Socialism which Kaiser advocated during his tenure as CDU chairman from December 1945 to December 1947 was not merely an attempt to preserve the educational and charitable role of the churches, but to apply their teachings to the creation of a new political, social, and economic order in the Soviet zone of Germany. Given the SVAG and SED domination of the levers of political power in the Soviet zone, this attempt was doomed to failure, as evidenced by Kaiser's removal by the SVAG in December 1947 and his replacement with the more compliant Otto Nuschke. Nevertheless, the CDU from the summer of 1945 to the winter of 1947 provided one of most visible symbols of resistance against the plan of the SVAG and their German allies to implement a red dictatorship in the place of a brown one, a role the leadership of the churches took on once the independence of the CDU in the Soviet zone had been neutralized.

With Germany's surrender in May 1945 the titanic struggle between the two totalitarian dictatorships came to an end. The Soviet Union had suffered terribly to bring about its victory over Nazi Germany, but with this victory Soviet power was extended to the heart of Central Europe, and one-third of Germany was now under Soviet control. The Soviet victory gave Stalin the opportunity to finish the work left undone in the Russian Civil War and the Soviet-Polish War, to extend Soviet-style socialism throughout Europe. The Soviet zone of Germany, like Hungary, Poland, Czechoslovakia, Romania, and Bulgaria, would be transformed into a Stalinist dictatorship from 1945 to 1949. The fact the Soviet zone of Germany followed a slower pace on this process than its Eastern neighbors did not negate the view in Moscow that the Soviet zone of Germany was the greatest conquest of Socialism and would undoubtedly be remade on the Soviet model.

This view included policies regarding religious institutions, as the Soviet authorities and their German Communist allies had already decided the Catholic and Protestant churches would eventually be prevented from playing any role in the social and political life in an SED-led Germany. There was an inevitability to this process, given the intrinsic hostility to religious belief inherent in the ideology of the Soviet and SED authorities. It would not be for decades later, as historians such as Tat'iana Chumachenko for Soviet case and Bernd Schaefer for the East German case have demonstrated, that Communists reconciled themselves to a permanent, if sharply reduced and still harassed, presence of religious institutions in the societies under their control.

The experience of the Second World War demonstrated a greater flexibility on the part of the Soviet government towards religious institutions. For this first time since the early 1920s, the Soviet government began to consider policies which utilized the propaganda value of "religious freedom", and the cultivation of certain churches and their clergy as allies, as opposed to policies designed merely to violently suppress religious institutions and criminalize religious faith. Nowhere was this more evident than Stalin's reversal regarding the Russian Orthodox Church in 1943. In his meeting with the Metropolitans of Moscow, Leningrad, and Kiev, Stalin made a number of concessions to the Russian Orthodox Church, such as allowing them to re-open a number of seminaries and publish a church newspaper. Stalin also allowed for the creation of the Council on Orthodox Church Affairs, to serve as go-between of the Soviet and Orthodox leadership.[1] Historians such as Tat'iana Chumachenko and Steven Miner have argued that this decision resulted less from any openness on Stalin's part to the existence of religious institutions in the Soviet Union and more for its propaganda value in the West as well as the role the Russian Orthodox Church would play in suppressing independent Orthodox churches which were often centers of nationalist resistance to the Soviet government.[2] Stalin's actions did reveal a greater sophistication on the part the Soviet government in forming policies regarding religious institutions, which would also manifest itself in SVAG policies towards the Protestant and to a lesser extent the Catholic churches.

The German Communist Party (KPD-*Kommunistische Partei Deutschlands*) also appeared to have altered its earlier open hostility to religious institutions in Germany which had characterized its policies since the creation of the Weimar Republic. At the KPD's first exile conference in Brussels in 1933, the party for the first time recognized freedom of religious belief. In

1935 the KPD's Central Committee noted the resistance of religious Germans to Hitler's regime. The so-called "concentration camp effect" in which dissident Protestant and Catholic clergy shared imprisonment in Nazi concentration camps with members of the KPD led to a common belief among certain religious leaders the KPD would not become enemies of the churches but instead would work with to rebuild a new political and social order with equal commitment to freedom of belief and antifascism. This belief persisted once the KPD merged with the Social Democratic Party in the Soviet zone in April 1946 to form the Socialist Unity Party.[3]

Many Catholic and Protestant clergy, despite whatever hopes they had about the KPD not returning to its pre-1933 view of viewing the churches has obstacles in the path of creating a socialist and atheist society, were drawn to the Christian Democratic Union (CDU-*Christliche Demokratische Union*). Allowed to emerge in the Soviet zone in June 1945 to represent middle-class religious Germans, the CDU issued its founding proclamation on June 26 1945. The CDU's attempt to offer a fully-formed ideological alternative to the Marxism-Leninism of the SED would not emerge for another nine months, in the form of the second chairman Jakob Kaiser's doctrine of "Christian Socialism." From the very beginning, however, the CDU leadership rejected the introduction dictatorial methods of political or economic control by any future German government and forcibly insisted the churches would still play a vital role in Germany's public life.[4]

The Soviet military administration in Germany (SVAG-*Sovetskaia voennaia Administratsiia v Germanii*), was headquartered in the Berlin suburb of Karlshorst, but also had branches in the five provinces which made up the Soviet zone, Berlin-Brandenburg, Sachsen, Sachsen-Anhalt, Thuringia, and Mecklenburg. The Soviet authorities had more power to dictate political, economic, cultural, and religious policies in the Soviet zone of Germany than they did anywhere else in Central or Eastern Europe. Yet at the same time, the proximity of the Soviet zone to the Western zones of Germany served to delay, although not halt, SVAG plans to build a Stalinist economic and political structure in their zone. If the Stalinist transformation was implemented too rapidly, it would jeopardize long-term Soviet plans of controlling all of Germany, not just their own zone. As the occupation continued, SVAG authorities were often willing to delegate numerous decisions to SED representatives on the German organs of self-government.[5]

The Catholic and especially the Protestant leadership viewed the end of the war as a great opportunity to rebuild German society along Christian lines and to undo the damage of the Nazi and the Weimar eras. Leaders such as Otto Dibelius believed Germany had lost its moral foundations after 1918, paving the way for the rise of Nazism. Despite Dibelius's staunchly anticommunist views, he and the rest of the Protestant hierarchy in Berlin-Brandenburg were determined to pursue a generally conciliatory policy towards the Soviet authorities. The first priority of Dibelius and other leading members of the Confessing Church was the removal of members of the German Christian movement from the church administration and replacing them with their own supporters.[6]

Cardinal Konrad von Preysing, as the head of the Diocese of Berlin, was in a far more unchallenged position as the leader of the Catholic hierarchy in Berlin-Brandenburg than Otto Dibelius in the Protestant Church. Indeed, Preysing was the most prominent Catholic cleric in the Soviet zone; given the fact the Diocese of Berlin encompassed not only the German capital but also Brandenburg and parts of Sachsen and Mecklenburg. Preysing, like his counterparts in the Western zones, viewed the end of Nazi rule as an opportunity to restore religious freedom in Germany, and to end the conflicts between the Catholic Church and the German government which had continued since 1871. Preysing could demonstrate resistance to Nazism better than most other members of the Catholic hierarchy in Germany, yet he largely agreed with them the church would broke no interference in its internal affairs and would fiercely guard its prerogatives in religious education, youth work, and charitable activities. Although their anti-Communism was equally strong as that of Dibelius and most other Protestant clerics, Preysing and the rest of Catholic clerical hierarchy also hoped for a cooperative relationship with the Soviet authorities, if not their German "friends."[7]

HISTORIOGRAPHY

This book crosses over three different historiographical fields: that of the Soviet occupation zone, the German Protestant and Catholic churches in the Soviet zone and the GDR, and finally the small number of works that have combined the two fields. Sixty-five years after the Soviet occupation of Germany began, and twenty-five years after the opening of state and religious archives in Central and Eastern Europe, no historian on either side of the Atlantic has written about the development and implementation of Soviet religious policies in the zone from both the Soviet and German perspectives in more than a peripheral manner. Until the fall of the Berlin Wall in 1989 most historians and political scientists in Russia, Europe, and the United States largely neglected the history of the Soviet zone. There were a few works on the subject, such as by J. P. Nettl, a political scientist by training, and Grigorii Klimov, a former Red Army officer who served in Soviet Administration of Germany but then fled to the West in 1950. His book was based on his own experiences and others in the Soviet administration. Both Nettl and Klimov discussed the formation of the German political parties in the Soviet zone, and emphasized the formation of the Socialist Unity Party in 1946 and its rise to prominence over the other political parties from 1947 to 1949. But neither author examined religious issues in any great extent.[8]

Among the few histories of the Soviet zone of occupation written in the 1970s and 1980s are those by Henry Kritsch and Gregory Sandford. Both of these authors also chose to focus on either political or economic questions in the zone instead of those concerning religion, taking the same examination of their topic as the early works by Nettl and Klimov.[9] Later histories of the Soviet zone in German, Russian, and English written after the opening of German and Russian archives 1989–1991 such as those by Edward Peterson, Gareth Pritchard and A. M. Filitov also take the same general approach in emphasizing political, economic and social concerns in the Soviet zone.[10]

By far the most comprehensive studies on the Soviet zone in any language are those by David Pike and Norman Naimark. Pike argues that the Soviet military authorities worked closely with the German Communist Party (KPD) and later the Socialist Unity Party in devising and implementing cultural policies to encourage antifascism and support for the construction of socialism. Pike concludes that this effort proved to be unsuccessful due to the increasing rigid uniformity of Stalinist cultural norms shared by both party functionaries in the SED and military authorities in the SVAG.[11] Naimark expands on Pike's argument that the ideological and political background of the certain Soviet officials in Germany, when combined with their belief they were engaged in competition with the three Western powers for the fate of Germany dictated their decision to construct socialism within their zone with the leading role for the Socialist Unity Party. Naimark points to Colonel Sergei Tiul'panov, head of the Propaganda/Information Administration in the Soviet zone, as the primary representative of this group in the Soviet military administration. He argued that Tiul'panov, with the aid of valuable patrons in Moscow such as ideology chief Andrei Zhdanov as well as Joseph Stalin, defied the wishes of those in the Soviet military administration, such as its commander from 1946 to 1949, Major General (later Marshal) Vasilii Sokolovskii, who did not desire a rapid construction of socialism in the Soviet zone.

According to Naimark, the victory of the Tiul'panov faction, symbolized by the attempt to construct a Stalinist political and economic order in the Soviet zone, was a significant factor in the collapse of the four-power administration of Germany as a single unit between the Soviets and the western allies.[12] However, despite their extensive research, Pike and Naimark devoted little attention to the question of religion. While it would not be accurate to claim that neither historian mentioned religious issues, the topic was not explored extensively in these two definitive works on the Soviet occupation of Germany.

Another school of interpretation emerged in the late early 1990s, characterized by the works of Carolyn Eisenberg, Wilfried Loth, and Geoffrey Roberts. Eisenberg argues the fault for the division of Germany lay not with the Soviet officials but with their British and, especially, American counterparts, who refused Soviet entreaties to continue to govern Germany as a united nation.[13] Loth concurs with Eisenberg as he argues the determination by American and British officials in London, Washington, and Berlin to "solve" the German question by incorporating the western zones of Germany into an the Anglo-American sphere of economic and political influence, when combined with the determination of Soviet officials in Germany and the leadership of the Socialist Unity Party to create a socialist state in the Soviet zone led inexorably to the division of Germany against Stalin's wishes.[14]

In Roberts's more recent work, he argues the Soviet government, or more accurately Stalin himself, desired a united, neutral, antifascist German state under a left-wing government friendly to the Soviet Union. Unlike Eisenberg or Loth, Roberts does not make it clear what role the Soviet military authorities in Germany played in this process, although he does concur with Loth and Eisenberg that American and British stubbornness on the reparations question and their determination to link the western zones of Germany to their plans for the economic and military revival of Western Europe was the principal cause of the division of Germany.[15]

Where Eisenberg, Loth, and Roberts agree on is the Soviet authorities in Karlshorst and in Moscow had no intention of creating a German state based on the Soviet model, but were essentially forced into such a step by the policies of the British and American authorities who rapidly began remaking the Western zones of Germany into a liberal capitalist state directly integrated with the Western market economy, in direct defiance of Soviet wishes for a united and neutral Germany built on a order agreed upon by all four victorious Allied powers. Loth differs slightly from Roberts and Eisenberg as he also assigns some blame for the division of Germany on SVAG officials such as Colonel Sergei Tiul'panov as well as the leader of the SED Walter Ulbricht, who assisted the construction of Stalinism in the Soviet zone in direct defiance of Stalin's wishes for a neutral, united Germany.

This revisionist school was opposed by other recent neo-traditionalist works such as those by Hubertus Knabe, Gary Bruce, Dirk Spilker, and Vladislav Zubok. All four agree the creation of a Stalinist East German state was no accident, nor was it something Soviet officials were forced into by the policies of the Western Allies. Rather, it was the deliberate result of plans devised in Moscow and implemented by Karlshorst. According to Zubok,

Spilker and Knabe, Stalin always hoped for all of Germany under Soviet influence, but, failing that, the Soviet zone would be remade along Stalinist economic, political, and social lines. They argue it was simply unrealistic for any historian to assume, as Loth does, that Tiul'panov and Ulbricht built a Stalinist order in the Soviet zone against Stalin's wishes. Loth's argument reveals a fundamental misunderstanding of how decisions were made in Moscow regarding its newly acquired Empire in Eastern and Central Europe and how Soviet officials on the ground as well as their German allies in the SED followed them.[16]

My conclusions largely concur with the arguments made by Naimark, Knabe, Zubok, and Bruce with regards to the general tone and direction of SVAG policies. It is certainly true SVAG and SED authorities showed certain flexibility in their relations with the churches in regard to some issues, particularly regarding charitable activities. This position was based on power realities on the ground in Berlin-Brandenburg and a desire on the part of the Soviet authorities not to move too fast in creating Stalinism in the Soviet zone, lest they throw away a chance to influence the Western zones of Germany as well. Nevertheless, neither the SVAG nor the SED believed religious institutions would have any role in the Stalinist Germany they planned to create, and it was this Marxist-Leninist-Stalinist hostility to the churches as "reactionary" if not actively fascist institutions that guided the increasingly restrictive SVAG and SED policies to the churches as the occupation continued into the late 1940s.

The second historiographical field that my research crosses over is that of church histories that focus on the Protestant and Catholic churches in East Germany. Important works on the churches in the Soviet zone and the GDR in English and German, such as histories by Richard Solberg and Robert Goeckel, do not focus on the religious policies of the Soviet authorities to any great extent, although they do mention the internal reformation of the Lutheran churches in the Soviet zone during the 1945–1949 period.[17] Some of the most important German works on the Protestant Church in the Soviet zone and the GDR, in particular the works of Gerhard Besier, do not examine the formation and development of Soviet religious policies concerning the Protestant churches in their zone. The overarching theme of Besier's book is that many clergy in the Protestant Church all too willingly collaborated with the East German Communists in their political and social goals, just as they had done during the Nazi period, and writes that this extended to their relationship with the Soviet authorities during the occupation period as well.[18]

There have been a few German historians who have written extensively on policies of the SED and the SVAG in the zone, such as Horst Dähn, Stefan Kreuzberger, Jan Foitzik, Volker Stanke, J. Jurgen Seidel, and Wolfgang

Tischer, whose work composes the third historiographical field, which attempted to merge histories of the zone with those of the Protestant and Catholic churches during the period. Foitzik's, Dähn's, and Creuzberger's works are histories of the Soviet military occupation in Germany and how it operated at the zonal, provincial, and local levels, much like those of Naimark and Pike. Creuzberger provides one example of a religious policy implemented by the Soviet occupation authorities during this period, which was their attempt to discourage Protestant clergy from taking a "political" role in provincial elections in the Soviet zone of Germany in 1946.[19] Dähn's work discusses evolving position on the religious question by the KPD/SED from one that accepted the churches as a valuable partner in the construction of an antifascist Germany to one that rejected any visible role for religious institutions in a German state under their leadership. However, he did not focus the role of the Soviet occupation authorities in these processes nor the religious policies made by Soviet authorities.[20]

Three works by German historians that do delve into my topic to a considerable extent are those by J. Jurgen Seidel, Martin Georg Goerner, and Volker Stanke.[21] But none of these authors based their research on material from Russian archives, which were not completely opened when Seidel and Stanke wrote their specific works. Seidel's work deals with the relations between leaders of Protestant churches within the Soviet zone and the head of the Propaganda Administration, Colonel Tiul'panov. Without access to Russian archives, however, he provides no real discussion of how Soviet religious policy was formed in Karlshorst and implemented by the Soviet authorities. Stanke's work provides a detailed history of the Evangelical churches in Saxony during the Soviet occupation, but he does not discuss the formation and implementation of Soviet religious policy to any great extent. Stanke chose instead to focus on the relations between the churches and the SED and the CDU. Goerner devotes that majority of his attention to the post-1953 period in relations between the SED-regime and the Protestant Church, and, like Seidel and Stanke, he did not have access to Russian archival material. However, Goerner is largely correct in description of the close collaboration between the SED and SVAG authorities on religious questions, and how their policies moved from attempts to co-opt the church to attempts to deny it any role in East German society.

In terms of the Catholic Church in the Soviet zone, two major works concerning my topic were written by the historians Bernd Schaefer and Wolfgang Tischner. Schaefer's work analyzes in detail the relationship between the Catholic authorities and the SED in the Soviet zone during the post-war period. The early chapters of Wolfgang Tischner's historical monograph discuss the policies of the Catholic bishop of Berlin, Konrad von Preysing during the Soviet Occupation, particularly his gradual turn to open opposition to anti-religious policies of the Soviet and German authorities after originally planning to implement a strict non-involvement in the political life of the Soviet zone.[22] Much like Stanke and Seidel, Schaefer and Tischner focus largely on the relations between the Catholic Church and the SED, with less attention paid to the SVAG authorities. Neither author utilized Russian language archival material.

I argue that Besier's argument was fundamentally correct, as the open collaborationist stance of Protestant clerics such as Kurt Rackwitz and Theodor Werner as well as the cooperative policy of officials such as Heinrich Gruber and Kurt Krummacher did little to mediate the policies of the SVAG or the SED. Even the emergence of a confrontational and anticommunist stance of clergy such as the Protestant Bishop Otto Dibelius and the Catholic Cardinal Konrad von Preysing was simply an acknowledgment of the reality of SVAG and SED plans for religious institutions in a future SED-led Germany. While Dibelius and Preysing's actions failed to halt the plans of the Soviet and German authorities to minimize the social and economic role of the churches, their opposition made the church leadership one of the most visible symbol in the Soviet zone of resistance to the Communist authorities, especially once the political independence of the CDU ended with the removal of Jakob Kaiser in December 1947.

There exists a considerable gap in the current historiography on the Soviet zone on both sides of the Atlantic with regards to the formation and implementation of religious polices by the Soviet military authorities towards the Protestant and Catholic churches in their zone of Germany, especially in English. This is particularly obvious with regards to the religious policies of the Soviet authorities, as most works on this topic did not use Russian archival material. I add to the existing historiography of the Soviet occupation of Germany and the experience of the German churches under Communism. No previous historical work on these topics uses the same perspective I provide, which analyzes how the Soviet and East German authorities treated the Evangelical and Catholic churches during the occupation, as well as how the churches responded, using extensive archival evidence from each major actor in this process

STRUCTURE OF THE BOOK

The eight chapters of the book are divided along thematic and chronological lines. Each chapter discusses a specific theme throughout the history of the

Soviet occupation, rather than chapters which attempt to focus on all important religious issues during a set amount of time. The first chapter provides a brief overview of the experience of the Catholic and Protestant churches under the Nazi regime from 1933 or 1945. Particular attention is paid to Nazi religious policies and the mixed responses of the churches toward them. The second and third chapters discuss the relationship between the Protestant and Catholic churches and the Christian Democratic Union in the Soviet zone. The chapters examine how the SVAG and SED authorities viewed the controversial issue of cooperation between the churches and the CDU, and what type of relationship existed in reality. The second chapter concerns the period of the CDU's relative political independence under its first two chairmen Andreas Hermes and Jakob Kaiser from 1945 to 1947, while third chapter analyzes the removal of Kaiser as CDU chairman during the *Volkscongress* controversy and the end of the CDU's freedom of action under the leadership of Otto Nuschke.

The focus of chapter four is the most intense conflict between the religious and secular authorities, the question of religious education in the secondary schools in the Soviet zone of Germany. Chapters five and six discuss the issues of religious charitable activity and religious youth and women's organizations, respectively. In all of their conflicts with the SVAG and SED, the churches strove to preserve their independent role in the social, cultural and economic life of the Soviet zone, with varying degrees of success. Undeniably, as the occupation continued and a Stalinist order was introduced in the Soviet zone, the opportunities for the churches to operate freely were sharply reduced. The anti-religious policies of the early 1950s after the founding of the GDR merely continued policies which had been put in place by the Soviet authorities and their German allies.

Chapter seven discusses the attempt by the SVAG and the SED, despite their increasingly hostile policies towards Protestant and Catholic churches, to present themselves as champions of "religious freedom." This was part of an effort both to win over religious Germans in the Soviet and Western zones and also to split the Catholic and Protestant clergy into "progressive" and "conservative" camps, in order to prevent them from creating a unified front against the SVAG and the SED. The eighth and final chapter concerns the Allied Religious Affairs Committee (ARAC), a low level committee of the Allied Control Council (ACC), composed of representatives from each occupation zones. While it failed in its objective of recommending common religious policies for all four zones of Germany, the actions of its Soviet representative, Lt. Colonel Vsevolod Ermolaev, demonstrate how seriously the Soviet authorities viewed cooperation with their Western allies to create uniform religious policies for all four occupation zones of Germany.

THE MAJOR HISTORICAL ACTORS

This story told in this book revolves around the five main institutions in the history of church-state relations in Berlin-Brandenburg. They were the Soviet Military Administration in Germany, both its headquarters in Karlshorst and its Brandenburg branch in Potsdam, the Socialist Unity Party (and by extension the German organs of self-government they controlled) the Protestant Church, the Catholic Church, and the Christian Democratic Union. In terms of historical figures, certain individuals play a major role in nearly each chapter while others play a significant role in one specific chapter given its subject matter. For example, future GDR leader Erich Honecker features prominently in chapter five, concerning religious youth and women's organizations, as he was the leader of the SED youth organization the Free German Youth (FDJ-*Freie Deutsche Jugend*). He does not show up in other chapters as do SED leaders Otto Grotewohl, Wilhelm Pieck, and Walter Ulbricht, who were involved in all of the SED religious policies during the period of occupation when it gradually seized power.

The principal officers in the SVAG who were involved in religious affairs were the leader of its Propaganda/Information Administration, Colonel Sergei Tiul'panov, and his religious affairs deputy Lieutenant Colonel Vsevolod Ermolaev. The arguments of Norman Naimark in particular which place Tiul'panov in central role in SVAG policy-making in the zone were borne out by my research as well. Tiul'panov took a very active role in deciding what type of relations the Soviet authorities should have with the churches, as well as later the decisive turn to a more hostile anti-religious policy from 1947 to 1949. Also vital were the various heads of the Propaganda/Information Administration in the urban and rural districts of Brandenburg, who were in charge of implementing SVAG religious policies and reported to Tiul'panov on the activities of the Protestant and Catholic churches. The two most prominent SVAG officers who worked directly under Tiul'panov in the implementation of religious policies in Berlin-Brandenburg were the two leaders of the Propaganda/Information Administration in Berlin-Brandenburg during the occupation, I. I. Mil'khiker and K. V. Martem'ianov.

Regarding most issues involving the churches the SVAG usually took the lead. The SED leadership of Pieck, Grotewohl, and Ulbricht, played a less prominent role, although this began to change by the end of the occupation.

Also of vital importance were the various SED party members who administered the German organs of self-government in Berlin-Brandenburg, who, much like the regional heads of the SVAG's Propaganda Administration, were in charge of implementing the SED's religious policies and dealing with the Protestant and Catholic clergy and laity at the ground level. Easily the most prominent was SED member Heinrich Steinhoff, head of the Provincial Administration for Brandenburg.

In the CDU, the three key figures were Otto Nuschke, Andreas Hermes, and especially Jakob Kaiser. During his brief tenure as the first chairman of the CDU from June to December 1945, Hermes established the CDU's commitment to preserve the unique role of the churches in German society as well as a strong opposition to the rebuilding of the Soviet zone of Germany on the Stalinist model. His successor, Jakob Kaiser, was the dominant CDU leader during the occupation. Although anxious to avoid identifying the CDU too closely with the churches or religious-based politics, Kaiser strove to combine moderate socialist economics with Christian humanism to present a genuine alternative to the Marxism-Leninism of the SED. The result was the CDU's official ideology of "Christian Socialism", which, from 1946 to the end of 1947, was the clearest alternative to the dominant ideology of the SED in Soviet zone. Kaiser welcomed the support of religious Germans and the churches in the Soviet zone, but he also successfully attempted to broaden the base of the party to include segments of Germany's population which had not supported Christian political parties in the pre-1933 era. Otto Nuschke was the other dominant CDU leader in the Soviet zone during the time period. Believing that only if the CDU followed a subservient line to the SVAG and SED authorities could it hope to survive as a political movement, Nuschke forcefully rejected Christian Socialism as the process of Stalinization rapidly accelerated from late 1947 to 1949.

The two key religious leaders in Berlin-Brandenburg during his time period were Bishop Otto Dibelius of the Protestant Church and Cardinal Konrad von Preysing of the Catholic Church. Much like certain SED officials, a number of Catholic and Protestant clergy play an important role in certain chapters, such as the Protestant minister Robert Hanisch and the Catholic priest Domvikar Lange in the chapter on religious youth and women's work, but were not directly involved in other issues regarding SVAG and SED religious policies. Other prominent Protestant clerical figures in this dissertation include Hans von Arnim, the General Secretary of the Protestant Church in Brandenburg, who largely agreed with Dibelius on his anti-Communist stance. Kurt Krummacher and Heinrich Gruber, head of the Protestant Church Chancellery and Provost for Berlin, respectively, sought a greater cooperative stance vis a-vis the SVAG and SED authorities.

SOURCES

In order to address the major questions raised in my research for this book, it was necessary to consult a broad variety of primary source materials from state, religious and political archives in Russia, Germany, and the United States. These sources allowed for a clear picture to emerge regarding how each side perceived each other, how close these perceptions were to the reality, and how they affected the course of church-state relations during this time period.

In the State Archive of the Russian Federation (GARF- *Gosudarstvennyi arkhiv Rossiisskoi Federatsii*) I used the records of the Soviet Military Government in Germany, both its central headquarters in Karlshorst and its Brandenburg branch in Potsdam. The record groups for both depositories contained the correspondence between the main Soviet official in charge of religious policies in Germany, Tiul'panov and his lieutenants in the cities and districts Brandenburg who implemented his orders. These consist before of reports Tiul'panov's men in the Propaganda/Information Administration sent to him on a monthly basis, as well as orders Tiul'panov sent to them concerning SVAG religious policies. I also worked in the Russian Archive for Social and Political History (RGASPI- *Rossiiskii gosudarstvennyi arkhiv sotsial'no-politicheskoi istorii*), which contained the records of the Council of Russian Orthodox Church Affairs and the Foreign Department of the Communist Party of the Soviet Union's Central Committee. Both of these institutions received occasional reports on religious life in the Soviet zone of Germany from Tiul'panov.

The Archive for Parties and Mass Organizations of the German Democratic Republic in the Bundesarchiv (SAPMO- *Stiftung Archiv der Parteien und Massenorganizationnen der DDR im Bundesarchiv*) formed the base of my research on the religious policies of the Socialist Unity Party in the Soviet zone, especially the policies of its leaders Grotewohl, Pieck, and Ulbricht. The provincial archive for Brandenburg (BLHA- *Brandenburgisches Landeshauptarchiv*) and the city archive of Berlin (LAB- *Landesarchiv Berlin*) were also crucial in understanding how the SED-controlled German organs of self-government implemented the SED's religious policies during the Soviet occupation, particularly concerning religious education, charitable activity, and youth and women's organizations.

In order to analyze the religious policies of the Christian Democratic Union I used the main archive for the records of the CDU's branches in West and East Germany, the Archive for Christian-Democratic Politics, held in the Adenauer Institute in Saint Augustin (ACDP- *Archiv fur Christliche-*

Demokratische Politik). I consulted both the records of the CDU's Executive Committee and also the official papers of its first three chairmen Andreas Hermes, Jakob Kaiser, and Otto Nuschke.

Other archives in Germany I examined were the three central Church Archives for Berlin-Brandenburg. The first was the Central Archive of the Protestant Church (EZA- *Evangelisches Zentral Archiv*) which contains materials from the Protestant Church Chancellery for the entire Soviet zone. The second was the Provincial Protestant archive for Brandenburg (ELAB- *Evangelisches Landesarchiv Brandenburg)* which contains the official records of the leading Protestant clergy in Brandenburg, Otto Dibelius, Heinrich Gruber, and Kurt Krummacher, as well as the records of the Protestant Church in Brandenburg. The third was the Archive for the Catholic Diocese of Berlin (DAB- *Diosezän Archiv für Berlin)* where I examined the official papers of the Catholic Cardinal Konrad von Preysing, the central Catholic leader in the Soviet zone.

Finally, I used a number archives in the United States, including the National Archives II in College Park, Maryland, which contained the records of the joint Allied Religious Affairs Committee, which attempted to recommend unified religious policies to the Allied Control Council for all four zones of Germany, but fell apart due to differences between the Soviet representative, Vsevolod Ermolaev, and his Western counterparts. I also examined materials from the Archives of the University of Notre Dame, which contained extensive records concerning Konrad von Preysing's tour of the United States in 1947 and how he attempted to explain to American Catholics the status of religious and political life in the Soviet zone.

Notes

1. Tat'iana Chumachenko, *Church and State in Soviet Russia: Russian Orthodoxy from World War II to the Khrushchev Years*. London: M. E. Sharpe Publishers, 2002. 15.

2. Steve Miner, *Stalin's Holy War: Religion, Nationalism, and Alliance Politics, 1941–1945*. Chapel Hill: University of North Carolina Press, 2003. 315. Chumachenko, 16.

3. Robert Goeckel, *The Lutheran Church and the East German State: Political Conflict and Change under Ulbricht and Honecker*. Ithaca: Cornell University Press, 1990. 41.

4. Gary Bruce, *Resistance With the People: Repression and Resistance in Eastern Germany 1945–1955*. New York: Rowman & Littlefield Publishers, 2006. 25.

5. Norman Naimark, *The Russians in Germany: A History of the Soviet Zone of Occupation, 1945–1949*. Cambridge: The Belknap Press of Harvard University Press, 1995. 11.

6. Goeckel, 42. The main priority for Dibelius and other prominent clergy in Germany such as Martin Niemoller was to preserve the church's independent role in reforming itself, with no outside interference by the Allied authorities

7. Wolfgang Tischner, "Die Kirchenpolitik unter Konrad Kardinal von Preysing 1945–1950" *Katholische Kirche in SBZ und DDR*. Wolfgang Tischner and Christoph Kösters, eds. Munich: Ferdinand Schönigh, 2005. 37–61. 41. There were, however, a small but vocal minority of Catholic and Protestant clergy who argued for more than mere toleration of the Soviet authorities, but rather to merge Christian belief with the Marxist-Leninist ideology of the SVAG and the SED. Some were influenced by the theology of Karl Barth, which rejected any policies by the Protestant Church which resembled those of the Weimar and Nazi eras.

8. J. P. Nettl, *The Eastern Zone and Soviet Policy in Germany 1945–1950*. London: Oxford University Press, 1951; Grigorii Klimov, The Terror Machine: The Inside Story of the Soviet administration in Germany. New York: Praeger, 1953.

9. Henry Kirsch, *German Politics under Soviet Occupation*. New York: Columbia University Press, 1974; Gregory Sandford, *From Hitler to Ulbricht: The Communist Reconstruction of East Germany, 1945–1946*. Princeton: Princeton University Press, 1983.

10. Edward Peterson, *Russian Commands and German Resistance: The Soviet Occupation 1945–1949*. New York: Peter Lang, 1999; Gareth Pritchard, *The Making of the GDR 1945–1953: From Antifascism to Stalinism*. Manchester: Manchester: Manchester University Press, 2000; A. M. Filitov, *Germanskii vopros: ot raskola k ob'edineniiu*. Moscow: Mezhdunarodnye otnosheniia, 1993.

11. David Pike, *The Politics of Culture in Soviet-Occupied Germany, 1945–1949*. Stanford: Stanford University Press, 1992.

12. Norman Naimark, *The Russians in Germany: A History of the Soviet Zone of Occupation, 1945–1949*. Cambridge: The Belknap Press of Harvard University Press, 1995, 468. More the most part, there does not appear to be a "Tiul'panov faction" in the SVAG with regards to religious policy, acting against the wishes of the overall commanders of SVAG.

13. Carolyn Eisenberg, *Drawing the Line: The American Decision to Divide Germany*. Oxford: Cambridge University Press, 1996. 287.

14. Wilfried Loth, *Stalin's Unwanted Child: The Soviet Union, the German Question, and the Founding of the GDR*. New York: St. Martin's Press, 1994. 10.

15. Geoffrey Roberts, *Stalin's Wars: From World War to Cold War 1939–1953*. New Haven: Yale University Press, 2006. 352.

16. Bruce, 49. Hubertus Knabe, *Tag Der Befreiung?: Das Kreigsende in Ostdeutschland*. Berlin: Propyläen. 2006. 13. Vladislav Zubok, *A Failed Empire: The Soviet Union in the Cold War From Stalin to Gorbachev*. Chapel Hill, NC: University of North Carolina Press, 2007. 62. Dirk Spilker, *The East German Leadership and the Division of Germany: Patriotism and Propaganda 1945–1953*. Oxford: Oxford University Press, 2006. 5.

17. Richard Solberg, *God and Caesar in East Germany: The Conflicts of Church and State in East Germany since 1945*. New York: The Macmillan Company. 1961; Robert Goeckel, *The Lutheran Church and the East German State: Political Conflict and Change under Ulbricht and Honecker*. Ithaca: Cornell University Press, 1990.

18. Gerhard Besier, *Die SED-staat und die Kirche*. Munich: C. Bertelsman, 1993.

19. Stefan Creuzberger, *Die sowjetische Besatzungsmacht und das Politische System der SBZ*. Weimar: Böhlau, 1996; Jan Foitzik, *Sowjetische Militäradministration in Deutschland (SMAD) 1945–1949: Struktur und Funktion*. Berlin: Akademie Verlag, 1999, 24–26. Foitzik's book is also extremely useful in that it provides a complete listing of each department of the Soviet occupation as well as which officers staffed them. Foitzik writes that the highly influential Propaganda Administration under Colonel Sergei Tiul'panov made religious policies. The head of the liaison office between the Soviet military administration and the churches was Lt. Colonel Vsevolod Ermolaev, who was also the Soviet representative on the Allied Religious Affairs Committee.

20. Horst Dähn, *Konfrontation oder Kooperation? Das Verhältnis von Staat und Kirche in der SBZ/DDR 1945–1980*. Düsseldorf: Westdeutscher Verlag, 1982.

21. J. Jurgen Seidel, *"Neubeginn" in der Kirche? Die evangelischen Landes-und Provinzialkirchen in der SBZ/DDR im gesellschaftspolitischen Kontext der Nachkriegszeit 1945–1953*. Göttingen: Vandenhoeck & Ruprecht, 1989. Volker Stanke, *Die Gestaltung der Beziehungen zwischen dem Land Sachsen und der Evangelisch-Lutherischen Landeskirche Sachsens von 1945 bis 1949*. Frankfurt am Main: Peter Lang, 1993. Martin Georg Goerner, *Die Kirche als Problem der SED: Strukturen kommunistischer Herrschaftsausübung gegenüber der evangelischen Kirche 1945 bis 1958*. Berlin: Akademie Verlag, 1997.

22. Bernd Schaefer, *Staat und katholische Kirche in der GDR, 1945–1989*. Berlin: Berghahn, 1999. Wolfgang, Tischner, "Die Kirchenpolitik unter Konrad von Preysing 1945–1950" *Katholische Kirche in SBZ und DDR*. Munich: Ferdinand Schöningh, 2005. 37–62.

Chapter One

The Brown Dictatorship before the Red

The German Churches under National Socialism, 1933–1945

INTRODUCTION

In many respects the experience of the Protestant and Catholic churches under the Nazi regime is quite similar to that of the Soviet occupation and later, the rule of the Socialist Unity Party. In both cases there was a strong divide among the church leadership regarding how to approach the totalitarian regime in Germany. This was especially prominent in the leadership of the Protestant Church. Some Protestant leaders, such as Ludwig Müller, favored overt collaboration with the Nazi regime, to the point of attempting to merge Protestant Christianity with the doctrines of National Socialism. Others, who joined the *Bekennede Kirche* ("Confessing Church") movement, tried to keep the Protestant Church and its theology free from Nazi influence and continue what they saw as the traditional spiritual, educational, and charitable role of the Church. Only a small minority of the *Bekennede Kirche* advocated overt resistance to the Nazi regime, although certain senior Catholic and Protestant clergy loudly protested over specific Nazi policies.

Furthermore, the Nazi regime's religious policies veered from attempting to co-opt the churches as part of the spiritual and intellectual pillars of the regime, to moving to minimize any role the churches could play in public life in Germany. While the later was almost certainly the long-term goal of Hitler and his chief ideologists Joseph Goebbels and Alfred Rosenberg, the Nazi persecution of the churches tended to be sporadic and fixated on outspoken Protestant and Catholic opponents of the regime. This contrasted sharply to Soviet policies towards the Russian Orthodox Church during the same period, whose immediate purpose was to wipe religious institutions entirely and permanently.

Even among Protestant and Catholic clergy who later became staunch opponents of the Nazi regime, such as Protestant leaders Martin Niemöller and Otto Dibelius or Catholic Bishops August von Galen and Konrad von Preysing, very few mourned the passing of the Weimar Republic in 1933. The majority of the senior Catholic and Evangelical leadership tended to be politically conservative, strongly anticommunist and despised the political and especially the moral chaos that characterized Germany's first experiment in democracy. This led them to briefly give Hitler's government the benefit of the doubt in restoring "order" to Germany.[1]

Although these men would eventually move into opposition to National Socialism, those in the Protestant Church would soon enter into an drawn out and painful struggle with the *Deutsche Christen* ("German Christian") movement for the leadership of Protestants in Hitler's Germany. The German Christians, led by former naval chaplain Ludwig Müller, wanted to pledge the Protestant Church's active, as opposed to tacit, support of the Nazi regime. Sharing not only the Nazi hatred of political liberalism but also their virulent anti-Semitism, the German Christians made it their main theological goal to bring Lutheran theology in line with National Socialist ideology. This meant in practice purging the church's theology and rituals of any "Old Testament" or "Jewish" influence, as well as proving spiritual reinforcement for the Nazi emphasis on German ethnic superiority over all the races of Europe.[2]

The highpoint of Nazi support for the German Christian movement was from 1933 to 1937. During this time, the German Christians, who in June 1932 had declared their goal of creating a new *Volkskirche* (People's Church) for all Protestants in Germany, were directly supported by Hitler and his religious affairs lieutenant, Hans Kerrl, in creating a new *Reichskirche* (Imperial Church), with Ludwig Müller as its head as *Reichsbischof*. Believing the older Evangelical Kirchenbund as too soft in its struggle against Communism and Judaism, the German Christians succeeded in seizing administrative control over most of the twenty-eight regional churches in Germany, and ordered to coordinate them directly under Müller's leadership. The regional churches which came under German Christian control were located in provinces which would later be part of the Soviet occupation zone, such as Prussia, Mecklenburg, Sachsen, and Thuringia.[3]

Ultimately, the German Christians and the Nazi regime failed in their objective to create a united *Reichskirche* for all of Germany's Protestants, although they remained a force within German religious life until 1945. There were two central reasons for this. The first was Hitler's waning interest in the movement after 1937, due largely to his disappointment with Müller's leadership skills and political acumen. The second was the stalwart resistance of the group of Protestant clergy known as the *Bekennende Kirche* or the Confessing

Church, who rejected the Nazi theology of the German Christians as heretical and who attempted to keep the Protestant churches free from the control of the Nazi regime. The leadership of the Confessing Church consisted of two groups, the theological radicals such as the German pastors Diedrich Bonhoeffer and Martin Niemöller and the Swiss theologian Karl Barth, and conservative theologians such as Bishop Theophil Wurm of Württemberg and Bishop Otto Dibelius of Berlin-Brandenburg. Two declarations written by the Confessing Church in 1934, the Barmen Declaration in June 1934 and the Dahlem Declaration in November 1934 outlined the theological opposition on the part of the Confessing Church to the German Christians and, more controversially for its members, the Nazi regime.[4] The Barmen declaration denounced the theology of the German Christians as heretical, specifically its equation of Hitler with Jesus and its attempt to completely disavow the Old Testament. The Dahlem declared staunchly proclaimed only members of the Confessing Church were fit to lead the Church at all of its administrative levels, and any attempts by the Nazi regime to force the appointment of German Christians to leadership positions had to be strenuously resisted.[5]

The opposition of the Confessing Church to the Nazi regime and its theological puppets involved a great deal of personal courage. Many leaders of the Confessing Church, such as Niemöller and Bonhoeffer, were imprisoned in concentration camps by the Nazi regime.[6] Others who were fortunate to avoid a conviction of attempting to subvert the regime after having been brought to trial, such as Bishop Otto Dibelius, still found themselves confined to house arrest.[7] Outspoken Catholic clerical opponents of the Nazi regime, such as Cardinal August von Galen of Münster and Cardinal Konrad von Preysing of Berlin, were fortunate to avoid arrest despite a handful of close calls with the Nazi authorities. Other lower-ranking clerics from Protestant and Catholic churches were not so lucky.[8]

Nevertheless, most of the opposition of Protestant and Catholic clergy to the Nazi regime was quite similar to that towards the Soviet and later SED authorities after 1945, in that it criticized specific government policies rather than directly attacking the government's political legitimacy. There were exceptions to this, such as the "radical" wing of the Confessing Church movement led by Barth, Niemöller, and Bonhoeffer, which did attempt to forge a broader resistance to Hitler's government that moved beyond its anti-clerical policies. Yet this remained a minority in the Confessing Church, which at most consisted of a third of Protestant clergy and even less of the laity.[9] As the historian John Conway described it, the policy of most Protestant clergy, outside of the openly pro-Nazi German Christian movement, could be largely characterized by accommodation and compromise, as opposed to outright resistance to the regime.[10]

Much like the Protestant Church, the central issue which defined relations between the Catholic Church and the Nazi regime occurred in its early years, namely, the controversy surrounding the Concordat. Unlike the Protestant Church, there was no equivalent to the German Christian movement in the Catholic Church. During the rise to power of the Nazis in the late 1920s and early 1930s, a number of high-ranking Catholic clergy, such as the archbishops of Breslau and Mainz, publicly warned their parishioners that Nazism and Catholicism were incompatible.[11] Nevertheless, Preysing's declaration that "we have fallen into the hands of criminals and fools" when the Nazi regime came to power was not shared by many among the Catholic laity or some of the clergy.[12] Indeed, certain Catholic politicians from the Center Party, the predecessor of the post-1945 Christian Democratic Union, such as Heinrich Brüning and Franz von Papen, played a substantial role in the fall of the Weimar Republic and its replacement with Hitler's regime, particularly regarding the Center Party's support for the Enabling Act of 1933, which gave Hitler the right to rule by decree without calling upon the Reichstag.[13]

Many Catholic clergy shared the same dislike of the Weimar Republic held by the Protestant counterparts, and hoped that a long-lasting accommodation with Hitler's regime was not only possible, but desirable, This was shared by the Vatican, despite its dislike of the National Socialist movement in Germany. Fearing another *Kulturkampf* and hoping the accommodation worked out between Mussolini and the Catholic Church in Italy could be replicated in Germany, the Catholic leadership in Rome and Berlin agreed to work with the Nazi regime for a broad-ranging Concordat. Still, there was little sense of optimism among Catholic Bishops concerning long-term relations with the Nazi regime, exemplified by Cardinal Faulhaber's quote: "With the Concordat we are hanged, against the Concordat we are hanged, drawn, and quartered."[14]

The Concordat supposedly recognized the freedom of religion in Germany for its Catholic population, as well as providing for the instruction of Catholic theology in secondary schools and the right of the churches to collect taxes for administrative and charitable means. In return, Catholic priests and bishops renounced participating in political parties and promised to recognize the "constitutional government" of Germany and to instruct their parishioners to do the same. While the Concordat appeared to recognize that there were areas of life in Germany that were not directly under the Nazi Party's control, the regime never intended to respect the Concordat if it interfered with their totalitarian goals in Germany.[15]

Following the announcement of the Concordat, many Catholic lay organizations enthusiastically offered their support to the Nazi regime. Many, although that all, Catholic youth and student organizations offered their support to Hitler's new government. Numerous Catholic newspapers did the same, while both the Catholic Trade Federation and the Catholic Teachers' Federation dissolved themselves, and some of their members entered Nazi front organizations.[16]

While the Nazi regime did not engage in a general assault on the Protestant or Catholic Church, it did embark on sporadic attempts to limit the churches' social and youth activities. The work of lay organizations, particularly those involved in youth and charitable work, was sharply restricted by the Nazi regime. Religious services were placed under close supervision by the Gestapo and the regime's domestic political police, the *Sicherheistdeinst* or the SD. Clergy who were outspoken in their opposition to the Nazi regime could and did find themselves arrested, tried, and imprisoned, often in concentration camps. Others were simply murdered outright.[17] Some key examples include Erich Klauser, the general secretary of Catholic Action, murdered by the SA on Hitler's explicit orders, as was Adalbert Prost, the head of the Catholic Youth Sports Association.[18]

Even after the Nazi regime embarked on its war of conquest throughout Europe, a handful of courageous Catholic and Protestant clergy and laity continued to speak out against the regime, although, as previously mentioned, this was usually limited to specific policies as opposed to a fundamental attack on the regime itself. In addition to the actions of the Confessing Church, especially its leaders such as Diedrich Bonhoeffer, Martin Niemöller, and Otto Dibelius, the Catholic Bishop of Berlin Konrad von Preysing remained a staunch opponent of the Nazi regime, famous denouncing its euthanasia policies towards the mentally handicapped:

> No justification and no excuse can be found for taking away the life for the weak or the ill for any sort of economic or eugenic reasons. . . . With the same determination as she has protested the institution of marriage . . . the church will protect the right of every individual to live. [19]

These actions and statements unfortunately remained the exception as opposed to the general rule, as the majority of the Protestant and Catholic clergy, even though they did not necessarily support the Nazi regime, preferred not to interfere in "political" affairs.

The Protestant *Innere Mission* and the Catholic charitable organization *Caritas* also faced sustained pressure to submit to the Nazi regime. This was especially prevalent due to the Nazi euthanasia and sterilization policies of the late 1930s and early 1940s, as both the *Innere Mission* and *Caritas* administered rest homes and hospitals for the elderly and infirm, which of course were obvious targets for Nazis policies designed at eliminating less "productive" members of German society. Given the united opposition to these policies among the Catholic clerical hierarchy in Germany, something the Protestant clerical hierarchy lacked, the Catholic Church was able to keep a tighter control over the activities of *Caritas* than the Protestant Church had over the *Innere Mission*.[20]

Despite promises made by Hitler, Rosenberg, Goebbels, and others that the Nazi regime would not interfere with religious education in German schools, the regime proceeded to do just that during its 12 years of rule. In the state of Prussia, secondary schools were administered on a strictly denominational basis, with separate schools for Lutherans and Catholics; in both cases religious education classes were offered throughout the curriculum. In Sachsen and Thuringia, schools were non-denominational, but both Lutheran and Catholic religious education was offered by Church-approved teachers.[21] Ironically, the Nazi regime disliked the German educational system, particularly regarding religious instruction, for the same reason as the SED educational authorities; that it hindered "national unity." Hitler himself declared in 1937:

> There is but one German people, and there can therefore be but one German youth. This Reich will hand over its youth to no one, but will take its education and formation upon itself.[22]

Hitler's Party Secretary Martin Bormann made this more explicit in his directive to all regional Party offices in 1939:

> The creation of an ideologically objective school system is one of the most important tasks of the Party and the State. In order to achieve this goal, the remains of the denominational influence must be completely removed from our German educational system wherever it still appears. Even though the official responsibility for carrying out the necessary measures belongs to the State and its responsible authorities, the Party, of course, and its local branches, is called upon to be the champions of political renewal, to point out circumstances which can no longer be tolerated on political or ideological grounds, and if necessary to bring about their alteration.[23]

Again, much like the later campaign waged against religious education by the Soviet authorities and their allies in the SED, the Nazi regime began by emphasizing in party propaganda the "un-Germanic" character of separate religious education, which posed a direct threat to the unity of the German nation. This was followed by measures designed to gradually bring an end to religious education for German children, often through fraudulent plebiscites at the town or city level.[24] By November of 1938, the Nazi regime's chief ideologist Alfred Rosenberg felt confident enough to announce: "The curriculum of all categories in our schools has already been so far reformed in an anti-Christian and anti-Jewish spirit that the generation which is growing up will be protected from the black swindle."[25]

With the advent of the Second World War in 1939, and especially after Nazi Germany entered into its life or death struggle with the Soviet Union in 1941, Nazi campaigns against the Protestant and Catholic churches were substantially reduced, particularly with regards to the churches' educational and charitable work. In a report sent from Hitler's party deputy Rudolf Hess (a few months before his ill-fated flight to Scotland in May 1941) to Hermann Goering, Hess admitted that the Nazi campaign against religious education in German schools had to come to an end. Synthesis between National Socialism and either Protestant or Catholic theology remained impossible, however, and once the war had ended the Nazis could fully "settle accounts" with the German churches, with political indoctrination completely replacing religious education in all German schools.[26]

This is not to say that Nazi policies designed to weaken religious institutions ended during the war. The Nazi regime continued to seize substantial amounts of church property, especially from the Protestant Church. This, of course, was not a policy the Nazis used towards the churches. Hitler's regime had, from its very beginning, seized property from Social Democrats, Communists, and Jews after depriving them of their civil liberties and political rights. After 1939, using the excuse that the wartime situation justified it, the Nazi regime, especially its authorities in Prussia, moved confiscate Church buildings and facilities. A report from the Tenth Confessing Synod of the Church of the Old Prussian Union revealed that from the years 1941 to 1942, the government seized the rest home of Karlshof in East Prussia, the rest home of Kückenmühle in the Mecklenberg capital of Schwerin, and the headquarters of the Church Periodical Society in Berlin. Catholic and Protestant kindergartens, hospitals, and rest homes were popular targets of the regional Nazi authorities. Furthermore, the government demanded, and received, "voluntary donations" of 1,000,000 marks from the Protestant Church and 800,000 from the Catholic Church.[27]

The struggle continued between the German Christians and the Confessing Church regarding the Nazis' increasingly violent and ultimately genocidal policies towards the Jews of Europe, including the Jews of Germany. Following the national law of September 1 1941, which demanded the all Jews wear the Star of David in public, the Protestant churches in Mecklenberg and Sachsen, among others, declared that even Jews who had converted to Christianity could not count on the protection of the church. The declaration stated: "A German Protestant Church has to care for and further the religious life of German fellow countrymen; racial Jewish Christians have no place or rights in it."[28] The Confessing Church leaders, of course, rejected this as contrary to the very core of Christian belief, Bishops Theophil Wurm and Otto Dibelius were particularly outspoken in this regard.[29]

Although the leadership of the Catholic Church was broadly supportive of the war effort, at least during the early period of the conflict, the Catholic bishops tried to draw a sharp distinction between praying for Germany's soldiers and its civilians and praying for its *Fuehrer* and the regime he led. Emblematic of this was Bishop of Münster August von Galen's rather ambiguous remarks in 1941:

> Bravely we continue to fight against the foreign foe; against the enemy in our midst who tortures and strikes us we cannot fight with weapons. There is but one means available to us in this struggle: strong, obstinate, enduring perseverance.[30]

Much like the Protestant Church, the Catholic Church also experienced the seizure of Church property, especially kindergartens, rest homes, hospitals, and monasteries. As relations between Berlin and the Vatican continued to sour over the Nazis' brutal wars against Catholic France and Poland as well as numerous violations of the Concordat in Germany, the regime also began making preparations for a final reckoning with the Catholic Church that would occur as soon as the war had reached a successful conclusion. This occurred at the very latest by the spring of 1940. Himmler's deputy, the SD leader Reinhard Heydrich noted in a report sent to Alfred Rosenberg that certain Catholic clerical leaders were becoming dangerously outspoken against the Nazi regime. Heydrich specifically noted Bishop Galen of Münster, Cardinal Faulhaber of Munich, and Bishop Konrad von Preysing of Berlin as particularly threatening opponents.[31] In the meantime, the regime continued to place barriers in the path of Catholic charitable work, such as preventing it from offering religious services for Polish slave laborers who had been deported to Germany, done over the protests of Von Preysing and Von Galen.[32]

The end of the war not only brought the fall of the Nazi regime but also the complete eclipse of the German Christian movement, at least regarding its attempts to lead the Protestant Church. It was left to the leadership of the Confessing Church that would try to direct the Church in the postwar Germany under Allied occupation. Both the Catholic and the Protestant churches were in a unique position in May 1945, as among the few German institutions that had survived the war and the rule of the National Socialists. As such, they had become extremely important institutions for the Soviet and

Western Allies, especially since they promised to alleviate the material and spiritual devastation that was prevalent through all of Germany.[33] Many of the churches leaders had either tacitly or openly supported Hitler's regime, but others had shown great courage in resisting the Nazi dictatorship. This mixed record would be replicated during the history of the Soviet occupation.

Under both the Nazis and the Communists, there was no one, uniform policy on the part of the churches in their relations with the totalitarian authorities. Regarding the Protestant Church, the leadership was deeply divided on the question of how much compromise and how much resistance should be offered to the state authorities. Except in a few rare exceptions, when opposition to the political authorities from church leaders did emerge, it concerned specific policies and did not attempt to directly challenge the legitimacy of the state.

There was a general consensus among the clerical leadership, particularly individuals such as Otto Dibelius, not to allow the church's theology and liturgy to be contaminated by the ideology of the regime. There is, of course, the considerable exception of the German Christian movement, which would have its equivalent in the Soviet occupation zone, the League of Religious Socialists, led by Berlin pastor Kurt Rackwitz. The experience of the German churches under the Nazis and the Communists was not one merely of spineless cowardice or courageous heroism. There was, and would be, a great deal of both.

Likewise, the Nazi authorities, like the SVAG and SED authorities who followed them, did not embark on policies designed to immediately and permanently suppress religious institutions, preferring instead to vary between attempts at co-opting the churches and restricting the roles they could play in political and social life in Germany. In that sense, the Protestant and Catholic churches in Germany did not face the same challenge as the Orthodox Church in the Soviet Union before the Second World War or the Greek Catholic Church afterwards, when the Communist regime made unrelenting attempts to destroy them entirely on an institutional basis.

Although the Nazi regime would try to recreate the Protestant Church along the lines of National Socialist ideology by supporting the German Christian movement, this should not be seen as a recognition of religious institutions by Hitler's regime as having a legitimate place in the Germany it hoped to create. Just as the Communists after them, the Nazis hoped to gain the collaboration of Protestant and to a lesser extent Catholic clergy who shared elements of their ideology to aid in minimizing the churches' capacity to resist them. Both Adolf Hitler and Walter Ulbricht believed that, once their government's primary political social goals had been achieved, the regime would turn on the churches, first suppressing their administrative independence, and then ultimately destroying them entirely. National Socialism and Communism were alike in that they tolerated no spiritual rivals for the allegiance of German hearts and minds.

Notes

1. Shelley Baranowski "Consent and Dissent: The Confessing Church and Conservative Opposition to National Socialism" *The Journal of Modern History*. Volume 59, No. 1, March 1987, 53–78. 57.

2. Doris Bergen, *Twisted Cross: The German Christian Movement in the Third Reich*. Chapel Hill: The University of North Carolina Press, 1996. 22.

3. Matthew Hockenos, *A Church Divided: German Protestants Confront the Nazi Past*. Bloomington: Indiana University Press, 2004. 18. Prussia as an administrative unit was formerly dissolved by four-power Allied decree in 1947, its territory that did not become part of Poland or the Soviet Union was thereafter referred to as Berlin-Brandenburg.

4. Hockenos, 29. The Barmen declaration was written by Karl Barth, while Martin Niemöller wrote the Dahlem declaration.

5. Ibid., 35.

6. Baranowski, 73. Niemöller would be released at the end of the war, while Bonhoeffer was executed shortly before the fall of the Nazi regime.

7. Conway, 212.

8. Beth Griech-Polelle, "Image of a Churchman-Resister: Bishop von Galen, the Euthanasia Project and the Sermons of Summer 1941" *Journal of Contemporary History*. Volume 36, Number 1, Jan 2001. 41–57. 41.

9. Hockenos, 33.

10. Conway, 231. The division among the Protestant Church leadership concerning how to approach the new dictatorial authority and the tendency to resist the certain egregious policies would be repeated under the Communists after 1945.

11. Michael Burleigh, *Sacred Causes: The Clash of Religion and Politics from the Great War to the War on Terror*. New York: Harper Collins Publishers, 2007. 170.

12. Conway, 61.

13. Burleigh, 171. In the case of Brüning, it can be argued his role in the rise of the Nazis was accidental, it the case of von Papen, it was far more deliberate.

14. Burleigh, 175.

15. Ibid., 176.

16. Conway, 61. The decision by the Catholic Trade Federation to dissolve itself was enormously unpopular with certain leaders who later became active in the CDU in the Soviet zone, such as Jakob Kaiser.

17. Conway, 69.

18. Burleigh, 177.

19. Conway, 270. While it would be inaccurate to say clerical opponents of the regime such as Konrad von Preysing, Otto Dibelius, or Martin Niemöller never mentioned the monstrous persecution of Europe's Jews by the Nazis, it was not the most frequent issue of contention between themselves and Hitler's government.

20. Burleigh, 181. This is not to say either Church was able to continue its charitable work entirely free from the interference of the Nazi regime, particularly the SD and the Gestapo.

21. Conway, 177. Prussia, of course, would later compose much of the Soviet occupation zone, particularly the provinces of Berlin-Brandenburg and Mecklenburg, although the state of Prussia itself was formally dissolved in 1947.

22. Ibid., 178.

23. Ibid.

24. Ibid., 180.

25. Ibid., 185.

26. Ibid., 191. Alfred Rosenberg drew up plans for these exact policies in the summer of 1941, when German victory over the Soviet Union, and thus permanent domination of Europe, appeared assured.

27. Helmreich, 323.

28. Helmreich, 329.

29. Ibid., 330.

30. Ibid., 347.

31. Ibid., 347.

32. Ibid., 355. Ultimately, the Ministry of Church Affairs relented in September 1942 and allowed one religious service per month for Polish laborers, although the use of Polish in the services was to be sharply limited.

33. Hockenos, 38.

Chapter Two

The Question of the CDU and the Churches during the Period of the "Antifascist Transformation," 1945–1947

INTRODUCTION

Throughout the history of the Soviet zone of Germany, no issue involving the churches, and the Communist authorities proved to be more divisive than the relationship between the churches and the Christian Democratic Union (CDU). For most officials in the SVAG and the SED, the churches and the CDU represented the least progressive elements of German society, mired in antiquated convictions, who would stop at nothing to undermine each and every attempt made at creating a socialist, antifascist Germany. Furthermore, they would do so with the active assistance of hostile foreign powers and "reactionaries" within the western occupation zones of Germany.

These perceptions of both the churches and the CDU also affected the SVAG's and the SED's understanding of the relationship between them. Soviet and German authorities in the Soviet zone had little doubt that the shared reactionary views of all three organizations meant that political collaboration between the churches and the CDU was a certainty. This collaboration was designed to attack the policies implemented by the SVAG and their allies in the SED with the intention to prevent the emergence of an antifascist German state built on the Soviet model.[1]

Nearly every work concerning the process of the transformation of the Soviet zone of Germany into a Stalinist German state, such as those by Naimark, Pike, Hubertus Knabe, and Gary Bruce, mention the destruction of the political independence of the CDU as a part of the gradual political and ideological *Gleichstaltung* that the SVAG accelerated in 1947 and had nearly completed by the time of Berlin Blockade in June 1948. However, with the exception of Gary Bruce's recent work, *Resistance with the People: Repression and Resistance in Eastern Germany 1945–1955*, none of the them discuss in any great detail the activities of the CDU in the Soviet zone and its attempt to provide a viable alternative to the Soviet-style socialism advocated by the SED. Even Bruce does not examine the relationship between the CDU and the Catholic and Protestant churches, despite the fact that the CDU was allowed to emerge by the Soviet authorities to represent religious Germans in the political process. The next two chapters of this study examine this neglected issue. Only by understanding the connection between the CDU and the churches, both in reality and how it was perceived by SVAG and SED authorities, can Soviet policies towards the CDU be properly understood, especially the decision to remove its influential second chairman, Jakob Kaiser in December 1947.[2]

The main branch of the SVAG that dealt with religious questions, which included the question of the relationship between the CDU and the churches, was Colonel Sergei Tiul'panov's Propaganda Administration (later renamed the Information Administration in January 1947). In January 1946 A. A. Sobolev, the assistant to the head of the Political Council of SVAG, Vladimir Semenov, suggested to the supreme commander of SVAG, Marshal Georgii Zhukov, to create of separate branch of the Soviet military government to deal exclusively with religious affairs. Sobolev claimed that this was necessary due to the diversity of religious issues in the Soviet zone and their political importance.[3] His advice was not followed, likely due to Tiul'panov's preference to deal with religious issues through the Propaganda Administration. Consequently Tiul'panov and his religious affairs deputy Lieutenant Colonel Vsevolod Ermolaev exercised the largest influence on SVAG's religious policies, only rarely coming into conflict with other authorities in the SVAG apparatus regarding their decisions.

The churches and the CDU in the Soviet zone did maintain a close and occasionally collaborative relationship, especially during the first three years of the occupation. The number of shared concerns between the zonal and provincial leadership of the churches and the CDU, such as the return to prominence of Christian religious belief within German culture, the continuation of religious education in the school system, administering charitable aid to the refuges expelled from Poland and Czechoslovakia, clear limits on land reform, and a shared conviction to resist the re-emergence of one-party rule in Germany, guaranteed this. At the highest levels of the church and CDU leadership during the tenure of the CDU's first two leaders in the Soviet zone, Andreas Hermes (June 1945–December 1945) and Jakob Kaiser (December 1945–December 1947), there was a common desire to work towards these goals.

Active collaboration for clearly defined political goals between the CDU and the churches was never as extensive as the SVAG and SED authorities alleged both in their internal communications and their public pronouncements. There were four important reasons for this. The first resulted from the decision of both the leadership of the CDU and the churches to generally pursue a cautious policy during the first few years of the occupation that attempted to avoid open confrontation with either the SVAG or the SED. The second was the decision of the Protestant and Catholic churches to openly proclaim political neutrality between the parties within the Soviet Zone. The third was CDU leader Jakob Kaiser's attempt to introduce "Christian Socialism" as the guiding ideology of the CDU in February 1946, which aimed to make the party more than one that merely represented the interests of religious Germans in the Soviet Zone. The fourth was the CDU's pursuit of a policy of greater collaboration with the SVAG and the SED from January 1948 to October 1949 following the removal of Kaiser on the orders of the SVAG in December 1947 and his replacement with Otto Nuschke.

While public and private cooperation between the CDU and the churches did exist during the Soviet occupation, it was cautious, limited, and generally failed to reach the objectives sought by both groups. In fact, they usually pursued their own interests independently. Perhaps the strongest example occurred during the early period of the occupation, when the CDU under the leadership of Andreas Hermes and Jakob Kaiser proved to be among the most vocal of critics of the actions of the SVAG and the SED, while the churches proved to be quite cautious in their rhetoric and actions. After the removal of Kaiser in December 1947 and his replacement with the more compliant Otto Nuschke, the Protestant and Catholic churches, especially leaders such as Otto Dibelius and Konrad von Preysing, became publicly critical of what they saw as the creation of a new totalitarian order in the Soviet zone.

THE ESTABLISHMENT OF THE ANTIFASCIST POLITICAL PARTIES AND FIRST CONFLICTS WITH THE CDU LEADERSHIP JUNE 1945–DECEMBER 1945

SVAG general order number two, issued by its Supreme Commander Marshal Georgii Zhukov on June 10, 1945, permitted the establishment of antifascist political parties and "mass organizations."[4] While the German Communist Party (*Kommunistische Partei Deutschlands* or KPD) formally proclaimed its existence the next day, the CDU did not issue its founding proclamation until June 26, Dr. Andreas Hermes was appointed as its chairman and Dr. Walter Schraiber as vice-chairman. Among other prominent members were future leaders Jakob Kaiser and Otto Nuschke. The CDU in the Soviet zone was founded before the CDU in the Western zones, which did not occur for a few months later. Historians have continually debated why the SVAG authorities allowed the CDU and the other bourgeois party, the LDP (*Liberale-Demokratische Partei*) to emerge in the Soviet zone. The most likely explanation, proposed by Gary Bruce, was that the Soviets desired to endear themselves to the entire population of their zone in order to have the broadest possible social base for their policies. Bourgeois parties, just like the working class parties of the SPD and KPD, would eventually be relied upon to support SVAG goals and to head off middle class discontent to the creation of a German state on the Soviet model.[5]

The CDU in the Soviet zone maintained a loose unity with the CDU in the Western zones, as the leadership of the both parties pledged to work together to maintain German unity and support the reconstruction of democracy. Numerous joint conferences were held between CDU leaders in the Western zones to create a unified ideology for the Western and Eastern CDUs. Yet this relationship was rather testy during Jakob Kaiser's tenure as head of the CDU in the Soviet zone, as the Western CDU leader Konrad Adenauer rejected Kaiser's ideology of Germany serving as bridge between East and West, belonging to neither, as Adenauer firmly supported a German state firmly entrenched with the rest of Western Europe. Following Kaiser's removal as CDU leader by the SVAG in December 1947 and his replacement with Otto Nuschke, any cooperation between the two CDUs was dropped as Nuschke denounced Adenauer as a reactionary working with the Americans and British to undermine German unity.[6]

A Catholic, Hermes had served as a former Reichsminister for Agriculture and had been a member of the Center party before 1933. Implicated in the July 20 assassination plot against Hitler, Hermes had been arrested by the Gestapo and sentenced to death but Hermes's wife continually worked to delay his execution. Liberated from the prison in Berlin-Moabit by Soviet authorities in May, Hermes was appointed to head the Food Office in Berlin.[7] KPD leader Walter Ulbricht had pushed for Hermes's appointment believing that he could be easily manipulated, even going so far as to secure ration cards for his wife and obtaining a new home for the couple to live in.[8]

Also appointed to serve in the Food office was Jakob Kaiser, also a Catholic, former member of the Center party. Active in the Catholic Trade Union movement from 1912 to 1933, Kaiser was also implicated in the assassination plot against Hitler and survived only by hiding in a friend's house in Babelsberg until the end of the war.[9] The other signatories of the CDU's founding proclamation were Walter Schraiber, Ernst Lemmer, and Otto Nuschke, all members of the Protestant Church, and veterans of either the Center Party or

German Democratic Party before 1933, although none could point to anti-Nazi credentials as could Hermes and Kaiser.[10]

The founding proclamation of the CDU promised a limited commitment to land reform and the nationalization of key industries which dealt with raw materials. It emphasized support for private property, the rule of law, cooperation with the other antifascist parties in rebuilding German democracy, and a commitment to restoring religious freedom.[11] On July 14, the CDU joined the four other legal political parties in the Soviet zone, the KPD, SPD (*Sozial-Demokratische Partei Deutschlands*) and LDP to form the *Einheitsfront der antifaschistich-demokratischen Parteien* or the united front of antifascist democratic Parties, commonly known as the antifascist-block. The leaders of all four parties pledged their devotion to a common front at local, provincial, and zonal levels to create an antifascist German democracy and rebuild from the ravages of Nazism.[12]

In a speech given in Berlin to assembled party members on July 27, Hermes focused on the themes of the CDU's founding declaration, and promised the CDU's commitment to cooperate with the antifascist-block. He also announced an intention to work with both the Catholic and Protestant churches to restore Christianity to the center of Germany's culture, as it had been perilously discarded during the Weimar and Nazi eras.[13] Hermes stated the CDU could only complete its work through the combined strength of all Christian forces in Germany. Yet he also emphasized the CDU membership was open to all religious believers as well as non-believers and that the party had no theocratic intentions for a future German state.[14]

Political pamphlets and flyers designed by the CDU in June and July of 1945 continued the same message, promising the CDU could most effectively unite the "Christian, Democratic, and Social strength of the German people" in creating a new German democracy rooted in the rule of law and Christian belief, while also safeguarding the free exercise of religion of all German citizens and protecting the church's special role in charitable and educational work. None of these political advertisements solely talked about religious concerns. The protection of private property and the return of German POWs were also popular themes.[15]

The self-identification of the CDU with religious Germans, if not specifically with the churches themselves, was also prominent in the CDU party newspaper, *Neue Zeit*, which began publishing in August 1945. Under the editorial direction of Otto Nuschke, the newspaper frequently discussed religious topics as well as restating the CDU's commitment to preserving religious freedom. On September 6, an article appeared entitled "Der evangelische Christ in der Union" (The Protestant Christian in the Union) that emphasized the CDU was substantially different from the Center party during the Weimar era. It represented both German Catholics and Protestants and was committed to protecting their religious freedom.[16] Another article from September 14, by a Protestant minister from Berlin named F. Bucholz, promised that out of the destruction of the Second World War, a new era of religious revivalism would sweep through Europe, including Germany. Both German Catholics and Protestants would participate in this revival.[17]

Neue Zeit continually published articles throughout the summer and fall of 1945 concerning the formation of the new Protestant Church federation in the Soviet and Western zones, the Evangelische Kirche Deutschlands (EKD) as well as stories concerning the relations between the Catholic churches in Germany and the Vatican. The September 4 edition of *Neue Zeit* discussed in detail on page one both the conference of Protestant bishops in Treysa from August 28 to September 1 and the conference of Catholic bishops in Fulda from August 21 to August 24.[18] In keeping with the CDU's determination to revive Christianity's central presence in German culture, *Neue Zeit* published numerous articles which emphasized the common links between German artists and their Christian religious beliefs. An article on November 15 examined numerous German painters who used their artwork to demonstrate religious themes.[19] As the year progressed the CDU newspaper published a number of articles pointing to the resistance of individual Protestant and Catholic clergymen to Nazism, which demonstrated the churches' ability to assist in the task of rebuilding an antifascist, democratic Germany.[20]

This is not to say the primary focus of the CDU party newspaper was religious issues. The majority of articles in *Neue Zeit* focused on the political and economic issues of the day, with particular attention to relations between the four victorious allies and the status of refugees from East Prussia and Silesia as well as the fate of POWs held in the Soviet Union. Front-page articles focusing on religious concerns were the exception rather than the rule, and the majority of issues of the newspaper did not mention religious issues at all during the first six months of *Neue Zeit*'s publication. Nevertheless, during the first six months of the Soviet occupation the CDU clearly attempted to appeal to all religious Germans in the Soviet Zone, while at same avoiding identification solely with religious issues. Hermes and the remainder of the executive leadership of the CDU were convinced that the party could not be a viable political force unless it moved beyond confessional politics, although it would not be until Jakob Kaiser's leadership that the party moved more definitively in this direction.

Neither the SED nor the SVAG planned to let the CDU stake out a position as the sole voice for religious Germans in the Soviet zone. The SED's predecessor, the KPD, was rather slow in staking out a position on the religious question in its party newspaper, *Deutsche Volkszeitung*. This was especially important due to the official recognition of the legal right to religious freedom by the KPD in its exile conferences in Bern and Brussels during the Nazi era as well as the guarantee of religious freedom in a future German state by the Soviet-sponsored National Committee for a Free Germany during the Second World War. Many KPD members in Soviet exile, such as Wilhelm Pieck and Walter Ulbricht, who would later lead the Socialist Unity Party, were prominent leaders in this movement.[21]

The first issue of *Deutsche Volkszeitung* which mentioned religious issues was June 23 1945. It contained an article that mentioned the need to create entirely secular "unity" schools free from confessional divides as well as chauvinistic and militarist propaganda.[22] The first issue that discussed religious issues in greater depth was on July 31. The article concerning religious affairs was dedicated entirely to attacking statements made by the Catholic Archbishop of Munich Cardinal von Faulhaber, who rejected the notion of collective German guilt for the crimes of Nazism. The article claimed Faulhaber's opinions had to be rejected by all Germans if they hoped to make a genuine transition to democracy.[23]

The only religious theme that occurred regularly in the pages of *Deutsche Volkszeitung* in 1945 was in relation to the issue of educational reforms, specifically the need to secularize the curriculum of the newly reformed educational system in the Soviet zone. Such stories criticized the opposition of those in the CDU or the Catholic and Protestant churches who continued to push for the inclusion of religious education in the schools. Pieck and SPD leader Otto Grotewohl issued a joint statement in the October 27 issue of *Deutsche Volkszeitung*, which called for a clear break between the churches and the educational system in order to serve the democratic unity of Germany.[24]

The official newspaper of the Soviet military government, *Tägliche Rundschau* (Daily View), was far more ambitious in attempting to draw religious Germans away from the CDU to identify with Soviet-style socialism, especially during the early period of the occupation. One of the first issues of the newspaper contained an article which detailed how the Red Army worked to reopen the churches of St. Gotthardt and St. Katharinen within the city of Brandenburg, noting that they were now open for services for the first time since the end of the war.[25]

Another example comes from the June 12 issue, in an article entitled "Die Kirche: Heute and Morgen" (The Church: Today and Tomorrow) by a Catholic priest named Karl Fischer, from the province of Mecklenburg. It mentioned that while the Nazis certainly planned to eradicate religious institutions and religious belief throughout all of Germany, the Soviets had no such intentions. Since the occupation began, they had not engaged in a campaign of closing churches and imprisoning clergymen, contrary to what the Nazis had warned. Fischer wrote that all the Soviets desired was that the German Protestant churches purge themselves of the influence of the "German Christians." They also desired that the Evangelical Church join with the Catholic churches in creating an antifascist, democratic order throughout Germany.[26]

During this early phase of the occupation, *Tägliche Rundschau* reported on developments within the CDU in the Soviet zone without editorializing on its ideology or its members, reporting on the formation of the CDU on June 26 and the formation of the antifascist block on July 24, with Andreas Hermes, Walter Schraiber, and Jakob Kaiser as the CDU representatives at the zonal level.[27] This soon ended with an article published on September 27 attacking CDU member Emil Dovifat, who had criticized the formation of the antifascist block. The unnamed author claimed that Dovifat, who continued to teach journalism at the University of Berlin for a few years after the Nazis came to power, demonstrated his Nazi sympathies with his attempt to undermine the antifascist block. The author concluded that he could only hope that the other members of the CDU, especially its leaders, did not share Dovifat's opinions.[28]

These articles would proved to be only the tip of the iceberg in what became a broad propaganda offensive by the SVAG through its Information Administration and *Tägliche Rundschau* to prove to the German people that the Soviet government was no enemy to religious institutions and its ideology no threat to religious belief. The SVAG publicly attempted to prevent the CDU from gaining the support of religious Germans in through its official German-language newspaper. Following the legalization of antifascist parties in the Soviet zone it quickly began an ambitious effort to monitor and occasionally prevent extensive cooperation between the Catholic and Protestant churches and the CDU, especially between the "reactionary" elements of all three institutions. This will be dealt with in greater detail in chapter seven.

The Propaganda/Information Administration, led by the influential Colonel Tiul'panov, headed this operation at the local, provincial, and zonal levels, but was not the sole actor within the SVAG in this process. Sergei Tiul'panov was a teacher of political economy at Leningrad State University before the war; afterwards, he served in the Seventh Section of the Main Political Administration of the Red Army. This particular section made use of Tiul'panov's fluent German and knowledge of German culture, as it was responsible for counter-propaganda among Wehrmacht soldiers and recruiting them for the National Committee for a Free Germany.[29] The KPD and SED also eventually became involved in this process, especially during the later years of the occupation.

In an early report dated July 29 1945, from the Assistant to the Political Council of the Supreme Commander of SVAG, I. I. Filippov, to a Full Member of the Political Council of the USSR, Andrei Vyshinsky, illustrates this point. Filippov wrote the SVAG authorities at all levels of the Soviet zone should exercise greater control over the activities of the CDU, as it had already developed a significant following from diverse groups among the German population, such as the young, women, and devoutly religious Germans. Filippov recommended the SVAG authorities limit the number of rallies that the CDU could hold, and to only permit them if they were informed in advance of the speakers and the topics on which they would speak.[30]

A later report sent to Colonel Sergei Tiul'panov by his chief religious affairs deputy within the SVAG's Information, Lieutenant Colonel Vsevolod Ermolaev, provides further evidence of the Soviet authorities intentions towards "political" activities by the churches. Ermolaev wrote the goal of the SVAG's Information Administration from mid-1945 onwards had been to work towards the political neutrality of both the Protestant and Catholic churches in the Soviet zone. At the same time it assisted the "progressive" elements in the churches to aid the anti-fascist democratic transformation of Germany. Authorities at all levels of the Information Administration actively pursued this policy.[31] The report also mentioned the Information Administration wanted at the early stages of the occupation to prevent active cooperation between the CDU and the churches, although this did not become a major concern until the zonal elections in the fall of 1946.[32]

Throughout the first six months of the occupation, the provincial and local authorities in the SVAG's Propaganda Administration showed a growing concern about the relationship between the churches and the CDU, claiming that it was increasing in strength and providing a focal point for political reactionaries throughout the Soviet zone. They were considerably less active in suggesting policies to prevent the growth of this relationship.

An October 15, 1945, report concerning political conditions sent to Tiul'panov from his chief of the Propaganda Administration in the province of Brandenburg Lieutenant Colonel I. I. Mil'khiker, mentioned that throughout the cities of Brandenburg, the CDU and prominent clergy and laity within both the Evangelical and Catholic churches were drawn together due to shared "reactionary" sentiments, especially their dislike of the SVAG and their rivals in the KPD and the SPD.[33] At the end of the year, Mil'khiker reported to Tiul'panov both the churches and the CDU had become bastions of reactionary strength within the Soviet zone. He warned this would continue for some time, although they would eventually lose the support of the German population as the democratic transformation continued.[34]

The fact that officials in the SVAG's Propaganda Administration were so quick to find "reactionaries" in the ranks of both the churches and the CDU meant that they were certain to view them as implacable enemies to the SVAG plans to implement Soviet-style socialism in the Soviet Zone. The inability of the officials in the SVAG to take any measurable steps to resolve this problem does not point to a lack of will or strength on the part of the Soviet authorities. Rather, it is emblematic of the cautious SVAG policies of the first eighteen months of the occupation. The SVAG did not want to risk closing off a chance to influence political developments in the Western zones by immediately introducing a Stalinist political and economic order in the Soviet zone. Once the process towards the transformation of the Soviet Zone accelerated in 1947, the Soviet authorities did not hesitate to take steps to limit political cooperation between the CDU and the churches.

The leaders of the KPD also expressed concern about the relationship between the CDU and the churches, but like the authorities within the SVAG, they did not propose extensive solutions to combat it. The issue of collaboration between the CDU and the churches was raised infrequently in the private correspondence of future SED leaders Wilhelm Pieck, Walter Ulbricht, or Otto Grotewohl. Pieck and Ulbricht did receive reports from KPD functionaries in the German PVs who complained about the unity of the CDU and the churches on certain issues. An example of this is a report received by Pieck from the head of the Berlin *Abteilung Volksbildung* (Department of the People's Education), Otto Winzer, dated October 27. Winzer noted that both Protestant and Catholic clergy as well as members of the CDU made unfavorable comparisons between the similarities of the education policies proposed by the SVAG and those made by the Nazi regime. This occurred after the SVAG's Department of the People's Education and its German equivalent had announced plans to secularize the education system at the beginning of October.[35]

Reports like these proved to be the exception rather than the rule. Neither the SVAG nor the KPD according to their official records appeared overly concerned with the prospect of an alliance between the CDU and the churches during the chaotic first few months of the Soviet occupation. There were, however, early clashes during the fall of 1945 between the SVAG and the KPD and the churches and CDU concerning the question of religious education within the new primary and secondary schools for German children, which will be examined in greater detail in chapter four. The political ramifications of collaboration between the CDU and the churches only became a more prominent concern for both the SVAG and the KPD as the zonal elections approached in the fall of 1946.

The reason that neither the SVAG nor the KPD noticed extensive collaboration between the CDU and the Protestant and Catholic churches was that throughout most of 1945 the leaders of all three institutions had not sought out an open or secret alliance that would jointly govern their activities. Neither Cardinal Konrad von Preysing nor Bishop Otto Dibelius, the respective heads of the Catholic and Protestant churches in Berlin-Brandenburg, made entreaties upon the CDU to intercede for them with the Soviet authorities. They preferred to do these themselves. Konrad von Preysing wrote to the Supreme Commander of SVAG Marshal Zhukov on numerous occasions in the later summer and early fall of 1945, asking him to redress such grievances as SVAG travel restrictions placed on priests traveling to or from parishes who resided in different provinces.[36] Throughout the four-year occupation Preysing rarely met with Tiul'panov or his religious affairs deputy Ermolaev, and these meetings generally were brief, curt and inconclusive, as Preysing raised concerns about the educational reforms in German schools, charitable work and the restoration of church property. In response, Tiul'panov and Ermolaev made non-committal promises to look into matters.[37]

Dibelius and his staff in the Protestant Church Chancellery also wrote to the Soviet authorities on numerous occasions throughout the occupation, although they usually appealed to the SVAG's Information administration as opposed to its supreme commanders. Throughout most of 1945 the principal concern of the Protestant Church was creating a new organizational structure for all Protestant churches in Germany, the Evangelische Kirche Deutschlands (EKD), and to a lesser extent, purging German Christian clerics from the church administration. Appeals written in 1945 were far less in number than those in the following years, although the topics they focused on were generally the same: assistance with alleviating the refugee crisis, freedom to continue charitable activities, restoration of church property, release of German POWs, and ending restrictions on religious education.[38]

Just as the Catholic and Protestant churches had shown little interest in depending on the CDU to be its spokesman to the Soviet authorities, the CDU in the Soviet zone under Andreas Hermes avoided tying its entire identity to religious issues. In a speech given to CDU party leaders representing the entire Soviet zone on September 28 1945, Hermes noted that any potential member of the CDU could be Catholic, Protestant or Jewish, or of no religious persuasion at all, as long as they ascribed to the CDU's dedication to the rule of law and to harmony along class and religious lines.[39] One month later, Hermes wrote an article in *Neue Zeit* informing members of Germany's surviving Jewish community that membership in the CDU was open to them as well. They should not be dissuaded from joining because of the use of the word "Christian" in the party's name as the CDU did not have any theocratic intentions. Hermes also admitted in the article that while many members of Germany's Christian community had not done enough to assist the German Jews, the CDU would work for improved understanding between the two groups.[40]

Hermes's tenure as the first leader of the CDU in Soviet zone was destined to be short-lived. He clashed repeatedly with the SPD, KPD and the SVAG authorities over the issue of land reform (*Bodenreform*), especially what Hermes viewed as the politicized methods by which it was implemented. This ultimately led to his removal as head of the CDU under the orders of the SVAG's Propaganda Administration in December 1945 and his replacement with Jakob Kaiser. The CDU under Hermes's leadership was far more vocally resistant to the land reforms than the leadership either of the Protestant and Catholic churches, despite numerous misgivings expressed through their private correspondence. Neither the CDU leadership nor that of the churches opposed the concept of land reform in principle, but they objected to the often brutal methods used to implement it by the SVAG and the German PVs. They also opposed the political, as opposed to economic goals that land reform was intended to accomplish.[41]

While land reform occurred in all four occupation zones of Germany, nowhere was it a more visible or important process than in the Soviet zone due to the extensive number of large land estates within the zone and the openly social and political goals behind it. For both the SVAG and the KPD, land reform was of paramount importance for their long-term goals of creating the proper social and economic conditions for the later-imposition of socialism on the Soviet model. Under KPD chairman Wilhelm Pieck's famous slogan: "*Junkerland in Bauernhand*" (The Junker's land in the farmers' hands), the KPD party members in the German PVs worked actively with the SVAG authorities within the agricultural departments to expropriate landed estates with over 100 hectares of land. They expropriated over 8,000 estates in all. Another 4,000 of smaller size were similarly treated under the guise of seizing the property of Nazis and other war criminals.[42] *Tägliche Rundschau* and *Deutsche Volkszeitung* printed numerous articles attesting to the benefits that land reform would bring to the German people, especially the breaking of economic the arch-reactionary Junkers, who had led Germany down the path of disaster on numerous occasions.[43]

This had very little to do with settling accounts with the Junkers. Nearly all those who had not already fled to what became the Western zones of occupation had been driven off their estates and in some cases murdered outright. Only in the eastern regions of Brandenburg and in much of Mecklenburg were the remaining Junkers affected by the land reform. Nor did the land reform assist the "new farmers" of the Soviet zone, which included many former Wehrmacht soldiers and ethnic German refugees expelled from Poland and Czechoslovakia. They generally had enough land but lacked proper equipment, farm animals, seed, or any experience working in large-scale farming. Land reform did help to drive out the remainder of the upper and upper-middle class landowners, whom the SVAG and the KPD viewed as among the forefront of social, economic, and political reaction. Many had no Nazi ties but often had their land seized regardless, and nearly always without compensation.[44]

The reaction of the Catholic and Protestant Church leadership to these events was quite reserved, especially since both churches' sizeable land holdings were largely exempted from the process, in yet another example of general restraint exercised by the SVAG in their religious policies during the first years of the occupation. Many religious leaders privately disapproved of the process, especially as it seemed to sweep up Nazis and non-Nazis alike. Preysing expressed his sharp disapproval of land reform, and the political goals behind it, in a letter to the commander of the American zone, General Lucius Clay, in July 1946.[45] Otto Dibelius also expressed his misgivings in private correspondence towards the end of the Soviet occupation, stating that the land reform pursued by the Soviet authorities and their German allies was primarily political in nature, and subsequently failed to alleviate the pressing economic problems in the Soviet zone and to help German farmers recover from the effects of the war.[46] Other prominent clergymen, such as the Evangelical bishops of Mecklenburg and Thuringia, Wilhelm Beste and Moritz Mitzenheim, voiced their unreserved support for the land reform measures, believing it to be an essential economic measure to support the reconstruction of German democracy.[47]

The issue was not an important one among the internal discussion of the Protestant Church leadership in the Soviet zone. The records from their meetings on September 25 and November 27, while mentioning the need for creating a new organizational structure for the church, as well as dealing with the problems of the restoration of church buildings and considerable refugee crisis, the controversy over land reform was hardly discussed.[48] This lack of attention to this issue is representative of the initial decision made by the leadership of the Protestant Church to stay out of political developments in the Soviet Zone, as it hoped to avoid conflict with the Soviet authorities while the church continued to reform its internal administrative structure and struggled to come to terms with the legacy of Nazism.

The CDU leadership was also divided about what position to adopt towards the SVAG's land reform proposals. But the tactics of the land reform's implementation, especially the seizure of land from non-Nazis without compensation, left much of the leadership of the CDU in the Soviet zone deeply uncomfortable. No one in the senior leadership was more disturbed than Hermes, who saw land reform as directly counter to the CDU's goals of mediating class conflict in post-war Germany. Despite warnings from other party leaders such as Ferdinand Friedensburg that his open opposition could lead to trouble with the SVAG authorities, Hermes persisted in his vocal criticism of the implementation of land reform.[49]

When the KPD put forth their initial land reform proposal in late August, Hermes protested that landowners who were not involved with the Nazi party should receive compensation for their land if it had been seized, although he agreed that land reform was desirable in principle. He later voiced his concerns in a newspaper published in the American zone of occupation, the *Frankfurter Allgemeine Zeitung*, that the land reform should be implemented in the Soviet zone in such a manner that it would not affect Germany's economic unity. In an interview with *Tägliche Rundschau* on October 25, Hermes also expressed concern that the KPD was using its cooperation in the antifascist block to dominate certain policies, including land reform.[50]

Officials in the SVAG's Propaganda Administration viewed Hermes's defiance on the issue of land reform with serious concern. Following a meeting with a leader of the CDU in Brandenburg Wilhelm Wolf, I. I. Mil'khiker reported to Tiul'panov that the conversation with Wolf convinced him that Hermes was clearly a reactionary, as were his supporters in the CDU party organizations in Berlin and Brandenburg.[51] Of particular concern for the Propaganda Administration was Hermes's constant traveling to the other Allied sectors of Berlin and the other occupation zones of Germany to make public criticisms concerning political and economic developments in the Soviet zone. According to Tiul'panov's later reports to his superiors on the Central Committee of the Communist Party, the only option for the SVAG by December 1945 was to remove Hermes from his leadership position within the CDU in the Soviet zone, although he denied any involvement by the Soviet authorities in choosing Hermes's replacement as leader of the CDU.[52]

The central CDU leadership in Berlin often had no ability to convey its specific opposition to the KPD's and SVAG's plans for land reform to the regional party organizations, due to the fact that the telephone and telegraph system had not been repaired since the end of the war. This meant that an internal split regarding the land reform question emerged in the CDU, as the leadership of the CDU party organizations in Sachsen and Mecklenburg, two of the provinces most affected by the land redistribution, voiced criticism of Hermes's opposition to land reform. They claimed that that the CDU's support of land reform would help it gain the political support of the "new farmers." The leadership of the CDU in Sachsen even passed a resolution calling for Hermes's deputy Walter Schraiber to resign, as he was known to be even less enthusiastic about land reform than Hermes.[53] The KPD ratcheted up the pressure on Hermes by changing tactics in the pages of *Deutsche Volkszeitung*. Rather than attacking Hermes as a reactionary for opposing land reform, it emphasized the internal divisions within the CDU in the Soviet zone and suggested that this indicated that Hermes could not be a proper leader of the party.[54]

With Zhukov's approval Tiul'panov had Hermes and Schraiber removed from their leadership positions with the CDU in the Soviet zone. Tiul'panov met with both leaders and informed them, as he would inform Jakob Kaiser at a private meeting two years later, the SVAG would no longer legally allow "reactionaries" to lead an antifascist party in the Soviet zone.[55] In a report sent two and one-half years later to the Central Committee's International Department, Tiul'panov stated Hermes "collaboration" with the "Anglo-Americans" and his inability to control the extreme reactionaries within the party made his removal inevitable. Tiul'panov did not mention any close ties between Hermes and the leadership of the Protestant and Catholic churches as a pressing reason for his dismissal.[56]

In January 1946, Tiul'panov instructed Mil'khiker and the other regional heads of the SVAG's Propaganda Administration to work to minimize the influence of Hermes's former supporters and to covertly assist former opponents of Hermes to obtain leadership positions within the regional CDU party apparatus, as well as continue to work towards the isolation of the CDU in the antifascist block.[57] Clearly the letter Tiul'panov had received a week earlier from the new CDU leader in the Soviet zone, Jakob Kaiser, which promised that the CDU would strive for a better relationship with the SVAG authorities, did not have a great effect on him. Kaiser was elected as CDU chairman by the Executive Committee of the CDU despite his reluctance to take the position, which believed his background in the Catholic Trade Union movement would make him more acceptable to the SVAG authorities.[58]

Despite the fact that Hermes's removal clearly indicated that the SVAG authorities would not tolerate open political opposition, the response of both the Protestant and Catholic churches in Brandenburg was silence, as their leadership strove to avoid an openly confrontational approach to either the SVAG or its allies in the KPD. Dibelius and Preysing avoided any public statements with regards to political developments involving the antifascist parties, including being identified too closely with the CDU. This did not change perceptions of the churches by either the Soviet or SED authorities, who remained convinced that both religious institutions were inherently reactionary, despite any resistance to the Nazi regime they may have shown or any later expressions of limited culpability such as the Stuttgart declaration of the Evangelical bishops in October 1945.

THE EMERGENCE OF CHRISTIAN SOCIALISM UNDER JAKOB KAISER, JANUARY 1946–AUGUST 1946

Jakob Kaiser's two-year tenure as head of the CDU in the Soviet Zone brought the tense issue of the political relationship between the CDU and the Protestant and Catholic churches to the attention of all political actors in the Soviet zone, especially after Kaiser adopted "Christian Socialism" as the guiding ideology of the CDU. Kaiser, whose political hero was the anti-Nazi mayor of Leipzig, Carl Gordeler, had stated shortly after the end of the war that "the era of bourgeois dominion is over." In describing his experience in the anti-Nazi movement in Germany, he noted that "we were all convinced that the future of the German people would be largely determined by socialist ideas." Kaiser moved the CDU towards a socialist direction, and away from the direction favored by the leader of the CDU in the Western zones, Konrad Adenauer, which was decidedly friendlier to free market capitalism.[59]

Kaiser's eventual proclamation of Christian Socialism aimed to move the CDU away from identification as a political party that focused on religious issues and appealed to religious Germans in the Soviet zone. Yet he insisted Christian religious institutions would continue to play a visible role in the public, educational, and cultural life of the Soviet zone. He held the CDU should not abandon its duty to address the concerns of religious Germans.

The political independence of the CDU in the Soviet Zone was always strictly limited. The SVAG repeatedly demonstrated a willingness to remove leaders of the CDU in the Soviet zone when they became too critical of SVAG and SED policies. The expulsion of Hermes in December 1945 and of Kaiser two years later demonstrates this beyond any doubt. Despite his likely awareness of the limited tolerance of the Soviet authorities, Kaiser continued to push the CDU along an independent political path that rejected both identification solely with religious issues and also a dedication to the Soviet model articulated by the SED. His hope was that Christian Socialism was would enable the CDU to do this exactly this.

On February 14 1946, Kaiser revealed his concept of Christian Socialism for the first time in the pages of *Neue Zeit*.[60] Kaiser stated the CDU rejected both the doctrine of class struggle and the need to create a party-based dictatorship. Rather, it wished to create a new German state dedicated to the rule of law and preservation of basic civil liberties. While

Christian Socialists, much like the Social Democrats under the leadership of Kurt Schumacher in the Western zones, supported the nationalization of key industries relating to living standards, such as public utilities, coal, and steel production, they rejected a centrally planned economy. The CDU under Kaiser called for a mix of the Western and Eastern economic models, so as not to create a disparity between the economic reforms in the Soviet zone as compared to the Western zones of Germany. Thus, this doctrine of "Christian Socialism and Unity" argued Kaiser could lift Germany out of the ravages of war and lead it to economic and political recovery. Christian Socialism would ultimately make Germany, in Kaiser's words, an economic and political bridge between East and West, adapting aspects of the political and economic structure of both models, yet conforming to neither. Looking at the text of the article, the Western political, cultural, and even economic model looms far larger than the Soviet; the bridge to be constructed by the Christian Socialists had far stronger foundations on its Western side.[61]

Kaiser tried to perform a delicate balancing act by stating that the CDU rejected any forms of theological dogmatism, which led only to "fanaticism and radicalism" and was not interested in "propagandizing" for either the Catholic or the Protestant churches. At the same time the CDU rejected the claims by the KPD that religious belief was something that must be entirely restricted from the public sphere. Instead it held religious institutions had a vital role to play in the reconstruction of the Soviet zone, especially in charitable and educational work. Christian Socialism, while accepting the need for the state structure to remain secular, would continue to push for an active public role for the Christian churches, and would continue to be guided by Christian social teachings.[62] A few weeks later, CDU party leader Friedrich Lutge returned to these themes of the economic foundations of Christian Socialism, arguing forcefully that while the CDU under Kaiser's leadership rejected centralized economic planning, it also did not advocate a return to the unrestricted free market economics, which caused of so much *"ungluck"*(unhappiness) within the nineteenth and early twentieth centuries.[63]

In February Kaiser and *Neue Zeit* editor Emil Dovifat, who had replaced Otto Nuschke a few months earlier, sent out an eighteen-page report to CDU members throughout the Soviet zone outlining the new cultural policies of CDU under its new ideology of Christian Socialism. In the section of the document "Staat und Kirche," the authors mentioned that the state bore an obligation to protect religious freedom and that *Neue Zeit* would continue to promote the Christian heritage in German culture. In addition, they advocated that the churches should be allowed a "special position" to articulate their message through the press, film and radio, and that parents be allowed the right to ensure that their children receive a religious education. The internal autonomy of the churches would be respected and preserved, the church tax would continue, and other religious groups, such as Germany's remaining Jewish community, would have the same rights as the Catholics and Protestants.[64]

Catholic and Protestant clergymen responded favorably if discretely to Kaiser's doctrine of Christian Socialism. Otto Dibelius sent a letter to CDU leader Otto Heinrich von der Gablentz on January 7, 1946, stating that he approved of Kaiser's ideology of Christian Socialism. He declared that it offered the best hope for Germany's political, cultural, and economic recovery. Dibelius stated while the Protestant Church as an institution must remain politically neutral, nearly all Protestant clergy and most individuals identified with the CDU and its goals, as did he. "We Christians must all fulfill our secular duties," he wrote "and in the political situation today the German Protestant Christian finds a positive understanding only with the CDU."[65] Preysing did not send an equivalent declaration of preference to the CDU leadership, but his own preference for the CDU and its Catholic leader Kaiser was well known.[66] Kaiser also received declarations of support for the adoption of Christian Socialism from clergy and laity throughout the Soviet zone. Among the most notable was from a Catholic priest in Mecklenburg, Karl Fischer, who began a regular correspondence with Kaiser during his tenure as head of the CDU. Fischer praised the CDU's declared ideology of Christian Socialism, stating that it best expressed the hopes of Germans who had resisted the Nazi regime due to their religious convictions.[67]

While Christian Socialism demonstrated an ability to appeal to clergy and laity in the Soviet zone in the minds of the CDU leadership, its electoral appeal had not yet been tested in the spring of 1946. *Neues Deutschland* (the newspaper of the newly formed Socialist Unity Party, created through the forced merger of the KPD and SPD in the Soviet zone in April 1946) and *Tägliche Rundschau* printed numerous editorials throughout the year which were harshly critical of the new ideology of the CDU. One article from *Tägliche Rundschau* by a Gustav Holt claimed Kaiser's Christian Socialism was merely a repetition of Hermes's open reactionary policies under a new name, and, if implemented, would imperil not only Germany's democratic transformation but also its economic and political unity.[68]

In an article in one of the first issues of *Neues Deutschland* entitled "Wohin Geht die CDU?" the unnamed author made largely the same argument, stating that the progressive rhetoric of Christian Socialism was merely designed to mask the reactionary designs of Kaiser and the rest of the CDU leadership. Their arch-conservative nature had been proven by Kaiser's continued attempt to maintain the unity between the CDU in the Soviet zone and the openly reactionary CDU/CSU (Christian Social Union, the Bavarian equivalent to the CDU) in the Western zones.[69]

Privately, officials with the Propaganda Administration expressed concern for the new direction of the CDU under Kaiser, especially as it opened up the possibility of greater collaboration between the CDU and the Protestant and Catholic churches. Tiul'panov argued this repeatedly, and claimed that Christian Socialism was designed by Kaiser to gather the strength of the disparate reactionary political, economic, and cultural elements within the Soviet zone, with the long-term goal of assisting the Anglo-American imperialists in overturning the "democratic antifascist transformation" of the Soviet zone.[70] In a report dated April 16 1946, Mil'khiker reported to Tiul'panov the CDU, with the assistance of both the Protestant and Catholic churches succeeded in reaching out to considerable numbers of German youths, women, and religious members of the working class with their claim that Christian Socialism had successfully merged the religious and political aims of the vast majority of Germans who were religious believers. Furthermore, the CDU's expansion had to come at the expense of the SED.[71]

Mil'khiker largely repeated to Tiul'panov the same arguments made by his subordinates at the provincial levels. On June 1 1946 Mil'khiker received a report from Major V. A. Rosenzweig, the head of the Propaganda Administration in the city of Eberswald. Rosenzweig stated the CDU's ability to appear as the defender of religious traditions while also emphasizing it would control the reforms proposed by the SED and the SVAG appealed to the largely rural and conservative population outside of the cities and towns of Brandenburg.[72]

Such expressions were not limited to Brandenburg. In a report dated June 24 1946, the head of the Propaganda Administration for the province of Sachsen-Anhalt, N. S. Rodionov, reported to Tiul'panov that the CDU's propagandizing of Christian Socialism with the aid of compliant Catholic and Protestant clerics, had proven to be very successful in winning over new members. This was especially clear among the working class and even the "new farmers" who had benefited from the SVAG's land reform policies. The CDU's growth in membership had come at the expense not only of the LDP but also the SED.[73]

In response to this rising concern regarding the political appeal of the CDU under Kaiser's leadership, officials throughout the Soviet military government recommended a number of solutions. Vladimir Semenov, head of the Political Council of SVAG, in a report concerning developments in the CDU sent on June 15 to Soviet Foreign Minister Vyacheslav Molotov, Deputy Foreign Minister Andrei Vyshinsky, and the new head of SVAG Marshal Vasilii Sokolovskii, stated the political mood of the CDU was considerably diverse, divided between "leftist-progressives," "reactionaries" who supported Kaiser and "extreme reactionaries" who continued to adhere to the views of Andreas Hermes. Semenov proposed that the SVAG should work in cultivating "leftist-progressive elements" in the regional CDU leaderships, noting certain figures such as Otto Nuschke and Georg Dertinger. The alternative was to allow Kaiser to build a power base among religious and bourgeois Germans with the covert assistance of the Protestant and Catholic churches, just as Adenauer had done in the Western zones of Germany.[74]

Shortly thereafter, Sokolovskii received a report from Colonel Tiul'panov concerning the first all-zonal CDU party conference in Berlin. Dated June 18, Tiul'panov wrote the SVAG should attempt to undermine any notions of Christian Socialism by publishing articles in party newspapers critical of it, to increase the inter-party struggle within the CDU by favoring the progressives against the "reactionaries", and to strengthen the SED's position in rural areas. He argued Kaiser's ideology of Christian Socialism could not be allowed to challenge the SVAG's own interpretation of how the antifascist transformation of Germany would be carried out.[75]

Tiul'panov also directed the heads of the Propaganda Administration to take a number of measures to limit the political role the churches could play. Sent on July 9, the directive stated the churches could play a part in the democratic development of Germany, such as urging support for land reform and informing the laity that they must participate in elections. However, clergy should not be allowed to agitate for any kind of political party. Finally, the churches must allow their parishioners to support any kind of political organizations, and not accuse members of the SED as abandoning their Christian identity.[76]

These policies implemented by SVAG at the behest of Tiul'panov in response to reports from his worried subordinates shows that the Soviet authorities viewed the CDU's use of Christian Socialism as its guiding ideology as a considerable threat. The SED had failed to come up with a better alternative that could appeal to Christian Germans who had socialist leanings. Kaiser's attempt to forge a genuine alternative to Stalinist-style socialism, which allowed for a strong public role for Protestant and Catholic churches, made it easier for clergy to assist the CDU while disguising their true "reactionary" nature to the German population. Yet the SVAG refused to implement heavy-handed policies of blatantly suppressing the CDU, preferring instead to win a propaganda battle with it. The fall of 1946 was still too early to fully implement a one-party dictatorship in the Soviet Zone. The Soviet leadership hoped an electoral sweep by the SED in the Soviet Zone could allow them to extend its influence into the Western zones as well.

THE ZONAL ELECTIONS OF OCTOBER 1946 AND THEIR EFFECT ON THE SVAG POLICIES TOWARDS THE CDU AND THE CHURCHES

The SVAG and the SED newspapers stepped up their attack on the CDU and Christian Socialism in order to weaken it leading up to the zonal elections in October. On June 20, *Neues Deutschland* published an article attacking "Political Catholicism" throughout all four occupation zones of Germany, noting the reactionary activities of the Center party during the Weimar era, especially the role played by former Center party leader Franz von Papen in helping to bring the Nazis to a position of political power in Germany. This was an especially harsh charge in the Soviet zone as the two leaders of the CDU, Jakob Kaiser and his deputy Ernst Lemmer, were both Catholics.[77]

In an article that appeared in the SED newspaper one month later, the Protestant cleric Kurt Rackwitz of Berlin, noted for his involvement in religious socialist movements, wrote an article discussing a series of lectures given by the Swiss theologian Karl Barth at the University of Bonn during that month. Rackwitz used his discussion of Barth's lectures to subtly criticize Kaiser's concept of Christian Socialism, claiming that while Christians and Socialists could find common ground on many issues, Christians in Germany should no longer expect the churches to occupy a culturally prominent position in a new antifascist Germany. Nor should the churches protest the end of their educational role. This was anathema to Kaiser and his supporters, who still insisted on a visible role for both the Protestant and Catholic churches in public and educational life.[78]

Neues Deutschland stepped up its attacks the next month, as did *Tägliche Rundschau*, often printing articles from Protestant or Catholic clerics such as Theodor Werner or Kurt Rackwitz that either attacked Christian Socialism for a variety of reasons or emphasized the need for strict political neutrality of the churches, often using clergy sympathetic to the SVAG and the SED, most of which were the Protestant Church.

On August 7, the Provincial Superintendent of the Protestant Church in Mecklenburg-Vorpommern, Theodor Werner, wrote in *Tägliche Rundschau* that Christians in Germany should not assume any one church spoke for them, and they should feel free to support any candidate they wished in the zonal elections in the month of October. Werner urged his readers to remember in Soviet zone "complete religious freedom" existed. The church was allowed to publish its own newspapers and magazines, as well as Sunday radio broadcasts, its religious services and charitable work was unimpeded by the state. The SVAG and authorities in the German PVs permitted the churches to allow for optional religious educational in the schools after regular school hours. Werner emphasized the necessity of the churches in maintaining a positive relationship with the state. He explained that no one wanted to go back to the period of Church-State relations as under the Nazis, which tried to suppress and co-opt the churches for its own ends.[79]

The next week another article appeared in *Neues Deutschland*, attacking Jakob Kaiser for attempting to convince the German people that there existed a strong dichotomy between Christianity and Marxism. The unnamed author stated that any claims that Christian churches could not exist in a state that embraced Marxism was preposterous, given the existence of religious freedom within the Soviet Union and the benevolence of the SVAG to the Protestant and Catholic churches in the Soviet zone. The article concluded Kaiser was attempting to follow the reactionary path of the CDU in the Western zones and used the religious concerns of the German people for his own reactionary political ends.[80]

The most dramatic example of both the SVAG and the SED using their newspapers to stress the political neutrality of the churches, or more accurately the denial of a link between the CDU and the Protestant Church, appeared on the front page of both *Tägliche Rundschau* and *Neues Deutschland* on August 16 entitled "Die Evangelische Kirche bildet keine Partei" ("The Protestant Church supports no political party"). The article was written by Otto Dibelius but signed by him as well as Bishop Mitzenheim of Thuringia, Bishop Beste of Mecklenburg-Vorpommern, and Bishop Mueller of Sachsen. Dibelius wrote that clergy were forbidden from using their position to support one particular political party, clergy were neither allowed to obtain leadership positions in political parties nor to inform parishioners that it was their Christian duty to vote for certain candidates.

At the conclusion of the article Dibelius claimed the Protestant churches in the Soviet zone, which represented 85 percent of the population, had been among the most consistent supporters for the reestablishment of civil liberties following the end of the war. The Protestant Church believed its most important priority was its work with the social needs of the German population. However, the EKD did not identify with any one political party and only hoped all three of antifascist parties would continue to work together in the spirit of Christian brotherhood.[81]

Complicating the situation was the fact that, with the first zonal elections only two months away, the Socialist Unity Party had not clarified its own position on the religious question. The founding declaration of the SED in April 1946 stressed the need for the complete separation of church and state as well as the exclusion of the churches from any role in the educational process. This sharply opposed earlier declarations of the KPD and its members in the Soviet-sponsored National Committee for the Free Germany, which declared that the Protestant and Catholic churches were partners to the democratic transformation of Germany.[82]

Kaiser and the rest of the CDU leadership were quick to pounce on this perceived weakness in the ambiguity of the SED's position, stating in an article in the August 11 issue of *Neue Zeit* that German voters faced a decision whether the fate of Germany would be governed by the principles of Christianity or Marxism. Only Christian Socialism could lead Germany to the path to economic and political recovery without the harshness of class struggle or revolutionary upheaval.[83] Attempting to clarify its position the SED's Central Secretariat issued a public statement at the end of August which stated: "The Socialist Unity Party categorically rejects subordinating itself to the church, just as the church with justification rejects taking itself in a partisan sense."[84]

This apparently did not prove to the SED leadership to be an adequate enough measure. SED leaders Wilhelm Pieck and Otto Grotewohl published an article in *Neues Deutschland* on August 30, which re-stated the position the SED had announced three days earlier. It also attacked Kaiser's attempt to frame the issue as a struggle between Christianity and Marxism. Pieck and Grotewohl announced all true Christians were supportive of the creation of a democratic, antifascist Germany, and there was consequently no need to support a form of Christian Socialism, as the goals of the scientific socialism of the SED and that of Christianity were already in harmony.[85]

Shortly before the elections in the Soviet zone in October 1946, Pieck and Grotewohl received a letter from the Protestant cleric Kurt Rackwitz, representing himself as the leader of "The Conference of Socialist Clergy" from all the provinces of the Soviet zone. Rackwitz informed them that clarification of the SED's position towards religious freedom would greatly assist them in their work to convince other Protestant clergy and laity to no longer act as obstacles to political and social progress in Germany. Rackwitz assured them the Protestant Church could prove to be a major ally of the SED, and that progressive clergy throughout the Soviet zone rejected Kaiser and the Christian Socialism of the CDU.[86]

During the last two months before the zonal elections in October, there were far more visible symbols of clerical support for the CDU than for the SED. This was especially prominent on the side of the Protestant Church, despite the SED leadership's statements and Dibelius's own promises of church neutrality. During a CDU party rally in Cottbus in southeastern Brandenburg on September 8, a Protestant minister named Heinrich Bucholz introduced Kaiser. In his remarks, Bucholz claimed the CDU under its ideology of Christian Socialism could successfully unite German Catholics and

Protestants in the construction of a prosperous, free and democratic Germany. The SED with its guiding principles of Marxism-Leninism would only serve to plunge Germany into endless social, political, and economic strife, the last thing Germany needed after the Nazi regime and the devastation of the Second World War.[87]

The CDU also attempted to clarify its stance regarding its identity in the period leading up to the elections. In a front-page article in *Neue Zeit* on September 7 entitled "Warum Christlich?" (Why Christian?), the unnamed author stated the Christian part of the CDU's name had three meanings. The first was to tie the CDU to antifascist resistance on the part of Catholics and Protestants to the Nazi regime. The second was to describe the CDU's economic policies under Christian Socialism. The third was to emphasize the CDU's commitment to the restoration of Christianity to a position of prominent importance in Germany's culture, and to ensure both the Catholic and Protestant churches would maintain prominent positions in public life.[88] A few weeks later, *Neue Zeit* printed a speech given by Kaiser in Berlin, where he again denied that the CDU represented any one particular religious group in Germany. Kaiser claimed the roots of Christian resistance to Nazism, such as a belief in political freedom, respect for the rights of the individual, a rejection of class struggle and party dictatorship, were also the foundations of Christian Socialism.[89]

Despite such outward manifestations of a strong link between the CDU and Catholic and Protestant churches, the records of the leadership of both the CDU and the Protestant Church on the eve of the zonal elections do not show any extensive discussion as to how to collaborate to ensure electoral victory for the CDU. At the meetings of the CDU party leadership on August 18, September 18, and October 15, religious issues were not discussed to any great extent, besides expressions of dissatisfaction concerning the issue of religious education in German schools.[90]

At the meeting of Protestant bishops in the Soviet zone in July 1946, the issue of the zonal elections was briefly discussed, and while the bishops did not relish the prospect of a sweeping SED victory, none mentioned how they could assist the CDU to prevent this. This is particularly revealing given the fact that Dibelius voiced concerns that the Soviet authorities and their SED allies in the German organs of self-government were making life very difficult for Protestant clerics throughout the Soviet zone, especially in regards to their efforts to provide for the spiritual needs of the refugee population and those imprisoned in the internment camps.[91]

Nor do the official papers of Preysing reveal any instructions to Catholic clergy to assist the CDU in their electoral campaigns, or any correspondence with Kaiser or the other CDU leaders concerning how to work together in the

Soviet zone to achieve shared political goals. However, during the summer of 1946 Preysing communicated in a series of letters sent to all diocesan clergy in the Soviet zone expressing his deep dissatisfaction with the policies of the Soviet authorities, especially on land reform and the exclusion of religious education from the curriculum of elementary and secondary schools.[92]

This was the result of the determination of the Protestant and Catholic churches' to maintain the institutional neutrality of the churches during the early phase of the Soviet occupation, despite the obvious distaste many of them felt for the Soviet and SED authorities. While Kaiser attempted to create a link between the ideology of the CDU and Christian humanistic and social thought, he and the rest of the party leadership also attempted to make the CDU more than just a church-based political party. The Soviet authorities in the Propaganda Administration did not see it that way, and as the elections approached they saw "collaboration" between the leadership of the CDU and the churches as a clear political threat.

Major L. L. Koloss, head of the Propaganda Administration for the SVAG in the Soviet sector of Berlin, reported to Mil'khiker on August 8, that both Catholic and Protestant clergy were actively engaged in political agitation for the CDU, often conducting these activities through the cover of religious charitable or educational work.[93] In a similar report at the end of August sent to Mil'khiker from Lieutenant Colonel Z. F. Rosenzweig charged that the CDU's ideology of Christian Socialism had succeeded in drawing away some religious German industrial workers from the "working class" SED. More importantly, the CDU was the more powerful of the bourgeois parties because of its religious identity. Nearly every Catholic and Protestant cleric, he observed, was a member of the CDU and worked relentlessly to improve the electoral fortunes of the party.[94]

At the end of September, Mil'khiker received a similar report from the head of the Propaganda Administration in the city of Brandenburg, Lieutenant Colonel A. A. Merzliakov, which made similar charges that the Protestant and Catholic churches were bastions of reactionary strength dedicated to recruiting new members and voters for the CDU. In all three reports, the Soviet officials declared that reactionaries in the CDU and in the Protestant and Catholic Church were drawn together in pursuit of common goals, and that their relationship had only strengthened over time.[95]

SVAG officials in Brandenburg were not the only ones concerned about the situation. On August 5 1946, the head of the Propaganda Administration in Erfurt, M. E. Shertinskii, conveyed to the head of the Propaganda Administration for the Soviet military government in Thuringia M. M. Variakin that nearly all prominent clergy and laity in the Protestant and Catholic churches were CDU party members. They had been quite successful in convincing religious Germans that the SED as an "atheist" party could never represent their interests.[96] On September 2, the regional heads of the SVAG's Propaganda Administration directed their subordinates to continue to support the SED against the reactionaries in the CDU. They urged greater vigilance in preventing any extensive collaboration between the churches and the CDU.[97]

Tiul'panov, in conversation with the SED leader Wilhelm Pieck, agreed with him that the churches could not be allowed to campaign for the CDU, and therefore it would be necessary for the SED to articulate repeatedly its own benevolent policies towards religious institutions as a method of limiting the appealing of the CDU's Christian Socialism.[98] Again, this would take the form of a propaganda offensive as opposed to the arrest and expulsion of the CDU's leaders. Tiul'panov, like many officials in SVAG, remained convinced that the SED would have little trouble emerging victorious in the zonal elections, and thus more repressive tactics were unnecessary.

Both the SVAG and the SED newspapers in October 1946 published a series of articles depicting the SED's views towards religious institutions in a highly positive light. At the same time, they attacked the CDU and its attempt to monopolize the religious vote. In the October 18 issue of *Neues Deutschland*, the Protestant cleric Kurt Rackwitz of Berlin-Neukölln, long known to be completely subservient to the SED, asked the readers to remind themselves the shared imprisonment of communists and Christians under the Nazi regime. He advised them to keep in mind the SED had worked with the SVAG to restore religious freedom to Germany and would continue to do so, guaranteeing that religious institutions would play an important role in the new socialist, democratic, and antifascist Germany.[99]

The next day, *Tägliche Rundschau* published its most scathing and lengthy attack on Kaiser and Christian Socialism. The article's author, Gustav Holt, wrote the meaning of the word "socialism" had frequently been twisted by reactionaries, but its true definition rested with the scientific socialism as interpreted by Marx and Engels. Holt argued the CDU, after it was formed in the Soviet zone in June 1945 and throughout the first six months of its existence, did not discuss any concept of "Christian Socialism." Instead, it was only conceptualized by Kaiser in order to refute claims that the CDU was a thoroughly reactionary party. The religious motivations behind Christian Socialism were irrelevant given the SED's own commitments to protecting religious freedom. Its true essence was nothing more than the preservation of the capitalist system within the Soviet zone. Holt concluded the CDU's adoption of Christian Socialism only demonstrated the CDU in the Soviet zone, like the CDU in the Western occupation zones, was in league with reactionary clergy, industrialists and businessmen, and was attempting to undo the democratic transformation of the Soviet zone under the leadership of the SED.[100]

Despite the best efforts of the various administrative branches of the SVAG, especially the Propaganda Administration, the results of the zonal elections on October 20, 1946, were far from what either the SVAG or the SED desired, especially since the SED received massive economic assistance from the SVAG during the electoral campaign. Already discouraged by the less than promising results of local elections in Sachsen and Thuringia, where the CDU did better than expected, the results of the district and provincial assembly elections throughout the Soviet zone as well as for Greater Berlin were even more disheartening. Nowhere did the SED receive a majority of the votes. In Berlin the SED, with 19.8 percent of the overall vote, placed third behind the SPD (which could not campaign anywhere else in the Soviet zone), which received 48.7 percent of the vote, and the CDU, which received 22.2 percent of the vote, surpassing the predictions of even the most pessimistic observers in the SVAG and the SED.[101] In all five of the provinces in the Soviet zone the CDU placed second to the SED. In Brandenburg and Mecklenburg-Vorpommern the CDU was far closer than in Sachsen, Sachsen-Anhalt, or Thuringia.[102] In Berlin, the SPD received 948,753 votes, the CDU 431,916 and the SED 383,192 votes. In Brandenburg, the SED received 634,786 votes and CDU 442,206. This contrasted greatly with the electoral predictions of *Tägliche Rundschau* and *Neues Deutschland,* which proclaimed that results would give the SED a mandate to complete the "antifascist democratic transformation" of the Soviet Zone and extend their influence over the Western occupation zones as well.[103]

The electoral results did not prevent the gradual but surely progressing Stalinization of the Soviet zone of Germany, given the continued domination of the German PVs by the SED and the fact that SVAG authorities could and did exercise veto power over decisions made by provincial and regional assemblies. Yet the electoral tallies robbed the SVAG and the SED of their primary goal, evidence of broad public support for the "antifascist democratic transformation" of the Soviet zone. This supposedly would have demonstrated the viability of the SED to compete in the electoral process in the Western zones to the British, American, and French authorities.[104] Due to their unsatisfying results for the Soviets and their German "friends" these were the last free elections in the five provinces that constituted the Soviet zone of Germany until the fall of 1989. Certainly the lingering suspicion of the Soviets and their German allies as militant atheists despite claims of the existence of "religious freedom" in the Soviet Union made many religious Germans vote for the CDU as opposed to the SED.

Tiul'panov, in a November 1946 report to one of his allies on the Central Committee of the CPSU Andrei Zhdanov regarding the electoral results in the Soviet zone, acknowledged that Kaiser's ideology of Christian Socialism had a beneficial effect for the CDU's electoral position, but repeated the common charge that Christian Socialism was merely a cover for the CDU's reactionary plans to re-establish capitalism in the Soviet zone.[105] Tiul'panov was merely repeating similar claims made by the regional heads of the Propaganda Administration. For example, Colonel M. M. Variakin, the head of the Propaganda Administration for Thuringia, reported to Tiul'panov the reactionary clergy who led the Protestant and Catholic churches had opposed every antifascist political, economic, and social reform introduced since the fall of 1945, and had actively campaigned for CDU candidates throughout the entire province.[106]

The CDU leadership certainly saw the results as a validation of their electoral strategy of reaching out to members of both the Evangelical and Catholic churches while also trying to broaden their appeal for Germans who did not put religious concerns as their primary motivating factor for voting in the elections. Articles celebrating the electoral results in the October 22 issue of *Neue Zeit* testified to this, although the CDU still pledged to cooperate with the SED and the LDP in the antifascist block.[107]

Throughout the remainder of the year, the CDU newspaper continued to return to the common themes of Christian Socialism. An article on November 7 by Kaiser declared the election results had validated the new path the CDU had taken since the beginning of the year, and would continue to promote Christian Socialism as the best hope for the recovery of Germany following the Nazi era and the Second World War.[108] Another article that appeared in *Neue Zeit* a few weeks later by one of the chief CDU ideologists Otto Heinrich von der Gablentz, returned to theme of the CDU's commitment to restoring Christianity to its primary role in German culture. Gablentz was somewhat vague as to how this would be accomplished, but stated it was impossible to imagine the revival of German culture following the war without a return to its Christian roots.[109]

At their post-electoral meeting on November 12 1946, the CDU executive committee, consisting of Kaiser, Lemmer, von der Gablentz, Nuschke, and Dertinger, proclaimed the success of their electoral tactics, particularly in Mecklenburg and Brandenburg. Committee members decided that they should continue their course with regard to a loyal relationship with the occupation authorities, working to preserve German unity while continuing support for the doctrine of Christian Socialism and acting as a voice for religious Germans throughout the Soviet zone.[110] Shortly thereafter, a series of new propaganda materials were released by the CDU for distribution throughout the Soviet zone. These claimed that the CDU placed a special importance on the role of religious women and youth in the party and supported an economically and politically unified Germany. Because the CDU remained explicitly a Christian party ("Weil die Union eine Christliche Partei ist") it rejected class struggle and dictatorship of any kind, while working for class and political reconciliation in Germany.[111]

The CDU took from their surprisingly successful results in the zonal elections that there existed considerable support for Christian Socialism among the inhabitants of the Soviet Zone. Kaiser embarked on more daring and riskier policies in 1947. This made authorities in the newly renamed Information Administration more suspicious than ever concerning Kaiser's role as a leader of "reactionary" religious and political sentiment in the Soviet Zone.

As for the leadership of the Protestant and Catholic churches, the promising electoral results of the CDU did not alter their behavior towards the Soviet authorities in the following fourteen months when the CDU still maintained its independence under Kaiser's leadership. Preysing never made any public comment on the electoral results of October 1946, and continued to act throughout 1947 as he did before, appealing directly to the highest levels of SVAG to redress grievances, as opposed to using the CDU as an intermediary. Preysing wrote a letter to Marshal Vasilii Sokolovskii on February 2 1947, in which he appealed to him to release German military chaplains who were still in Soviet custody. He also made a request for the release of elderly and female prisoners held at the Soviet concentration camp in Sachsenhausen in the northern suburb of Berlin, Oranienburg. Receiving no response from Sokolovskii, Preysing also appealed to the other military commanders of the three Western zones to use their influence on their Soviet opposite number to secure the release of prisoners from the Soviet "Special Camp Number One" at the former Nazi concentration camp at Sachsenhausen. Ultimately nothing came of this, although the American and British commanders Lucius Clay and Brian Robertson made promises to assist Preysing.[112]

The electoral results had little impact on the leadership of the Protestant Church and their decisions over the following three years. Neither Dibelius nor any of the other leaders of the Protestant Church appeared to believe the CDU, even while running on a platform of Christian Socialism, could ever act as their representative to the authorities in the Soviet zone. In the first meeting of the leadership of the Protestant Church in the Soviet zone on November 11 1946, the assembled leadership, including Dibelius, Mitzenheim, Beste, Mueller, and Superintendent of the EKD Kurt Krummacher, discussed how to continue religious educational work despite attempts by Soviet and SED members of the Departments of the People's Education to prevent it. They also considered how to assist in the release of German prisoners of war in

Soviet custody, especially the release of Protestant clerics who served as military chaplains. Not only did they fail to discuss the electoral results of the previous month but they also did not discuss how the CDU could assist them on the questions of religious education or the release of Germans prisoners of war.[113]

While his earlier letter to von der Gablentz left little doubt Dibelius was pleased with the lackluster showing of the SED combined with the success of the CDU, he made no public pronouncements following the elections, beyond calling for the antifascist parties to continue to work together towards improving material conditions and preserving the political unity of Germany.[114] Dibelius largely followed this general message in his public statements about political developments until the fall of 1948 despite private misgivings he revealed to other Protestant clergy. Then, he, like Preysing, made numerous public pronouncements concerning his opposition to the establishment of a Communist dictatorship in the Soviet zone. Dibelius also sent largely unsuccessful entreaties to the SVAG authorities on a variety of topics during the next two years, including the issues of religious education, charitable work, and the restoration of church property.[115]

As the negotiations between the Soviets and the Western powers over the question of German reparations broke down at the Moscow Conference of Foreign Ministers in April 1947, the SED began to move in the direction of remaking itself as a "party of the new type" (i.e. a Stalinist political party). This did not mean n immediate suppression of religious institutions, but it did mean that in a future German state led by the SED their role would be clearly limited.

SVAG and SED officials saw the CDU under Kaiser with its guiding ideology of Christian Socialism as a minor but not irrelevant threat, especially since it offered the possibility of greater collaboration between the Protestant and Catholic churches and the CDU. The decision to remove Kaiser the next year and replace him with the more pliant Otto Nuschke along with the subsequent abandonment of Christian Socialism is proof of this. The disappointing electoral results for the SED in October 1946 and the excellent showing of the CDU was, among other factors, due to the fact that for many religious Germans, the SED, much like their Soviet allies, represented the forces of communist atheism. Kaiser, with the aid of some clerical allies in the Protestant and Catholic churches, had been successful in framing the debate as one of "Christianity against Marxism."

Yet, as Tiul'panov's and Pieck's statements make clear, neither the Soviet nor the German officials feared any long term political challenge from Kaiser or believed that collaboration between the CDU and the churches could do much more than delay the antifascist democratic transformation of the Soviet

Zone. Even the most nervous reports from SVAG officials in the Propaganda Administration during the fall of 1946 concerning the CDU's relationship with the churches never expressed any belief that such "antiquated and reactionary" institutions could challenge their own political authority. Just as the elections failed to change the realities of power in the Soviet zone and likely encouraged the Soviet authorities to take greater steps in the creation of an East German state on the Soviet model, the CDU's electoral success and the appeal of Christian Socialism remained an annoyance that would be dealt with at the appropriate time.

Despite Dibelius's correspondence with von Gablentz concerning the tacit support of most Protestant clergy for the CDU and Preysing's own distaste for the Soviet and SED authorities, the repeated statements of the Protestant and Catholic Church in Berlin and Brandenburg declaring the institutional neutrality of the churches should not be seen in a cynical light. Both churches adopted this policy as a continuation of their actions during the Nazi era and also because the other issues confronting them during the first three years of the occupation were more important than the conflicts between the antifascist political parties.

The public statements of Dibelius and other clergy in the pages of *Tägliche Rundschau* and *Neues Deutschland* should not be seen as a craven attempt to win the approval of the SVAG or SED. Rather, the Protestant Church attempted to emphasize its institutional neutrality and its commitment to German unity and recovery from the war. It would not be until 1948, when the other independent political actors had been removed from the scene and the process of creating a Stalinist German state was almost complete, that the religious leadership, particularly Dibelius and Von Preysing, began to publicly voice their concerns over political developments in the Soviet Zone.

Notes

1. The German organs of self-government were first referred to as the Provincial Administration, *Provinzial Verwaltung*-PVs, and after early 1948 the State Government, *Landes Regierung*-LRs. In order to avoid repetition I will refer to the German organs of self-government as PVs or LRs, depending on the time period.

2. The sources used for the first two chapters include internal records from the SVAG's central headquarters in the Berlin suburb of Karlshorst as well as from the administrative branch for Berlin and Brandenburg. Of particular importance are the internal reports sent by local and provincial officers of the SVAG's Propaganda/Information Administration to its leaders in Brandenburg, as well as correspondence between the heads of the Propaganda/Information Administration for Brandenburg and the commander of the SVAG's Propaganda Administration, Colonel Sergei

Tiul'panov. Other important records used for this chapter include the German-language newspapers of the SVAG, the KPD, and the SED, as they were among the principal means these organizations used to disseminate party propaganda. The correspondence between the leadership of the Protestant and Catholic churches and members of the CDU help to reveal what type of relationship existed between them, as do the internal communications among the executive leadership of the CDU. The meetings of the Protestant Church leadership in the Soviet zone from 1945 to 1949 and the official records of the Protestant and Catholic bishops of Berlin, Otto Dibelius and Konrad von Preysing, discuss the limited priority political developments had for the leadership of the churches during the first few years of the Soviet occupation. The CDU newspaper, *Neue Zeit* and many of the speeches given by CDU party leaders help to illustrate how the CDU viewed its relationship with the Protestant and Catholic churches, given the fact it was founded to represent religious Germans in the Soviet zone.

3. *Die UdSSR und die Deutsche Frage 1941–1948: Dokumente aus dem Archiv für Aussenpolitik der Russischen Föderation Volume 2*: 9 Mai 1945 bis 3. October 1946. Eds, Jochen Laufer, Georgii Kynin and Viktor Knoll. Berlin: Duncker & Humbolt, 2004. 241–242.

4. Pike, 4.

5. Bruce, 24.

6. Ibid., 32. Kaiser and Adenauer also disagreed on where the CDU's headquarters should be located, as Adenauer rejected Kaiser's proposal the Berlin CDU serve the leading role. Despite these disagreements, Kaiser joined Adenauer's first cabinet in West Germany in 1949 as a minister for all-German affairs.

7. Ibid., 25.

8. Paul Steege, *Black Market, Cold War: Everyday Life in Berlin, 1946–1949*. Cambridge: Cambridge University Press, 2007, 69.

9. Archiv für Christliche-Demokratische Politik (ACDP) Signatur 07–011-CDU Ost, 2993. Personnel files from the CDU Landesverband Berlin.

10. ACDP, Signatur 07–011-CDU Ost, 2993.

11. Bruce, 26.

12. Ibid., 27.

13. ACDP, Signatur 07–010–CDU Ost, 672.

14. Ibid.

15. ACDP, Signatur 07–011, 2376.

16. Neue Zeit. 6 Sept. 1945, 2. As in many of the articles from newspapers in the Soviet zone, the authors were not listed. The article also mentioned that the CDU was dedicated to preventing the political misuse of the churches, continuing the work of the Confessing Church during the Nazi era.

17. "Die Religiose Lage" *Neue Zeit*. 14 Sept, 1945. 3.

18. *Neue Zeit*. 4 Sept. 1945. 1. Both articles also mentioned the commitment of the Evangelical and Catholic bishops to assisting the construction of an antifascist German democracy.

19. *Neue Zeit*. 15 Nov 1945. 3.

20. *Neue Zeit.* 29 Nov 1945. 3.

21. Robert Goeckel, *The Lutheran Church and the East German State.* Ithaca: Cornell University Press, 1990. 42.

22. *Deutsche Volkszeitung.* 23 Jun 1945. 2.

23. *Deutsche Volkszeitung.* 31 July 1945. 2.

24. Wilhelm Pieck and Otto Grotewohl, *Deutsche Volkszeitung.* 27 Oct 1945. 1.

25. "Kirchliches Leben in Brandenburg" *Tägliche Rundschau.* 9 Jun 1945. 2. *Tägliche Rundschau,* much like *Neue Zeit, Neues Deutschland* and *Deutshce Volkszeitung,* only occasionally mentioned the authors of articles within the newspaper.

26. Karl Fischer, *Tägliche Rundschau.* 14 Jun. 1945. 2. Fischer's remarks were especially relevant given the fact that the provinces of the Soviet zone, especially Thuringia and Sachsen, were hotbeds of the German Christian movement. As Doris Bergen notes her work, Twisted Cross: The German Christian Movement in the Third Reich, many leaders of the Protestant Church after 1945 in both the Western and Soviet zones were willing to quietly re-admit many prominent German Christians to the Protestant Church, although not yet in leadership positions.

27. *Tägliche Rundschau.* 26 Jun 1945 1, *Tägliche Rundschau.* 24 Jul 1945 1.

28. *Tägliche Rundschau.* 27 Sept 1945 2. The essence of Dovifat's criticism of the antifascist block structure was that since major decisions required unanimity on the part of representatives of all four parties, the KPD essentially had a veto power over any decision undertaken by the Block, but as the largest and most visible antifascist party in the Soviet zone, the KPD could still exercise great influence due to its numbers and its special relationship with the Soviet military authorities.

29. Naimark, 323. It was even rumored Tiul'panov had studied for a year at Heidelberg University in the early 1930s. His deputy for Religious Affairs Vsevolod Ermolaev was also a professor at Leningrad State University before the war, having taught Russian and European history.

30. *Die UdSSR und die Deutsche Frage 1941–1948: Dokumente aus dem Archiv für Aussenpolitik der Russischen Föderation Volume 2: 9 Mai 1945 bis 3. October 1946.* Eds, Jochen Laufer, Georgii Kynin and Viktor Knoll. Berlin: Duncker & Humbolt, 2004. 63–64.

31. Gosudarstvennyi arkhiv Rossiiskoi Federatsii (GARF- State Archives of the Russian Federation). f. 7317 (SVAG), op. 1 (Upravlenie informatsii), d. 19 (Correspondence June–December 1947), ll. 242. This report concerning religious affairs comes from a massive report sent to Tiul'panov from various members of staff within the Information Administration in early 1948, possibly because Tiul'panov was under pressure both from enemies in Moscow and within the SVAG apparatus to resign his position as head of the Information Administration, and desired a summary of accomplishments under his leadership.

32. GARF, f. 7317, op. 19, d. 1, l. 243. By the time the report had been written, the Propaganda Administration had changed its name to the Information Administration following the disastrous electoral results in October of 1946 in the Soviet zone.

33. GARF, f. 7077 (SVAG Brandenburg), op. 1 (Upravlenie propagandy), d. 179 (Correspondence August–December 1945) ll. 35–38.

34. GARF, f. 7077 (SVAG Brandenburg), op.1 (Upravlenie propagandy), d. 180 (Correspondence October–December 1945) ll. 3–4.

35. Stiftung-Arkhiv für Parteien und Massenorganizationen in der DDR. (SAP-MO-Institute and Archive for the Parties and Mass Organizations in the GDR, located in the Bundesarchiv). DY 30- SED Zentral Kommittee IV 2-ZK Secretariat, 12-Arbeitsgruppe für Kirchenfragen, 124- Juni-Dezember 1945.

36. Diozesänarchiv Berlin (DAB- Diocese archive for Berlin). Abteilung I- Bischöfliches Ordinariat Berlin Repositur 4–3. The letter sent from Preysing to Zhukov is dated 10/5/45. The file does not contain any response Zhukov may have sent.

37. Wolfgang Tischner, "Die Kirchenpolitik unter Konrad Kardinal von Preysing 1945–1949" *Katholische Kirche in SBZ und DDR*. Christoph Kosters and Wolfgang Tischner, eds. 37–62. 51.

38. Evangelische Zentral Archiv (EZA-The Central Archive for the Evangelical Church in Germany). Bestand 4-EKD Kirchen Kanzlei, Repositur 351. Unlike Preysing, who soon tired of sending appeals to the Soviet authorities, Dibelius and other members of the EKD were much more active, sending request after request until 1948.

39. ACDP, *Signatur* 07–010-CDU Ost, 672.

40. Andreas Hermes, *Neue Zeit*. 28 Aug 1945. 1.

41. Goeckel, 43.

42. Norman Naimark, 86.

43. *Tägliche Rundschau* 14 Dec 1945, 5.

44. Naimark, 144.

45. DAB, Abteilung I-Bischöfliches Ordinariat Berlin, *Repositur* 4–3.

46. Evangelische Landeskirckenarchiv Berlin-Brandenburg (ELAB- Provincial Archive of the Evangelical Church in Berlin-Brandenburg), Bestand 603-Nachlasse Otto Dibelius, A 7. From an essay sent to Evangelical clergy and laity dated 8/2/49, entitled "Das Kirchliche Leben im Deutschen Osten."

47. Goeckel, 43. Beste and Mitzenheim were publicly supportive of a cooperative relationship between the Evangelical Church and the SVAG authorities, and later after the founding of the GDR with the SED leadership as well.

48. *Die Protokolle der Kirchlichen Ostkonferenz 1945–1949*. Eds, Michael Kuhne, Gottingen: Vandenhoeck & Ruprecht, 2005. 65, 88.

49. ACDP, *Signatur* 07–010, 672. Letter from Friedensburg to Hermes dated 12/15/45, Friedensburg mentioned that while he had sympathy for Hermes's position, it was too risky to offend the KPD and more importantly the SVAG authorities.

50. Bruce, 29. Bruce also notes how Hermes had received information from the CDU's head for political and economic affairs, Heinrich von der Gablentz, that confirmed that numerous landowners in the provinces were being removed from their land without any compensation.

51. GARF, f. 7077 (SVAG Brandenburg), op.1 (Upravlenie propagandy), d. 186 (Correspondence June–October 1945), ll. 22–24. Hermes and his closest deputy, Schraiber, would be dismissed shortly thereafter.

52. GARF, f. 7317, op. 19, d.1, ll. 65–66.

53. Bruce, 30.

54. *Deutsche Volkszeitung.* 10 Oct 1945, 12 Dec 1945, 19 Dec 1945.

55. Naimark, 183.

56. GARF, f.7077 (SVAG-Brandenburg), op. 1 (Upravlenie informatsii), d. 238 (Correspondence August–December 1947), ll. 123–156. The report was sent on July 29 1948, after the CDU's political independence in the Soviet zone had been suppressed.

57. GARF, f. 7077 (SVAG-Brandenburg), op. 1 (Upravlenie propagandy), d. 187 (Correspondence January–July 1946), l. 28.

58. ACDP, Signatur 07–010, 701. The letter from Kaiser to Tiul'panov is dated December 22, 1945.

59. Bruce, 31. Kaiser remained in constant contact with Konrad Adenauer, the leader of the CDU in the Western zones of Germany. Both Kaiser and Adenauer agreed on preserving the unity of the CDU in all four zones of Germany, although the free-market oriented Adenauer rejected Kaiser's doctrine of Christian Socialism.

60. *Neue Zeit.* 14 Feb 1946. 1.

61. Ibid.

62. *Neue Zeit.* 14 Feb 1946.

63. F. Lutge, "Christliche Wirtschaftsgestaltung" *Neue Zeit.* 28 Feb 1946.

64. ACDP, Signatur 07–010, 2179. (From the records of the monthly meetings of the Executive Committee of the CDU in the Soviet zone).

65. ACDP, Signatur 07–010, 1848. Dibelius did express a concern that many of the executive leadership positions within the CDU in the Soviet zone appeared to have an inordinate number of Catholics given their minority status in the Soviet zone, but he also noted the CDU had a number of Protestant leaders as well, including von Gablentz.

66. Tischner, 51. Preysing had stated at numerous instances he concurred with the desire of Kaiser to preserve the special role of the churches in German society.

67. ACDP, *Signatur* 07–010, 6157.

68. *Tägliche Rundschau* 8 Aug 1946.

69. Neues Deutschland 7 May 1946. It is important to note that the majority of articles in both the SED and SVAG newspapers concerning political topics attacked not Kaiser and the CDU leadership, but rather the despised Kurt Schumacher, the avowed anti-Soviet leader of the SPD in the Western zones of Germany.

70. GARF, f. 7371, op. 19, d. 1, ll. 68–69.

71. GARF, f. 7077 (SVAG Brandenburg), op. 1(Upravlenie propagandy), d. 203 (Correspondence January–June 1946), l. 81.

72. GARF, f. 7077 (SVAG Brandenburg), op. 1 (Upravlenie propagandy), d. 204 (Correspondence June–September 1946), ll. 58–61.

73. *SVAG i religioznye konfessii Sovetskoi zony okkupatsii Germanii 1945–1949: Sbornik dokumentov.* (SVAG and Religious Confessions in the Soviet zone of occupation: A Chronicle of Documents). Eds, V. V. Zakharov, O. V. Lavinskaia, D. N. Nokhotovich, and E. V. Poltoratskoi. Moscow: Rosspen 2006, 444–455.

74. *Die UdSSR und die Deutsche Frage 1941–1948: Dokumente aus dem Archiv für Aussenpolitik der Russischen Föderation Volume 2: 9 Mai 1945 bis 3. October 1946,* 516–535. Semenov did note in his report, written shortly after the joint CDU

party conference in Berlin on June 15 1946, that Adenauer and his political supporters were far more reactionary than Kaiser's yet this did not mean that they could not
pursue similar political strategies.

75. GARF, f. 7077, op. 1,d. 204, ll. 68–73. Tiul'panov also noted in his report
that party speakers from the Soviet zone at the CDU congress tried not to appear
as reactionaries, but were unsuccessful in masking their true intentions. He did not
mention specifically how the SED was supposed to strengthen its position against the
CDU in rural villages.

76. GARF, f. 7077, op. 1, d. 204, l. 83.

77. *Neues Deutschland* 20 Jun 1946. 1.

78. *Neues Deutschland*. 26 Jul 1946. 2.

79. Theodor Werner Tägliche Rundschau. 7 Aug 1946. 2. The same article was
printed on the same day in Neues Deutschland. It would be unfair to refer to Rackwitz
and Werner as simply hired stooges of the Communist authorities, as they genuinely
appeared to believe in the possibility of merging Evangelical theology with Marxist-
Leninist political theory.

80. *Neues Deutschland*. 15 Aug 1946. 2.

81. Otto Dibelius, *Tägliche Rundschau* 16 Aug 1946. 1. No equivalent article
appeared from the Catholic bishop Konrad von Preysing, although he too made
attempts to stress the neutrality of the Catholic Church in the political conflict and
was quite careful in his criticism of the policies of the SVAG and the SED during the
first few years of the Soviet occupation.

82. Goeckel, 42.

83. Jakob Kaiser Neue Zeit. 11 Aug 1946. 1.

84. Goeckel, 42.

85. Wilhelm Pieck and Otto Grotewohl. *Neues Deutschland*. 30 Aug 1946. 1.

86. SAPMO, NY 4036/756-Nachlässe Wilhelm Pieck.

87. ACDP, *Signatur* 07–010, 842. Kaiser's speech was not nearly inflammatory,
discussing the economic, cultural, and political foundations of Christian Socialism.

88. *Neue Zeit*. 7 Sept 1946. 1.

89. *Neue Zeit*, 1 Oct 1946. 1. This article of course, ignored serious divisions
between Kaiser and Adenauer over whether Christian Socialism would be adopted for
the CDU in the Western zones as well, possibly the biggest division between the two
along with the issue over whether Berlin would remain Germany's capital.

90. ACDP, *Signatur* 07–010, 1846.

91. *Die Protokolle der Kirchlichen Ostkonferenz 1945–1949*, 122–136.

92. DAB, *Abteilung V-Nachlässe Konrad von Preysing, Repositur*, 16–1.

93. GARF, f. 7077, op. 1, d. 192, ll. 147–152.

94. GARF. f. 7077, op. 1, d. 201, ll. 66–72.

95. Ibid., 112–122. Merzliakov also noted that the CDU did a successful job in
convincing religious peasants in the rural areas around Brandenburg that the SED was
implacably hostile to religious belief and religious institutions.

96. SVAG i religioznye konfessii Sovetskoi zony okkupatsii Germanii 1945–
1949: Sbornik dokumentov, 175–178. Variakin, like Mil'khiker and the other

provincial heads of the SVAG's propaganda administration, passed on these concerns to Tiul'panov.

97. GARF, f. 7077, op.1, d. 201. ll. 12–14. Mil'khiker emphasized in his instructions the Propaganda Administrations in the other provinces of the Soviet zone would pursue the same policy.

98. Naimark, 291.

99. Kurt Rackwitz, *Neues Deutschland*. 18 Oct 1945. Presumably the SED leadership believed such an article on the eve of elections should be written by a clergyman as opposed to an SED party leader, despite the fact that Pieck and Grotewohl had made similar statements regarding religious freedom.

100. Gustav Holt, *Tägliche Rundschau*. 19 Oct 1945. 1.

101. Naimark, 329.

102. *Tägliche Rundschau*. 22 Oct 1946, 1.

103. *Tägliche Rundschau*. 18 Oct 1946, 1. 22 Oct 1946, 1.

104. Steege, 92.

105. *Die USSR und die Deutsche Frage 1941–1948: Dokumente aus dem Archiv für Aussenpolitik der Russischen Föderation Volume 3*: 6 Oktober 1946 bis 15 Juni 1948. Eds, Jochen Laufer, Georgii Kinin and Viktor Knoll. Berlin: Duncker & Humbolt 2004. 125–132. Tiul'panov never admitted any culpability for the disastrous electoral results on the part of the SVAG's Propaganda Administration, besides a vague statement that the SED's identification as the "Russian party" damaged its reputation among much of the German population.

106. *SVAG i religioznye konfessii v Sovetskoi zony okkupatsii Germanii 1945–1949: Sbornik dokumentov*. 181–182. This was a rather interesting charge, as the Evangelical Bishop of Thuringia, Moritz Mitzenheim, was even at that point interested in a more conciliatory approach towards the SVAG and the SED, unlike Dibelius.

107. *Neue Zeit*. 22 Oct 1945. 1.

108. Jakob Kaiser, *Neue Zeit*. 7 Nov 1946. 2.

109. Otto Heinrich von Gablentz, *Neue Zeit*. 30 Nov 1946. 2.

110. ACDP, *Signatur* 07–010, 2179.

111. Ibid.

112. DAB, *Abteilung V Repositur* 16–5.

113. *Die Protokolle der Kirchlichen Ostkonferenz 1945–1949*, 137–152.

114. Otto Dibelius, *Neue Zeit* 1 Jan 1947. Dibelius's stressed his constant public message that all German political parties should work in cooperation with each other and with those in the Western zones of occupation in order to preserve the political and economic unity of Germany, this was clearly a paramount goal.

115. EZA, *Bestand* 4, 351. The charitable work of the churches was generally subject to fewer restrictions than their other activities; see chapter 2.

Chapter Three

The *Volkscongress* Movement and the End of the CDU's Political Independence, December 1946 to October 1949

INTRODUCTION

Writing to CPSU Central Committee's Foreign Affairs section on July 29 1948, Sergei Tiul'panov expressed a great deal of confidence that the problem of CDU reactionaries attempting to prevent the antifascist transformation of the Soviet zone had been solved. He wrote the Christian Democratic Party was always a particular political problem for the Soviet authorities. It had been a center of reactionary strength in the Soviet zone and attracted the political support of the German churches, which were among the most reactionary organizations within the zone. Tiul'panov summarized that Hermes and Kaiser had been under the control of the "Anglo-Americans" and has been unable to control the activities of the reactionaries within the CDU, who came to dominate the party. Kaiser had naively believed that he could revive the CDU as a version of the old Center party through his plan of "Christian Socialism."

According to Tiul'panov, the CDU became a true participant in the antifascist block only after Kaiser was expelled in December of 1947. He claimed the goal of the Information Administration was always to remove any independent initiative from the CDU and place them under the control of the SED and prevent the CDU in the Soviet zone from coming under the control of the reactionaries in the CDU/CSU in the Western zones. While Tiul'panov did not claim reactionary Catholic and Protestant clerical and laity would not cause further problems for the SVAG and the SED, they would no longer be able to work with political reactionaries in the CDU.[1]

The "special problem" that Tiul'panov admitted was posed by the CDU during the first two years of the occupation was "solved" due to the SVAG

51

and the SED efforts, to demonstrate their popular political viability for all four zones of Germany in late 1947. This was manifested by the controversy surrounding the *Volkscongress* (People's Congress) movement, which by the end of the year ended the political independence of the CDU and moved the leadership of the churches to the forefront of political resistance in the Soviet zone.

During the third year of the Soviet occupation the CDU leadership continued to emphasize its special role of guiding Germany to serve as a bridge between East and West, which could only be brought about by Christian Socialism. This theme was discussed constantly in the pages of *Neue Zeit* as well as in speeches by CDU leaders and in party pamphlets and advertisements. The CDU also made a number of attempts to add a further religious dimension to Christian Socialism by stating in the pages of *Neue Zeit* the Protestant and Catholic faith as practiced in Germany could serve as a "spiritual bridge between East and West." Exactly how this was to be accomplished was rather vague. All the articles could offer was that, just as Christian Socialism would incorporate elements of both capitalist and socialist economic systems, the churches would retain a prominent social and cultural role unlike under Soviet atheism, yet neither would exist as a "state church."[2]

The CDU's attempt to continue on an independent political path quickly brought it into conflict with the SVAG authorities and the SED, which had rapidly begun to consolidate all remaining economic and political power in the Soviet Zone in their hands. There remained fewer impediments to the Stalinization of the Soviet Zone once relations with the Western Allies deteriorated over the reparations issue throughout late 1946 and early 1947. In March 1947 Kaiser gave a speech at the Mecklenburg capital of Schwerin in which he warned the assembled CDU party members that many in the Soviet Zone believed that the time was right for the full implementation of Communism. He insisted that the CDU must resist such measures with all their strength, as they would only bring about irreparable harm to the prospects of maintaining German unity.[3]

During the spring and summer of 1947, Kaiser and Ernst Lemmer continued to speak out against SED efforts to dominate the antifascist block. On July 12 1947 the CDU leader gave a speech to assembled party members in Berlin which came to be known among his supporters as the "opposition speech", symbolizing his opposition to further steps towards an SED dictatorship.[4] Kaiser discretely praised the Marshall Plan, noting that it could provide for the economic recovery of all of Europe, including Germany. However, he noted that all four zones of Germany would have to participate. Soviet refusal of Eastern European participation, however, meant the Soviet zone of Germany would also be left behind. He pointedly insisted the CDU would continue on an independent political path, guided by the principles of Christian Socialism. It would not allow itself to become a branch of the SED, so long as arbitrary arrests continued and citizens in the zone lived in a state of fear and insecurity.[5]

In a meeting with Tiul'panov on August 17, Kaiser and his party's leadership assured him that the CDU wanted to continue to have a cooperative relationship with the Soviet authorities and the antifascist block to maintain the unity of Germany. Kaiser insisted that the German people remained in a desperate situation, and needed assistance from all the Allied powers. However, Germany could never hope to recover under the burden of crushing reparations payments, as the Soviet government insisted. Furthermore, the majority of the German people in all of the zones wished to participate in the Marshall Plan. He warned Tiul'panov that the Soviet dismantling of factories and shipping them off to the Soviet Union was building political support for the Western Allies as opposed to the USSR. In his report concerning the conversation to A. A. Smirnov, the deputy chief of the European Section of the Soviet Union's Foreign Ministry, Tiul'panov informed him that he and the head of SVAG Marshal Sokolovskii had decided it was time to undermine Kaiser's position as head of the CDU in the Soviet zone and find more pliable CDU leaders.[6]

This tense meeting was followed by the CDU party conference in Berlin from September 4–8. This gathering was noteworthy for its pointed criticisms of SVAG and SED actions in the Soviet zone. Kaiser stated: "We must be, and we want to be, a breakwater against dogmatic Marxism and its totalitarian tendencies."[7] The head of the CDU in Sachsen, Robert Tillmans, went even further in his speech. He attacked Marxism-Leninism and the foolish attempts by the SVAG and the SED to implement it in the Soviet zone, and he pointedly ignored the presence of Tiul'panov during his speech.

Despite the overwhelming re-election of Kaiser and Lemmer to their leadership positions in the CDU following its party congress at the beginning of September, both served only for three more months. Following the slow progress at the Foreign Minister's Conference in London in the last two months of 1947 and the recognition that the failure among the four powers to reach agreement over the future government of Germany would likely lead to the indefinite economic and political division of country, the SED and SVAG leadership decided that a new tactic was necessary to secure SED influence over Germany.[8] This was the *Volkscongress* movement. In November of 1947, at the initiative of the Soviet government, the SED sent out invitations to all political parties, mass organizations, and factory and agricultural organizations in all four zones to send representatives to the Soviet sector of Berlin, for a conference from December 6–7. There they would draw up a provisional constitution for Germany and elect a group of representatives to submit the constitution to the Allied Foreign Ministers in London.[9]

Kaiser staunchly resisted CDU participation in the *Volkscongress*. He made a number of public statements in November stating his misgivings about the movement and at a meeting of party leaders of the antifascist block on November 24, he voiced his opposition to the *Volkscongress*. He stated it would never be truly representative for all of Germany, as the CDU and SPD in the Western zones were unlikely to participate in considerable numbers. According to Kaiser all the movement was likely to accomplish was to provide a pretense for the SED to present itself as representative of the political views of most Germans.[10] At the executive committee meeting of the CDU, Kaiser and Lemmer rejected official CDU participation in the *Volkscongress*, although they agreed at the insistence of Nuschke, Dertinger, and the head of the CDU in Sachsen-Anhalt Hugo Hickmann that individual CDU members could attend. Most of the regional leaders of the CDU supported Nuschke, but the former vice-chairman of the CDU in 1945, Walter Schraiber, now head of the CDU in West Berlin, strongly rejected any form of participation.[11]

The SVAG and SED press harshly attacked Kaiser for his opposition to the *Volkscongress* movement. In the November 16 issue of *Neues Deutschland,* the reliable pro-SED Protestant cleric Karl Rackwitz called upon all Protestants in Germany to resist the tide of "the torture of Humanity, Capitalism, and Militarism," and not to be swayed by the reactionary and nationalist statements by the CDU but to join with all socialist and antifascist elements to work towards German unity.[12] Three days later, another article appeared that accused Kaiser of peddling the "false doctrines" of Christian Socialism in order to mask his true, reactionary desires to join with the CDU and SPD leaders in the Western zones in order to assist the British and Americans in "colonizing" Germany. The article pointed to Kaiser's public criticisms of the *Volkscongress* movement, which the author deemed as the best hope of preserving German unity and independence.[13]

Tägliche Rundschau published an even more inflammatory article containing remarks by Tiul'panov which insinuated the American and British military governments, as well as CDU in the Western zones, were secretly working with Kaiser to undermine the *Volkscongress*. While he denied a specific rumor that British army intelligence officers were active in the Soviet zone working with CDU party members, Tiul'panov stated that Kaiser's reactionary positions had created a deep crisis within the leadership of the CDU.[14]

This "crisis" was resolved shortly thereafter, as Tiul'panov met with Kaiser and Lemmer on December 17 and informed them their "anti-democratic" stance with regards to the question of CDU participation in the *Volkscongress* meant the SVAG would deny them the leadership of the CDU in the Soviet zone. Kaiser and Lemmer protested this decision. They stated their opposition to the *Volkscongress* movement did not mean they did not desire to work with the SVAG and the SED to preserve German unity. Tiul'panov stated the CDU's consistently reactionary policies under Kaiser's leadership had made it impossible for the Soviet authorities to allow them to threaten the supposed democratic transformation of Germany. He concluded there was no possibility of either of them ever again leading a political organization in the Soviet zone.[15] Both left for the Western sectors of Berlin and continued their criticism of the encroaching Communist dictatorship in the Soviet zone. On January 13, Kaiser gave a speech to assembled CDU party members entitled "Um Demokratie und Freiheit" (Concerning Democracy and Freedom). He described the threat posed by the policies of the SED, specifically the *Volkscongress* movement, as well as his own disappointment with the CDU leaders in the Soviet zone who supported it. Kaiser stated he would continue his work to support German unity, despite the increasing political repression in the Soviet zone.[16]

The removal of Kaiser and Lemmer by the SVAG meant any future CDU leaders would have to abandon even the pretense of political independence and follow the SED's lead in creating a German state on the Soviet model. Kaiser's successor Otto Nuschke acted in this manner since he believed this would be the only way the CDU could continue to exist in any form the Soviet Zone. This meant Christian Socialism, as a viable alternative to the Marxism-Leninism, would have to be discarded by the CDU. This followed the SED leadership's decision to force its own members to renounce a special "German road to socialism" during the emerging conflict between Yugoslav leader Josip Tito and Joseph Stalin. The appeal of Christian Socialism for the Protestant and Catholic churches as well as for religious Germans appeared to SVAG officials in the Information Administration as an impediment to their long-term political goals in the Soviet zone. Yet since the churches maintained their policy of public institutional neutrality, removing the CDU leaders who supported Christian Socialism and a political identity independent of the SED could solve this problem. It would not be until Kaiser and Lemmer, the last remaining political leaders who did not follow the line of SVAG and the SED were removed and anti-religious policies intensified that the Protestant and Catholic church leadership in Berlin-Brandenburg began to speak out more openly concerning political developments in the Soviet zone

THE TRANSFORMATION OF THE CDU INTO A PARTNER OF THE "ANTIFASCIST TRANSFORMATION" AND THE EMERGING OPPOSITION OF DIBELIUS AND PREYSING, JANUARY 1948 TO OCTOBER 1949

The issue of collaboration between the CDU and the Protestant and Catholic churches, so dominant from 1945 to 1947, became far less important for Soviet authorities following Kaiser's replacement by Nuschke and the loss of the CDU's political independence during the last two years of the Soviet occupation. The new leadership of the CDU chairman Otto Nuschke and vice-chairmen Otto Heinrich von der Lobedanz and Georg Dertinger proved to be more compliant to the demands of the SVAG and the SED authorities. All three were official participants in the *Volkscongress* convention in the month of December. During the convention, Nuschke pledged the CDU's commitment to true cooperation in the antifascist block, and stated the CDU would always work with the SED and the Soviet Union to maintain German unity and would resist attempts by the political leaders of the Western zones to turn it into an Anglo-American colony.[17]

The reaction of the Protestant and Catholic churches to these statements was, unsurprisingly, rather muted. While leaders of the Evangelical Church in the Soviet zone, such as Dibelius, Mitzenheim, and head of POW affairs D. D. Asmussen, remained in constant contact with the SVAG authorities, none sent a letter of protest concerning Kaiser's removal. Most correspondence with SVAG officials during 1947 and 1948 concerned either the fate of German POWs, especially military chaplains who had been taken prisoner by the Red Army, or the spiritual status of inmates in the internment camps. At the first meeting of the Protestant Church leadership in the Soviet zone following the *Volkscongress* on January 10 1948, the main issue discussed was the successful petition to the supreme commander of SVAG, Marshal Sokolovskii, by the Protestant bishops to allow the distribution of religious literature and occasional religious services in the internment camps. Kaiser's removal as the head of the CDU and the *Volkscongress* was not even mentioned.[18]

Preysing also did not issue any public statements with regard to Kaiser's political fate, despite the fact that Kaiser was easily the most prominent Catholic politician in the Soviet zone. Five months after the *Volkscongress* in May 1948 Preysing sent a letter to be distributed to Catholic churches throughout the Soviet zone, which stated the *Volkscongress* was nothing more than a SED-front designed to spread its political control over all of Germany. Preysing stated the SED had to be opposed because it had shown itself to be the enemy of the Catholic Church in Germany. Otto Nuschke, the leader of the CDU since Kaiser's expulsion, publicly rebuked Preysing for his attempts to undermine the CDU's efforts to work with the SED and LDP to preserve German unity, claiming the Catholic bishop was following the same pattern of behavior of Catholic bishops in the Weimar era, placing the narrow interests of conservative clergy ahead of what was best for Germany.[19]

Many SVAG officials were not convinced that Kaiser's influence had dissipated over the CDU in the Soviet zone. Lieutenant Colonel K. V. Martem'ianov, who had replaced Mil'khiker as the head of the Information Department in Brandenburg in mid-1947, reported to Tiul'panov on December 31 1947 that much of the CDU leadership in Brandenburg and East Berlin had distanced themselves from Kaiser and his doctrine of Christian Socialism, but had only done so because they were afraid of sharing Kaiser's fate. He judged that "reactionary" strength remained strong in the CDU.[20] In a similar report sent in February, Martem'ianov wrote to Tiul'panov, informing him Erich Wolf, the leader of the CDU in Brandenburg, while loyal to Nuschke, had not been able to suppress the influence of reactionaries still loyal to Kaiser and the doctrine of Christian Socialism.[21]

It would not be until May that Martem'ianov reported to Tiul'panov that Wolf and the rest of the CDU leadership in Brandenburg had successfully suppressed "Kaiserite" elements as well as talk about the CDU implementing Christian Socialism. Nonetheless he still admitted to the presence of reactionaries within the CDU in Brandenburg, although they were less numerous and less vocal.[22] Other regional heads of the SVAG's Information Administration were far less optimistic. As late as September 1948 Tiul'panov received a report from Colonel N. S. Rodionov, the head of Information Administration in Sachsen-Anhalt, that the CDU in the province was still full of Kaiser's supporters, especially among Catholic members of the party as well as women and youths. Rodionov assured Tiul'panov the politically reliable party leadership of the CDU in Sachsen-Anhalt was gradually suppressing the influence of those who continued to support Kaiser.[23]

Tiul'panov and his lieutenants were largely proven correct with regards to CDU activity during the last two years of the Soviet occupation. Nuschke received a letter from SED head Wilhelm Pieck in March 1948 informing him that despite the success of the *Volkscongress* movement in uniting the progressive political forces in the Soviet zone, in the Western zone of Germany and in West Berlin CDU leader Konrad Adenauer and SPD leader Kurt Schumacher and their "reactionary" clique had embarked on policies certain to lead Germany down the capitalist path. Pieck also added that Adenauer depended on the assistance of the Anglo-Americans, and that the CDU, SED, and LDP in the Soviet zone had to work together in ensuring that none of Adenauer's or Schumacher's supporters in the Soviet zone gained any political influence.[24] In fact, the CDU had already implemented this policy.

Political agitation material from the CDU in the Soviet zone during this period made no mention of Christian Socialism or of religious concerns at all, but rather focused on how to best cooperate with the antifascist block to maintain Germany's unity and "democratic transformation" with the assistance of the SED and the SVAG.[25]

Stark evidence of this change in the CDU's position emerged during the midst of the Berlin Blockade in August 1948. In the background of the desperate attempts by the British and the Americans to hold their position in the Western sectors of Berlin in the face of seeming Soviet and SED dominance, Nuschke announced to assembled members of his party's leadership that the CDU would continue its cooperation with the SED in the antifascist bloc to preserve the unity of Germany against the separatist ideologies of Kaiser, Adenauer and Schumacher. Furthermore, it needed to direct their efforts towards this goal at all levels of the CDU party organizations in the Soviet zone.[26]

Religious concerns were barely mentioned at most of the meetings of the executive leadership of the CDU in 1949, and this proved to be the case in the provincial leadership as well. The CDU took more steps to limit its political independence, such as Georg Dertinger's February 1949 letter to the SED's head of women's organizations Kathe Kern. Here the CDU vice-chairman assured Kern the CDU youth and women's organizations would work in cooperation with the SED's to ensure the continuation of the antifascist democratic transformation of Germany and to marshal the strength of the Soviet zone's political parties to preserve German unity.[27]

As the final preparations towards the creation of an East German state on the Soviet model began in the fall of 1949, the CDU leadership abandoned even the pretense of political independence. Following the official proclamation of the Federal Republic of Germany in the Western zones, Dertinger and Nuschke joined with Pieck, Ulbricht, Grotewohl, and LDP leader Hermann Kastner in public statement on September 30, which announced that the division of Germany by the separatist Bonn republic a few days earlier allowed the antifascist progressive forces in the Soviet zone to proclaim the existence of the German Democratic Republic (GDR). The GDR was officially proclaimed seven days later with Nuschke serving as a deputy prime minister and Dertinger as Foreign Minister.[28]

Shortly thereafter, the final break with any Christian Socialist ideas occurred, as the executive leadership of the CDU issued a proclamation to the regional leaders of the CDU stating the CDU would seek a firm and long-lasting friendship with the Soviet Union and would work to accelerate the process of socialization in the GDR. The CDU instead sought to find common ground between Marxism-Leninism-Stalinism and Christianity. Marxism could only exist on a scientific basis, not a spiritual one, and thus the CDU proclamation held it was a Christian's job to support the creation of secular socialism rather than try to support compromises between Christianity and Marxism-Leninism.[29]

This transformation did not immediately manifest itself in the pages of *Neue Zeit* following the removal of Kaiser, but gradually emerged from January 1948 to October 1949. On January 1 1948, an article written by Otto Dibelius stated the German people should be optimistic in the hope that Germany would emerge as a united, democratic country. He called on the people of the Soviet zone not to fear that they would return to the atmosphere of denunciations and fear that characterized the Nazi era. Dibelius promised that the Protestant Church would continue its charitable activities and strive to preserve the unity of Germany.[30]

During the spring of 1948, articles which emphasized the importance of Christian humanism for German cultural development continued. One example was an article by a Protestant cleric from Brandenburg named Emil Dilschneider. Dilschneider argued Christian humanism had played a decisive role in the works of national German writers such as Goethe and Herder, and that this phenomenon extended to other "national writers" such as Shakespeare and Dostoevsky.[31]

Far more common, however, were articles such as "Der Weg der CDU in der Ostzone" (The Path of the CDU in the Eastern Zone) by an Evangelical cleric named Ludwig Kirsch from the city of Chemnitz in Thuringia. It appeared on May 6 1948, one month before the Berlin Blockade began. Kirsch stated the CDU in the Soviet zone continued to work towards a peaceful resolution of Germany's political and economic divisions. He rejected criticisms of the party by CDU politicians and clergy in the Western zones that it was nothing more than a puppet for the Soviets and the SED. Kirsch reminded readers that the Soviet authorities had allowed for free exercise of religion in the Soviet zone, and there was no reason to expect that they would rescind it.[32]

By the end of 1948, *Neue Zeit* moved towards a harshly critical position of those who opposed the "antifascist democratic transformation" of the Soviet zone. In an article in mid-October, an anonymous author attacked Otto Dibelius for his recent statements that Protestant clerics should not take part in acts of political or social upheaval, or even voice support for it. The article stated that Dibelius's statements only demonstrated the continued hold of "reactionaries" over the Protestant church in the Soviet zone.[33]

Ludwig Kirsch, who emerged as a popular Protestant writer for the CDU newspaper in 1948 and 1949, moved to a more conciliatory direction in his article on January 4 1949, claiming the Soviet Union was the only nation that had ever favored the maintenance of German unity. For him, the CDU had nothing to fear from further cooperation with the SED, which had no interest in establishing a new German dictatorship.[34] In the same spirit, during the spring of 1949, *Neue Zeit* published a series of articles, which argued that the Catholic and Evangelical churches should not involve themselves in the emerging class struggle in the Soviet zone of Germany, but should work to ameliorate its effects.[35]

By the fall of 1949, shortly before the end of the Soviet occupation and the founding the GDR, *Neue Zeit* also made its final break with Kaiser and any lingering support for the ideas of Christian Socialism. In a front page article on September 15 1949, the CDU renounced any attempts to create a "Christian" version of Marxism, while holding the Protestant and Catholic churches, through their charitable activities, could still assist the growth of socialism along the Marxist-Leninist path.[36] Despite this statement, the CDU newspaper continued to publish articles concerning the relevance of Christian thought to German cultural life, especially concerning Goethe's writings, as well as the importance of religious figures such as Martin Luther for Germany's historical development along the "progressive" road, an interesting development given the later harsh criticism of Luther by SED ideologists as the "gravedigger of German democracy."[37]

Reports from Tiul'panov's Information Administration also began to find less collaboration between the CDU and the churches in 1948 and 1949. K. V. Martem'ianov, reported to Tiul'panov in June 1948 while the CDU at the provincial and local levels remained continued to work with clergy to preserve religious education in the schools and continue church charity work, they no longer took an active part in political or economic life.[38] One month later, Martem'ianov informed him that, while there remained lingering support for Kaiser among some CDU members, the leadership of the CDU in Brandenburg remained solidly behind the new line of Nuschke and Dertinger.[39] By the end of the year, the regional heads of the Information Administration linked the CDU and the churches in "reactionary" activity less and less, although this did not mean that the churches were not working with anti-Soviet forces. In December 1948, Martem'ianov expressed worries to Tiul'panov that the Protestant and Catholic churches were working with the "Schumacherites" to undermine the activities of the SED's youth organization, the Free German Youth.[40]

This did not mean that heads of the SVAG's Information Administration abruptly stopped associating religious activities with political activism for the CDU. A report sent to Martem'ianov by the head of the Information Administration in the Beeskow region A. V. Gevorkian in January 1949 explicitly linked charitable activity by the Protestant and Catholic churches to supporting the political fortunes of the CDU.[41] Likewise, Martem'ianov, Rodionov, and the other provincial heads of SVAG Information Administration ordered their lieutenants at the regional and local levels to prevent collaboration between "reactionaries" among Catholic and Protestant clergy and the CDU.[42]

Other officials in the SVAG remained convinced that members of the CDU in the Soviet zone were still working with reactionary clergy against the Soviet authorities. In September 1949, shortly before the founding of the GDR, A. G. Russkikh, the deputy head of the SVAG Department for Political Affairs, informed his superiors in the Political Department of the Supreme Soviet of the USSR that the Protestant bishop Otto Dibelius was secretly holding meetings in his residence in West Berlin for CDU members from both halves of the city, meetings dedicated to finding ways to assist the Anglo-Americans in undermining SVAG and SED authority throughout the Soviet zone.[43]

Dibelius and Preysing had emerged by this point as vocal critics of political, social, and economic developments in the zone, effectively taking Kaiser's place as a voice for popular discontent in the Soviet zone from 1948–1949. Just as the SVAG's perceptions of Christian Socialism as having the potential of uniting the churches and the CDU against the Soviet authorities contributed to the decision to remove Kaiser as CDU leader, the increasingly public opposition of Dibelius and Preysing to SVAG and SED policies contributed to sharp attacks on them in *Tägliche Rundschau* and *Neues Deutschland*. Both the Protestant and Catholic leaders became easy substitutes for Kaiser as leaders of "reactionary" forces in the Soviet Zone.

Preysing had striven for much of Soviet occupation to avoid making public statements which might antagonize either the SVAG authorities or the SED, despite his frequent letters sent to SVAG protesting certain policies. During his goodwill tour of the United States in the spring of 1947, Preysing continuously refused to speak on political conditions within the Soviet zone, despite the fact that most of Catholic laity of Berlin lived in areas under Soviet administration. Capitalizing on his role as a prominent internal Catholic opponent of the Nazi regime, Preysing attempted to assure his American audiences that the German people had abandoned Nazism, and that American aid was still necessary to alleviate the desperate living conditions in all four of the occupation zones.[44] Preysing's speech at the University of Notre Dame on March 21 1947 contained a perfect summary of his message for the American people: "We are confronted in Germany with the aftermath of the terrible ideology of Nazism. Thank God it has been destroyed. But the war has left our cities, churches, and hospitals in ruins. Our people are freezing and starving. That is why we are appealing to generous Americans for help."[45]

By late 1947 and throughout 1948 and 1949, Preysing took an increasingly disparaging tone towards the SVAG and SED authorities in communication with his clerical subordinates and the Catholic laity in the Soviet zone. In September 1947 Preysing sent a pastoral letter (*Hirtenbrief*) to be read at Catholic churches in the Soviet zone as well as in the Western zones. In the letter he accused the SVAG of misusing land reforms to seize property from political enemies of the Soviets or the KPD/SED, attempting to end religious education in public schools, refusing to allow for the creation of confessional schools for children, and finally the administration of the former Nazi camp at Sachsenhausen as a new camp for political enemies of the Communists.[46] On the eve of elections to the second *Volkscongress* in May 1948, Preysing sent a pastoral letter to all Catholic clerics and laity in Berlin and Brandenburg denouncing the *Volkscongress* as a SED-front and urging all German Catholics not to participate. This in turn led to harsh criticism of Preysing as a reactionary not only by the SED but also by the CDU's leader Otto Nuschke.[47]

Following this dispute, most of Preysing's subsequent pastoral letters in 1948 were more subdued and did not mention political topics, although he urged German Catholics to continue with educational and charitable work, regardless of what obstacles were placed in front of them by state authorities. By mid 1949, however, the pastoral letters again took a critical tone, especially directed towards the CDU's loss of political independence, and the rapid construction of Stalinist-style socialism in the Soviet zone. One particular theme was the comparison of the new SED-led German *Volkspolizei* in the Soviet zone to the Gestapo.[48]

While Preysing was clearly the leading authority among the Catholic Church in the Soviet zone, the Protestant Church could not speak with one voice. However, a number of leading officials in the Protestant Church, especially Otto Dibelius, emerged as prominent critics of political developments in the last two years of the Soviet occupation. In a pastoral letter written in October 1948 and distributed to all Protestant churches in Berlin-Brandenburg, Dibelius wrote Berlin had become the battleground for two competing ideologies, one grounded in the ideals of intellectual and religious freedom, the other in atheism and materialism. He continued by arguing the Soviet side wanted to extend their ideology to the Atlantic ocean, and during this difficult time the German people, especially the inhabitants of Berlin, had to rely on their spiritual strength to resist.[49]

In Dibelius's famous pastoral letter distributed on June 1 1949 (and reprinted in several newspapers in West Berlin and Western occupation zones), he argued the Protestant Church must strive for political neutrality while at the same time it should resist the re-establishment of a dictatorship in the Soviet zone. Dibelius pointed to imposition of state censorship, the elimination of genuine multi-party democracy, and the brutal actions of the newly-created "special divisions" of the *Volkspolizei*, which Dibelius, like Preysing, explicitly compared to the Gestapo. Dibelius expressed hope that the continued unity of the Protestant Church between Western and Soviet zones would help to preserve the political unity of Germany, and for that reason the Church would never allow itself to be "divided between East and West." He concluded the letter by stating for Christians, the highest authority was God and his heavenly scripture, and the Protestant laity should resist any attempt by political authorities, especially the SVAG and the SED to supplant his divine role.[50]

For these statements, Dibelius came under direct attack by the SED. The party used an Protestant cleric to make their attack for them in the pages of *Neues Deutschland*. In this case, it was an Protestant cleric named Hans Schwartz from the Mecklenburg city of Ludwigslust. Schwartz wrote that the inhabitants in the Soviet zone were well aware of Dibelius's positions as friendly to NATO, which Schwartz referred as "an imperial military pact directed against the Soviet Union and the People's Democracies of Eastern Europe." He alleged it was inappropriate for a leading Evangelical Bishop to take a political position against the SVAG and the SED, especially since both had done so much to rebuild the antifascist democracy in the Soviet zone and had not attacked religious freedom. He finally warned Dibelius such reactionary positions would only hurt the churches in the long run, as both the majority of the clergy and the majority of the German people did not care for Dibelius's "imperialist friends" and would turn away from the churches if individuals such as him led them.[51]

Dibelius continued on this path until the very end of the Soviet occupation, writing in another pastoral letter on August 2 1949 that future of religious and political life in the Soviet zone looked grim indeed. The bishop wrote that both the land and school reforms were intended solely to serve the ideological ends of the SVAG and the SED, not the needs of the population of the Soviet zone. He noted a totalitarian state had been created in the Soviet zone over the past four years, and its politicizing of all aspects of life was a considerable threat to religious freedom in the zone. German Protestant Christians should prepare themselves for the continuation of dictatorship in East Germany.[52] Like Preysing, Dibelius continued after the founding of GDR in October 1949 to issue similar public criticisms of the regime, and while Preysing would die the next year, Dibelius would emerge as the most vocal religious critic of the East German regime during its first two decades of existence.

CONCLUSION

Understanding the relationship between the CDU and the Protestant and Catholic churches, both what it truly was and how it was perceived by SVAG and SED authorities, is vital to understanding the numerous other religious controversies which occurred during the Soviet occupation, such as the dispute over religious education, the charitable activities of the churches and the role played by religious youth and women's organizations. The Soviets and to a lesser extent the Socialist Unity Party were determined to limit cooperation between "reactionaries" in the CDU and the churches as well as prevent the CDU from realistically claiming to represent all religious Germans in the Soviet zone. This reached its peak during the lead up to the zonal elections in October 1946. The poor showing of the SED and the success of the CDU only magnified SVAG and SED insecurities regarding these issues, despite the fact that the electoral results did not alter the political control exercised by the Soviet authorities and their East German "friends."

Following the destruction of the CDU's political independence with the removal of Jakob Kaiser as its leader in December 1947, these fears subsided slightly, although both the SVAG and the SED authorities, especially Sergei Tiul'panov and Wilhelm Pieck, continued to fear the political influence of the churches. This did not stop them from enlisting clerical "progressives" such as Kurt Rackwitz and Theodor Werner to undermine "reactionary" clergymen. The relationship between the CDU and the Protestant and Catholic churches at the zonal, provincial, and local levels was far more complex than it was interpreted by the SVAG and the SED. Undoubtedly, certain clergy and CDU party members supported each other's goals of maintaining Christian religious institutions as vital public institutions in the Soviet zone, as public statements and private correspondence by figures such as Dibelius, Preysing, Hermes, and Kaiser indicate.

Yet both sides pursued their objectives independently. Certainly neither the Catholic nor the Protestant churches saw the CDU as their "voice" for the Soviet authorities. They preferred to resolve any issues they had with the Soviet authorities directly. Likewise, Kaiser's attempt to use Christian Socialism as the guiding ideology of the CDU after January 1946 was a clear attempt to win over all religious Germans in the Soviet zone. At the same time it was an attempt by the CDU to move away from a strictly confessional identity by emphasizing an economic and political alternative to the SED's

Marxism-Leninism that could appeal to religious German workers as well as the middle class.

Neither can it be claimed that Hermes, Kaiser, Dibelius, or Preysing were the sole voices for popular discontent with the "antifascist democratic transformation" in the Soviet zone, or that they represented all religious Germans. Nevertheless, both the CDU and the church leadership symbolized a significant element of the population who proved unwilling to trade one dictatorship for another. Given the eventual collapse of the German Democratic Republic in 1989 and the Soviet Union itself in 1991, it is easy to forget that it in the late 1940s it appeared to many clergy and laity that the order exemplified by the SVAG and SED, as harsh as it could be, was also extremely stable and permanent. Thus, the early opposition of figures such as Kaiser and Dibelius not only took considerable courage in the face of a totalitarian political authority but also a willingness to stand isolated from one's supposed allies.

Notes

1. GARF, f. 7077, op. 1, d. 238, ll. 123–156.

2. *Neue Zeit.* 9 Sept 1947. 2. The unnamed authors of the article reportedly came from Sachsen, Thuringia, and Brandenburg.

3. ACDP, *Signatur* 07–010- CDU Ost, #842-Jakob Kaiser. Kaiser also noted during the speech that divisions between the Allies over the German question was hardly surprising, given that much of the world still did not trust the Germans due to Hitler's "adventurism"

4. Bruce, 78.

5. ACDP, *Signatur* 07–010-CDU Ost, 1851.

6. *Die UdSSR und die Deutsche Frage 1941–1948: Dokumente aus dem Archiv für Aussenpolitik der Russischen Föderation Volume 3*: 6 Oktober 1946 bis 15 Juni 1948. 375–378. This discussion demonstrates that purely religious issues were not of primary importance for Kaiser, as he referenced the Soviet dismantling of factories as opposed to the their attempts to restrict religious education in the schools. Tiul'panov did not mention in his report what his own comments to Kaiser were.

7. Bruce, 79.

8. Ibid.

9. *Neues Deutschland.* 2 Nov 1947. This article announcing the SED's invitation to form the *Volkscongress* was soon followed by articles in subsequent days and weeks that unsurprisingly attacked the authorities in the Western occupation zones for refusing to allow the Germans there to organize efforts to participate in the movement.

10. Bruce, 79. Ultimately some delegates from the CDU in the Western zones did attend, but the majority of participants were members of the SED or SED-led organizations such as the Free German Youth and Free German Trade Union.

11. ACDP, *Signatur* 07–010-CDU Ost, 2073-Jakob Kaiser.

12. *Neues Deutschland.* 16 Nov 1947. 2.

13. *Neues Deutschland.* 19 Nov 1947. 1.

14. *Tägliche Rundschau.* 14 Dec 1947. 3.

15. Naimark, 341.

16. ACDP, *Signatur* 07–010, 2073. Kaiser later joined Konrad Adenauer's first government for West Germany in 1949, serving as the minister for All-German affairs.

17. *Tägliche Rundschau* 7 Dec 1947. 3.

18. *Die Protokolle der Kirchlichen Ostkonferenz 1945–1949.* 232.

19. DAB, *Abteilung I- Bischöfliches Ordinariat Berlin Repositur* 4–15–1.

20. GARF, f. 7077- (SVAG Brandenburg), op. 1 (Upravlenie informatsii) d. 221 (Correspondence August–December 1947), ll. 114–122.

21. GARF, f. 7077 (SVAG Brandenburg), op.1 (Upravlenie informatsii), d. 238 (Correspondence February–December 1948), ll. 70–73.

22. GARF, f. 7077, op.1, d. 238, ll. 105–117.

23. *SVAG i religioznye konfessii Sovetskoi zony okkupatsii Germanii 1945–1949*: Sbornik dokumentov. 472–474. Rodionov noted that the majority of the party members loyal to Nuschke were Protestants, while supporters of Kaiser tended to be Catholics, and expressed hope that the SED could capitalize on this theological divide.

24. ACDP, *Signatur* 07–010, 1843. From the official papers of CDU leader Otto Nuschke. Pieck also explicitly ordered Nuschke not to meet with his CDU counterparts in the Western zones during an upcoming meeting in Frankfurt am Main, given Adenauer's reactionary stance towards the SED.

25. ACDP, *Signatur* 07–010, 1848.

26. ACDP, *Signatur* 07–010- CDU Ost 2039-Jakob Kaiser.

27. Ibid. This was sharp contrast with CDU policies from 1945–1947, when the party under Hermes's and Kaiser's leadership reviewed its youth and women's organizations as major means of drawing support away from the SED. See also chapter 4.

28. Ibid. The other deputy prime ministers were Ulbricht and Wilhelm Kastner, head of the LDP, with Pieck as President and Grotewohl as Prime Minister.

29. ACDP *Signatur* 07–011- CDU Ost, 543.

30. *Neue Zeit.* 1 Jan 1948. 2

31. "Christeuntum und Humanisumus" *Neue Zeit.* 11 Jan 1948. 1.

32. *Neue Zeit.* 6 May 1948. 1.

33. *Neue Zeit.* 15 Oct 1948. 1.

34. *Neue Zeit.* 4 Jan 1949. 1.

35. *Neue Zeit.* 19 Feb 1949 2, Neue Zeit. 13 April 1949. 1.

36. *Neue Zeit.* 15 Sept 1949. 1.

37. *Neue Zeit.* 18 Aug 1949. 3.

38. GARF, f. 7077 (SVAG Brandenburg), op.1 (Upravlenie informatsii), d. 226 (Correspondence January–June 1948), ll. 141–163.

39. GARF, f. 7077, op.1, d. 226, ll. 281–298.

40. GARF, f. 7077 (SVAG Brandenburg), op.1 (Upravlenie informatsii), d. 242 (Correspondence August–December 1948) , ll. 216–222.

41. GARF, f. 7077, op.1, d. 254, ll. 23–24.

42. GARF, f. 7077, op.1, d. 254, ll. 42–43.

43. *Politika SVAG v oblasti kul'tury, nauki, i obrazovaniia: tseli, metody, rezul'taty, 1945–1949: Sbornik dokumentov.* Eds, H. Mueller, A. O. Chubar'ian, H. Weber, V. P. Kozlov, and S. V. Mironenko. Moscow: Rosspen 2006. 476–478.

44. DAB Abteilung V-Nachlässe Konrad von Preysing, Repositur 16–9.

45. Archives of the University of Notre Dame, UDIS 115/65.

46. DAB, Abteilung I, Repositur 4–15–1.

47. DAB, Abteilung V, Repositur 16–1. Preysing did note in a letter that the stated goals of the *Volkscongress*, the preservation of German unity and the securing of political independence, were admirable, but that did not justify cooperation with the SED.

48. DAB, Abteilung V, Repositur 16–7-2.

49. ELAB, Bestand 603-Nachlässe Otto Dibelius A 7 -1.1.

50. ELAB, Bestand 603, B 10. Dibelius would return to these arguments frequently during the next ten years, especially with his 1959 pastoral letter *Obrigkeit* (Obedience), which argued that Christians in the GDR no longer needed to follow the regime's laws, as it had attempted to exercise powers reserved only for God.

51. *Neues Deutschland.* 23 Jun 1949. 2.

52. ELAB, Bestand 603, A 7–1.1.

Chapter Four

"Unity Schools Are Secular Schools"

The Struggle over Religious Education in the Secondary Schools of Berlin-Brandenburg

"Long after the SVAG was gone, the USSR continued to control the East German educational apparatus. For there was seldom much difference between the contents of the DDR and the USSR schoolbook: What Hänschen learned to read was usually very similar to what little Ivan was learning to read. What East Berlin mandated had already been handed down from Moscow."

—John Rodden[1]

INTRODUCTION

Following the end of the Second World War, the SVAG and the SED were determined to radically change the secondary *(Gymnasium)* school system, which educated children from the ages of ten to seventeen. Since the Soviets and the SED as well as the leadership of the Catholic and Protestant churches viewed the educational system as an essential tool in their plans to rebuild Germany from the legacy of Nazism, the bitter conflict over the issue of religious education in the schools was inevitable.

The Soviet authorities and the members of the SED who controlled the German organs of self-government (PVs) believed the educational system during the Third Reich had cultivated racist and militarist beliefs in German children. Thus, secondary education helped to transform them into fanatical Nazis. Only an educational system that contributed to the development of an "antifascist and democratic spirit," which in reality meant support for Stalinist-style socialism, would be allowed to emerge under Soviet and SED leadership. This meant religious education had no place in the curriculum, nor would private religious schools be tolerated.

The leadership of the Catholic and Protestant churches in the Soviet zone, as well as the Christian Democratic Union was equally determined to return Christian religious education to the curriculum of secondary schools, after twelve years of attempts by Nazi educational authorities to restrict or ban it. Catholic and Protestant clergy and the CDU party leadership saw the unfettered presence of religious education in the secondary schools as essential to rebuilding Germany's Christian foundations, whose loss during the Weimar era had, in their minds, paved the way for the rise of Nazism.

The stage was set for the first and tensest conflict between the churches and their allies in the CDU on one side, and the Soviet and SED authorities on the other, which lasted from the fall of 1945 until the formal end of the Soviet occupation in October 1949.[2] This chapter examines this conflict from the formal announcement of the Soviet and SED plans for the secondary educational curriculum in September 1945 to the "compromise" on voluntary religious education in the schools in April 1946. It then explores the attempts by the Soviet and SED authorities over the next three years to circumvent this arrangement. The churches doggedly persisted in pushing the state authorities to honor their promises in allowing religious education in the schools, although they were often frustrated in their attempts, which in turn embittered many to the idea of any compromise with the SVAG and SED authorities.

More than any other issue, the conflict over religious education in secondary schools and, to a lesser extent, over the administration of private religious schools demonstrates how the differing plans of secular and religious authorities for Germany's future after the end of the Nazi era led inevitably to conflict. This, in turn, led to an increasingly anti-religious character of Soviet and SED educational policies in Germany.[3]

Naimark and David Pike are correct in claiming neither the SVAG nor the SED were monolithic in their policies and occasionally experienced sharp disagreements about how to bring about the "antifascist democratic transformation" of Germany.[4] Quarrels over which policies to implement and when to implement them were prevalent in the SVAG and SED leadership at the zonal, provincial, and local levels from 1945 to 1949. The chapters on the relationship between the churches and the CDU as well as religious charitable activity reveal the conflicting perceptions felt by officials in the SVAG Propaganda/Information Administration and the SED concerning the "threat" posed by religious charitable work in the Soviet zone and the relationship between the CDU and the churches.

At the same time, there was broad consensus on a number of issues regarding religion among both the SVAG and SED leadership. The determination to exclude religious institutions from the education system was shared by all leading officials who dealt with religious and educational affairs among the SVAG and SED. Since the secondary schools would be among the most important institutions involved in creating a German state on the Stalinist model, the state authorities would have to have absolute control over the education process. Any efforts by the Protestant and Catholic churches to offer religious education would be swiftly restricted, as this would only slow the process of the Stalinist indoctrination of the German population. All SVAG and SED religious education policies in Berlin and Brandenburg from 1945 to 1949 have to be viewed in this light.

Even though broad consensus existed from the very beginning on which policies would be pursued, political and social realities in the Soviet zone prevented the SVAG and the SED from achieving all of their goals with regards to religious education. The delicate four-power governance of Berlin and the SVAG determination not to immediately abandon their goal of influencing developments in the Western zones of Germany kept them from dealing with the Protestant and Catholic churches as harshly as would be the case elsewhere in Eastern Europe during this time period, such as in Western Ukraine, Romania and Hungary.[5]

Since the educational system in Brandenburg functioned differently from that of the Soviet sector of Berlin, due to the unique four-power structure in the German capital, Soviet and SED education authorities had a great deal more freedom of action to restrict religious education in Brandenburg than in the Soviet sector of Berlin. Only during 1948 in the background of the Berlin blockade did the Soviet authorities make greater attempts to end religious education in the Soviet sector, although these were generally less successful than their efforts in Brandenburg. For this reason, the history of Soviet and SED religious education policies and the reaction of the churches to them will be dealt with by discussing Brandenburg first, and then the Soviet sector of Berlin.[6]

THE DIVERSE PLANS FOR THE FUTURE OF THE EDUCATION SYSTEM IN THE SOVIET ZONE OF GERMANY

When the Soviet occupation began in the summer of 1945, the SVAG, KPD and SPD were optimistic that a new, "antifascist and democratic" school system could be created that rejected not only the Nazi educational system with its racist and militarist indoctrination but also the "blind obedience" of the Prussian educational system which remained during the Weimar era.[7] As the official record of the SVAG-ONO's activities from 1945 to 1948, written by its head A. D. Danilov put it: "the democratization of Germany means the democratization of the German schools."[8]

This meant the new "democratic" German schools would be thoroughly secular in their curriculum and in their identity. According to Danilov, the SVAG and KPD leadership were in complete agreement in the summer of 1945 on this point: "As to the question of religion, religious education would be excluded from the German schools, without question and without reservation." Studies in dialectical materialism would replace religious instruction in the curriculum of all secondary schools.[9] In mid-September 1945, KPD and SPD leaders Wilhelm Pieck and Otto Grotewohl, future leaders of the SED, made a joint statement to all party members concerning the role of religious education in the German schools. They stated the new antifascist and democratic German schools must strive to create and defend the democratic unity of the German nation. Therefore, they could no longer be divided by religious differences. The religious education of children would no longer be the affair of the schools, but rather that of their parents and religious communities.[10]

In their public statements, the KPD did not make any claims concerning the need for the new German schools to cultivate support for socialism or for the need to secularize the curriculum. On September 5, 1945, the four antifascist parties issued statements that were printed in all major newspapers in the Soviet zone which briefly outlined their positions on the education question. The KPD statement read: "We desire the cleansing from the schools of all reactionary and fascist misguidance. We desire a democratic, progressive and free spirit in all schools and teaching institutions." The declaration of the SPD in the Soviet zone was actually more forthright, claiming the new German schools would educate children in a "Democratic, Socialist spirit."[11]

In private correspondence, both SPD and KPD party leaders were clear with each other regarding their plans to secularize the school curriculum during the fall of 1945, when most schools had not yet re-opened. In a speech by made Otto Grotewohl to the Central Committee of the SPD in the Soviet zone, he rejected religious education even as a voluntary part of the school curriculum, and also the ability of the Protestant and Catholic churches to operate private confessional schools. Grotewohl insisted only "Unity" schools free of confessional divisions could create the conditions for the rebuilding of Germany on an antifascist, democratic model.[12] In a speech to the Berlin city government (*Magistrate*) on September 24 1945, KPD leader Anton Ackermann made a similar case, stating quite clearly there was to be no religious instruction in the curriculum of the new schools constructed in the Soviet zone, nor would school buildings be used for voluntary religious education after school hours. In addition, private confessional schools would never re-emerge, as education had to remain in the hands of secular authorities.[13]

SVAG officials agreed with this point of view, as Danilov expressed to the commander of SVAG in Brandenburg, Lieutenant General V. A. Sharov, in an official memorandum on September 20, 1945. Danilov insisted secondary schools in Brandenburg must exclude religious studies from the official curriculum, although it could temporarily allow the churches to use the school buildings for optional religious education if enough parents in a particular area insisted on it, in order to avoid immediately inflaming the churches regarding this delicate issue.[14]

The hopes of the CDU and the Protestant and Catholic churches in Berlin-Brandenburg for the secondary educational system after the fall of Nazism were quite different. In a front page article in the CDU newspaper *Neue Zeit* on August 14, 1945 CDU educational theorist Dr. Christian Caselmann wrote the CDU accepted the notion that the new German schools should not be used for political ends, but should serve to cultivate antifascism and democracy in Germany's youth. Caselmann also claimed the new political and social order in Germany should allow for religious schools as well as for optional religious education in secular schools.[15] In the CDU's official position on education reform in the four-party statement released on September 4, the party stated it was up to parents to decide whether or not children should receive religious education, and it was up to the Protestant and Catholic churches to provide it. The CDU statement conceded religious educational should still be a voluntary part of the school curriculum.[16]

Similarly, CDU party leader Andreas Hermes mentioned in a speech at the founding conference of the CDU in Berlin on July 22 1945 the importance of protecting religious education in the schools, as part of the CDU's overall goals of rebuilding Germany on Christian foundations. While religious education was the responsibility of the Protestant and Catholic churches, it would still be available to those parents who desired it in the schools. Hermes also stated that the CDU accepted that schools should be free of any "Weltanschauungs" or ideological manipulation of the curriculum. He counseled the Soviet authorities and the Germans in the *Abteilung Volksbildung* should not follow the example of the Nazis and attempt to ban confessional schools or prohibit religious education.[17]

The positions of the Protestant and Catholic churches in Berlin-Brandenburg were broadly similar to that of the CDU, although they were more unbending on the question of leaving religious education in the curriculum and making it a strictly voluntary course. On October 15, 1945, Konrad von Preysing sent a letter to every Catholic parish in the diocese of Berlin (which encompassed not merely Berlin itself but stretched all the way to the Oder river and the Baltic sea) urging them not to tolerate anything less the resumption of religious education in all German schools as a mandatory part of the curriculum. Preysing stated the Catholic church would be ready to fight against the Soviet authorities and their German allies to preserve religious education in the schools, just as they had been against the National Socialists. Any school with a purely secular curriculum would have an inherent anti-religious bias, which, in the minds of the church leadership, was the goal of the Soviet authorities all along.[18] Otto Dibelius made very similar statements to the Protestant population of Brandenburg during the fall of 1945, stating secular authorities had no right to tell religious Germans how they should raise their children. Like Preysing, Dibelius compared the removal of religious education from the curriculum of the new German schools to Nazi educational policies, and that likewise stated "secular" schools would necessarily take on an anti-religious identity.[19]

THE EARLY CONFLICTS OVER RELIGIOUS EDUCATION, NOVEMBER 1945 TO APRIL 1946

On November 4, 1945, KPD member and education specialist Max Kreuziger gave a major speech to assembled KPD and SPD educational specialists, in which he rejected the claims of Dibelius and Preysing that secular schools would have an inherent anti-religious bias. In addition, the KPD and SPD, as well as the Soviet authorities, rejected the position of the churches and the CDU to allow for the emergence of religious schools, since only state-run, democratic and secular "unity" schools could offer a complete education that would prepare German youths for life in an antifascist Germany. Religious instruction should be an affair solely of the churches, conducted on church property and only for those parents who desired it, since the churches would only use religious instruction to disseminate reactionary anti-communist propaganda among impressionable German youths. The churches should save themselves the trouble and realize all schools in the Soviet zone would follow this model.[20]

The Soviet authorities followed a similar propaganda line. One notable example comes from the October 23, 1945 issue of the SVAG German-language newspaper *Tägliche Rundschau*. In an article entitled "Aufruf zur demokratischen Schulreform" (Appeal for the Democratic School Reform) the unnamed author stated the SVAG-ONO, Otdal Narodnogo Obrazovaniiz (Department of the People's Education) authorities were completely convinced that in order to create and preserve the antifascist and democratic unity of the German nation, it was necessary to make a clear break between the churches and the Schools. Religious education would only be allowed as a private affair between students and the churches. Private schools, especially of a religious character, would never be allowed to emerge.[21]

Conflict between the Protestant and Catholic leaders and the CDU on one side and the SVAG and KPD/SPD leadership on the other over the issue of religious education was inevitable at this point. While the two sides could and did find areas of compromise on other issues, such as the necessity of religious charitable work to alleviate the suffering of the population, common ground was not possible over the need to create thoroughly secular German schools. For the SVAG and KPD/SED authorities, schools were simply far too important in their goal of eventually creating a German state on the atheist Stalinist model to allow the churches any possible role in the educational process. The KPD/SED leadership was careful not to proclaim this openly during the first year of the occupation, preferring instead to emphasize the need to create "unity" schools whose secularism would transcend Germany's confessional divisions.

The leadership of the CDU and the churches were just as convinced that Germany's recovery from the effects of Nazism had to have a religious element as well as a political and economic one. Therefore, religious education was an essential part of the school curriculum, since it was a vital element of rebuilding Germany on Christian foundations. This was a common theme in the writings and speeches of both CDU party leaders, such as Andreas Hermes and Jakob Kaiser, and prominent clergy such as Dibelius and Preysing.

A letter sent to all clergy by the chief office of the Protestant church for Brandenburg on September 12, 1945 reflected this attitude. Written by Hans von Arnim, the head of the Protestant church Chancellery for Brandenburg, the letter stated officials in the German organs of self-government, as well as German teachers' organizations and the KPD, had all been moving towards the complete division between the churches and the schools, denying both confessions in Brandenburg the opportunity to fulfill one of their most important missions, namely that of religious education. The Protestant Church saw the construction of an antifascist order as a possibility to bring about a religious revival in all of Germany. The conclusion of the letter stated the Protestant Church could not restrict itself to merely a private role in German society, especially since they believed a moral collapse on the part of the German people in the 1920s and early 1930s helped to precipitate the rise of Nazism. The letter asked all clerics not to allow religious instruction to be excluded entirely from the new schools system in Germany, and suggested they work to include it as a part of the official curriculum.[22]

During a meeting in Berlin of all of the Protestant Bishops in the Soviet zone, on February 2, 1946, Dibelius and the General Secretary of the Protestant Church in the Soviet Zone, Dr. Kurt Krummacher both stressed all Protestant clergy must maintain a unified position on pushing for the inclusion of religious education in the schools. Krummacher did note a slight modification of the earlier stance of the Protestant Church. He allowed that religious education as an optional course after schools hours was acceptable to the Protestant Church leadership. Krummacher justified this position by stating it was the best the church could hope for given the continued push by the Soviet and German educational authorities for thoroughly secular, "Unity" schools.[23]

Clearly by this point the leaders of both churches were determined to preserve religious education in the new secondary schools, although there were disagreements as to whether it should be a mandatory or optional part of the curriculum. The willingness of the Protestant and Catholic churches to challenge the Soviet and SED authorities on this issue at an early period demonstrates the importance they attached to it.

The struggle over the role of religion in the curriculum in the Germans schools continued through 1945 and into the spring of 1946, taking on an air of unreality as so few of the schools in the Soviet zone had even re-opened. State authorities continued to place obstacles in the way of any forms of religious education in the schools which had opened. On February 11, 1946, the (Department of the People's Education) *Abteilung Volksbildung* for the Soviet sector of Berlin issued a directive to all school administrators, which stated Protestant and Catholic clergy could not approach students or their parents on school grounds and inquire whether they desired religious education after school hours, or publicly recruit them to force secular authorities to accept religious education officially in the curriculum. The directive concluded the complete break between the churches and the schools was absolutely necessary and as such they could not allow religious education on public school grounds, since religious education was now "solely a matter for the churches."[24]

Since neither the KPD, the SPD nor the CDU were willing to bend from their positions regarding religious education, a series of meetings held from the fall of 1945 to the spring of 1946 between representatives of the antifascist parties intended to reach some form of compromise were unproductive. The dispute was finally resolved with the education compromise of April 16, 1946, when the CDU finally agreed with the democratic school reforms. The reason for CDU leader Jakob Kaiser's acquiescence was the fact that the new school law allowed the Catholic and Protestant churches to offer religious education courses in the school buildings as a voluntary course. The course could only be offered after school hours and would not be a part of the official curriculum. Regular school teachers could not offer religious education, as the churches would have to provide their own instructors, who still needed to be vetted by the local *Abteilung Volksbildung*. The SVAG-ONO approved the decree, and it was passed by the provincial *Landtags* (legislatures) in May and June.[25]

Although this compromise differed from the original goal of the CDU and the churches to include religious education as an official part of the curriculum, both CDU and church leaders saw it as a success, especially because it occurred against the opposition of the atheistic Soviet authorities and their German allies. An article in the May 22, 1946, issue of *Neue Zeit* entitled "Der Schulreform" proclaimed the compromise on religious education as a triumph for the CDU, given the strong opposition of the atheistic SVAG and SED opponents. The article also mentioned the CDU would continue to fight to preserve religious education in the schools and prevent authorities in the *Abteilung Volksbildung* from circumventing this compromise, since the preservation of religious education was absolutely essential to the democratization of Germany.[26]

Preysing also noted his approval of the concession, expressing in a letter to all Catholic parents in Berlin-Brandenburg on May 14, 1946, his thanks for making their feelings concerning the debate over religious education clear to state authorities. The ultimate resolution was not satisfactory since religious education was not made part of the official curriculum, but at least it had not been excluded entirely. Preysing noted the struggle for the preservation of Catholic religious schools would continue, as their status remained ambiguous, although the greatest challenge in this issue would occur in the Soviet zone. In the meantime, parents had to be absolutely sure to petition the local *Abteilung Volksbilung* to ensure the preservation of religious education in secondary schools, describing it as their *"Heilige Pflicht"* ("Holy Duty").[27]

At the party conference of the CDU from June 12–15, 1946, in Berlin, CDU leader Kaiser recognized the need for a secular curriculum for the schools, but not the prospect of one "unified" school for all of Germany, recognizing *"Frei Schule"* formed on private grounds should also exist in Germany. He reaffirmed the principle of voluntary religious education in the schools, which would be unimpeded by state authorities at any level. The schools' curriculum should be free of any ideological indoctrination and should not attack Christian religious beliefs. Kaiser also proclaimed the CDU would work to ensure the secular authorities honored the promise to allow religious education in schools after hours.[28]

In comparison, *Tägliche Rundschau* and *Neues Deutschland*, the newspapers of the SVAG and the SED, barely mentioned the religious education compromise. Both continued to rail against the idea of confessional schools or allowing religious education to have any place in the official curriculum. One example comes from the May 9, 1946, issues of *Neues Deutschland,* in an article by SED member Dr. Heinrich Dieters. Dieters attacked the decision by educational authorities in Hanover (in the British occupation zone) to allow the formation of Catholic and Protestant schools. According to him, this demonstrated the strength of "reactionary" sentiment in the British zone and such schools divided along confessional lines would only serve to threaten the national unity of Germany. Dieters concluded the Soviet zone was fortunate since the SVAG-ONO had only allowed for the creation of secular schools.[29]

Officials in the SVAG-ONO noted their own disapproval for the SED's agreement with the CDU on allowing religious education as a voluntary course in the schools, believing the SED had disregarded their advice to pursue a more aggressive anti-religious policy. In his review of the this decision, Danilov recognized it as necessary due to the temporary strength of the CDU in the Soviet zone and to remove the issue from possible use by the CDU in its electoral propaganda, especially in rural areas. He noted neither SVAG nor the SED education officials planned to allow for religious education in any form in the German schools.[30]

The SVAG's Propaganda Administration concurred with this viewpoint, as the head of the Propaganda Administration in Brandenburg, Lieutenant Colonel I. I. Mil'khiker, admitted to his superior Tiul'panov in a report dated April 16, 1946. Mil'khiker stated since the Catholic and Protestant churches would never accept a secular school system, the compromise which allowed optional religious education in the schools would be recognized in theory but not in reality. In his response a few days later, Tiul'panov stated that along with religious youth organizations, religious education was the main tool of the churches to win over German youths. Therefore, the SVAG and especially SED-controlled *Abteilung Volksbildung* had to work to prevent the churches from offering religious education.[31]

Internal SED party documents reveal a distinct lack of enthusiasm for the compromise of the part of the party leadership and rank and file members. They also looked for methods to circumvent the compromise. In an internal report sent out to all SED party members in Berlin and Brandenburg dated May 11, 1946, by the SED's department for Culture and Education, the party's education authorities Paul Wandel and Anton Ackermann admitted the religious compromise was merely an expedient measure. Religious education teachers would not be regular school teachers and would be excluded entirely from broader educational work in the Soviet zone. The report concluded it would be up to the *Abteilung Volksbildung* at the local level to make their own arrangements with religious communities to provide optional religious education for German school children whose parents desired it. SED members who controlled the local *Abteilung Volksbildung* would ensure no religious education teachers would be allowed to continue their work if they had belonged to the Nazi party or other illegal organizations.[32]

The statements by the SED and the SVAG officials reveal the reasons for allowing the religious education compromise in April 1946. Members of the

SVAG-ONO and the *Abteilung Volksbildung* remained determined to create an educational system which was thoroughly secular and anti-religious with its emphasis on dialectical materialism, the atheistic philosophical foundations for the SED's ideology. Since religious education was no longer a part of the official curriculum the infusion of dialectical materialism theoretically could still be implemented with relative ease.

In April of 1946, the Socialist Unity Party had just been formed and did not yet have the strength to seize power on its own. Aware of this, the Soviet authorities allowed the SED to make a gesture of cooperation with the other main antifascist party, the CDU, by compromising on the issue of religious education. As the next three years would demonstrate, what was promised at one point could easily be rescinded later. Neither the CDU nor the Protestant and Catholic churches saw the religious education compromise in this light, and they engaged in frequent attempts to prevent SED educational policies in the Soviet zone from circumventing it, although these were largely unsuccessful.

THE IMPLEMENTATION OF THE RELIGIOUS EDUCATION COMPROMISE IN BRANDENBURG FROM APRIL 1946 TO OCTOBER 1949: THE POLICIES OF THE SVAG AND SED AUTHORITIES

While only a slight majority of teachers in the Soviet sector of Berlin and Brandenburg were members of the SED, every single branch of the *Abteilung Volksbildung* in Brandenburg, over seventeen in all, was entirely staffed by SED party members by the spring of 1946.[33] This meant SED members could use their authority to circumvent allowing religious education in the schools, although this did not begin in earnest until after the zonal elections in October 1946. The SED tried to avoid giving the CDU clear evidence of their atheistic tendencies which it could use as an electoral weapon against them. In the city of Berlin, the unique four-power governing structure of the city allowed for a greater deal of freedom in religious education in the schools, as the *Abteilung Volksbildung* in the Soviet sector was not solely controlled by the SED until 1947. This unique circumstance broke down in the summer of 1948 following the Berlin blockade.

The fact that the SED and Soviet authorities allowed religious education to continue in the schools on a voluntary basis became an important element of SED party propaganda in the months before the zonal elections in October 1946. One notable example came from the August 7, 1946, issue of *Tägliche Rundschau* in an article by a Protestant pastor named Theodor Werner.

Werner reminded German voters religious education would not have continued in the schools of the Soviet zone had it not been by the agreement of the
SED.[34] In the October 18 issue of *Neues Deutschland*, a group of Protestant
clerics in the Soviet zone, led by Kurt Rackwitz, wrote German voters should
remember that the SED and the SVAG authorities had "given us back the task
of religious education, which only we can accomplish successfully."[35]

Even before the elections of October 1946, attempts by SED educational
authorities to restrict religious education in the schools emerged. This accelerated after the SED's unfavorable electoral results. Before the school year
began in September 1946, the head of the *Abteilung Volksbildung* for the
Soviet zone, Paul Wandel, sent a directive to the Brandenburg educational
authorities on July 28, 1946. It stated two hours of religious education could
be offered to children if their parents desired it, until the age of fourteen,
when German children would decide for themselves whether to continue.
Teachers who provided religious education did not have to be clergy, but had
to be paid and trained by the churches themselves. This approval rested on
the authorities in the local *Abteilung Volksbildung* who could remove teachers if they saw it as an appropriate action. The school buildings themselves
could be used for religious instruction, but only if no other adequate space
had been found and only if the church applied in advance to the local educational authorities and the provincial *Abteilung Volksbildung*. The wording of
this order gave local educational authorities a great deal of freedom to restrict
religious education by both the Protestant and Catholic churches.[36]

On August 20, 1946, Hans von Arnim sent a plea to the head of the Brandenburg Provincial Administration, Heinrich Steinhoff, regarding the situation involving religious education in the city of Bernau-Oranienberg. The
head of the *Abteilung Volksbildung* in the city, Georg Jaeger, decreed the
Protestant Church could use public schools for religious education only if no
other buildings in the city were available. Since Jaeger believed the churches
themselves could serve as suitable locations for religious education, he
effectively banned the Protestant churches from using the school buildings.
Apparently Steinhoff did not even answer Von Arnim's request, much less
take steps to resolve the situation.[37]

Another example of this policy comes from a protest sent to the head
office of the *Abteilung Volksbildung* for Brandenburg (located, along with
all other Brandenburg government offices, in Potsdam) from Protestant
authorities in the city of Gorlitz, dated September 2, 1946. The Protestant
clerics claimed educational authorities in the city had allotted only thirty
minutes for religious education during the school day, and had assigned it
during the middle of the day, when many students had gone home for lunch.
The author of the protest letter complained the SED educational authorities

had deliberately chosen the time of day in order to prevent religious education from occurring at all in school buildings.[38]

These tactics continued throughout the end of 1946 and into 1947. Preysing received complaints from throughout Brandenburg, such as from the cities of Eisenthal and Frankfurt am Oder, concerning obstacles placed in the way of allowing religious education in the schools, these included extending the school day in order to cut into the time used for religious education, either by lengthening classes or planning special activities after school hours. When teachers and clergy protested this, they were uniformly answered by the claim from local education authorities the *"Die Schule sind wichtiger als der Kirchen"* (The Schools are more important than the Churches). Preysing wrote a long article denouncing these practices to the head of the Provincial Administration Brandenburg in Potsdam in March of 1947, but this also had little effect.[39] In essence, the strategy pursued by the education authorities did not ban religious education but made it effectively impossible for the churches to offer classes in school buildings. This enabled the SED and SVAG to maintain their support of "religious freedom" for broader propaganda purposes in Germany, while continuing to move towards the goal of creating a Stalinist education system in the Soviet zone by preventing religious education from actually occurring.

Another popular tactic used by SED education authorities was to find or create evidence of membership in the Nazi party or its affiliated organizations in order to disqualify religious education teachers, who had to pass approval by the local *Abteilung Volksbildung* even though they were paid a salary by the churches. On December 12, 1945, five months before the compromise on religious education was even reached, all local *Abteilung Volksbildung* received a directive from education authorities in Potsdam, stating they should investigate teachers of religious education in the German schools for evidence of support for or membership in the Nazi party as a reason for excluding them from any chance to offer religious education to German youths.[40]

Education authorities in Brandenburg pursued this tactic aggressively over the next four years. One of the most notable examples comes from a prolonged struggle in the city of Brunn bei Wusterhausen that stretched from June to September of 1946. On June 7, 1946, the head of the local SED organization in the city informed his superiors in Potsdam that a Protestant pastor's wife, Ilse Kanitz, a former leader of the local branch of the Nazi women's organization the *National Sozialistische Frauenschaft*, (National Socialist Women's League) had been chosen to teach religious education in the schools by a church official named Richard Friederichs. The report mentioned Friederichs was a member of the Nazi party from 1934 to 1945 and was now the head of the Protestant charitable organization in Brunn bei Wusterhausen, the *Innere Mission*. The report also revealed her husband was in the Wehrmacht and was currently a POW in Soviet custody. Soon, the officials in the local *Abteilung Volksbildung* as well as the mayor (*Burger-meister*) of the city, Robert Schmeer, an SED party member, demanded her removal before the school year started.[41]

Von Arnim wrote a letter to the head of the Brandenburg *Abteilung Volks-bildung* justifying his decision to appoint Friederichs on July 17, 1946. He argued while it was true Friederichs was a Nazi party member from 1934 to 1945, he was never a particularly "active" one. Indeed, he had allowed members of KPD to assemble in his house for forbidden political discussions, and did not allow in his own school classes to begin with the "Heil Hitler" greeting. Von Arnim pleaded that Friederichs had joined the Nazi party under duress, and was simply too useful as a worker in the *Innere Mission* to be removed from his position. He also disputed rumors of a possible Nazi background on the part of Kanitz.[42]

Ilse Kanitz wrote to Vice-President of the Brandenburg government Karl Rucker in Potsdam on July 17, 1946, protesting the attacks made on her by local SED authorities in Brunn bei Wusterhausen. She denied being a Nazi party member, although she did admit her husband was a Wehrmacht officer. She also denied being a member or even a supporter of the *National Sozialistische Frauenschaft*. She sarcastically concluded that since she had three children and her husband was in a Soviet prison camp, she would have no time for fascist provocation even if she wanted to. She reminded Rucker to instruct Schmeer and the *Abteilung Volksbildung* authorities in Brunn bei Wusterhausen that since religious education was an affair for the churches, Evangelical officials should be able to choose who they wanted to teach religious education no matter what their background was. Rucker also received a letter from Hans von Arnim attesting to Kanitz's antifascist credentials shortly thereafter. Kanitz was allowed to take the position according to a letter sent to her by the education authorities in Brunn bei Wusterhausen on September 11, 1946, which also apologized half-heartedly for the problems the investigation has caused.[43]

Many others were not so lucky. On September 16, 1946, Von Arnim wrote a letter to education authorities in Potsdam defending another alleged Nazi whom the Protestant church had appointed as a religious teacher in the city of Linthe. This teacher, Karl Mertz, had been a member of the Nazi party in the 1930s but von Arnim claimed he too had joined under duress, and that he used his membership to work against the Nazis' anti-Christian tendencies. Von Arnim also argued the *Abteilung Volksbildung* and the Soviet education authorities were using the search for former Nazis to deny the church any role in providing religious education in the schools. Von Arnim's request was ignored and Mertz was removed from his position, and consequently the city did not have teacher of religious education for the school year of 1946–1947.[44]

Only when a religious education teacher could prove they were never members of the Nazi party could they hope to maintain their position in the school system. Even brief membership was grounds for dismissal, and religious education teachers who were dismissed were rarely replaced. An excellent example of this was the case of Else Laurisch, an Evangelical teacher of religious education in the city of Frankfurt am Oder. In March 1947, the city's *Abteilung Volksbildung* reported to the city government of Frankfurt am Oder that Laurish had been a member of the Nazi party from 1932 to 1945, and was appointed as religious educator for the city in order to spread her reactionary and anti-democratic ideology to the German youths under the guise of religious education.[45]

At the order of the Soviet commandant for the city and the local *Abteilung Volksbildung* in June 1947 Laurish was forbidden to work as a religious instructor in any educational institutions, despite the fact a number of different individuals, including the chief of police and the superintendent for the Protestant Church in Frankfurt am Oder, testified to the Soviet and SED education authorities Laurisch actually resisted Nazi attempts to gain influence over the Protestant churches in Germany. The Protestant Superintendent for Frankfurt am Oder wrote in an open letter to all parishioners the opposition to Laurisch's appointment had less to do with her background and more with preventing the churches from using school classrooms to offer optional religious education. Laurisch ultimately admitted to the local *Abteilung Volksbildung* that she had been a member of the Nazi party from 1932 to 1933, only to break with it due to disputes concerning their religious policies, especially towards religious education the schools. She was nevertheless removed from her position and the Protestant Church had no religious education instructor in many of the schools in the city during the next few years.[46]

THE IMPLEMENTATION OF THE RELIGIOUS EDUCATION COMPROMISE IN BRANDENBURG FROM APRIL 1946 TO OCTOBER 1949: THE RESPONSE OF THE CDU AND THE CHURCHES

These tactics of dismissing religious education instructors and denying the use of school building for instruction only increased in intensity during the final two years of the Soviet occupation, which proved to be a major problem for both the Protestant and Catholic churches as they often lacked adequate personnel to offer religious education in the schools, especially in rural areas and smaller towns. Paul Zimmermann, the leading Protestant religious education official in the Soviet zone, expressed the feelings of most of the assembled Protestant clergy and laity at their meeting in Greifswald on January 7, 1948, when he stated SED education officials were not interested in finding former Nazis but instead finding reasons to prevent religious education in the schools.[47]

Religious education instructors were frequently accompanied by local SED members in the classrooms to ensure they did not use religious instruction to engage in political agitation for the CDU. The use of these tactics was particularly notorious in the city of Königs Wusterhausen during March and April of 1948, and once again the protests of Preysing, von Arnim and Otto Dibelius had little effect on education authorities.[48]

While both religious leaders were generally careful to avoid overt confrontation with the SVAG and SED authorities during the early years of the occupation, as SVAG/SED policies towards restricting religious education in Brandenburg became more stringent von Preysing and Dibelius responded in kind. In a letter written to all Catholic parishioners in Brandenburg on January 18, 1948, Preysing expressed the hope that they would continue to strive to protect religious education in the German schools, as it was absolutely necessary for the formation of their children's moral character. He stated this would be exceedingly difficult given the SVAG and SED policies towards religious education, which von Preysing likened to those of the Nazis.[49]

Otto Dibelius and Zimmermann used similar tactics to those of Preysing, although both were more likely to intercede with SED authorities regarding particular disputes over religious education. This often did little good, as Zimmermann admitted to the assembled Protestant Bishops of the Soviet zone on April 14, 1948 in Berlin. He noted the Protestant Church faced increasing pressure from SED authorities to end religious education in school buildings, even as an optional class after official school hours.[50]

As the situation worsened during the final sixteen months of the Soviet occupation, Zimmermann admitted to the Protestant leadership on September 13, 1949, he had received assurances from the head of the SVAG-ONO A. D. Danilov informing him the Soviet authorities still recognized the Protestant and Catholic churches' right to offer two hours of optional religious education each week after school hours. Danilov added the Soviet authorities had left it up to the German authorities in the *Abteilung Volksbildung* to make their own arrangements with the churches, and would not interfere with or overrule decisions made by the SED officials. Zimmermann concluded this meant policies which prevented the use of school buildings and attempts to remove religious education teachers on the basis of specious claims of Nazi party membership would continue indefinitely.[51]

Towards the end of the Soviet occupation, Dibelius struck a similar tone with regards to the religious education question. In an essay distributed to all Protestant clergy in both the Soviet and Western zones on August 2, 1949, entitled "Das Kirchliche Leben im Deutschen Osten." (The Church Life in the German East), Dibelius offered a grim picture of Protestant opportunities to offer religious education in the German schools. In the new "unity" schools the influence of dialectical materialism permeated every aspect of the curriculum, although Dibelius stated this was unsurprising given it was prevalent in all aspects of Soviet and SED propaganda in the Soviet zone. Dibelius noted that it had been able to turn some German youths away from religious belief, but that its success was still quite limited.[52] The second major problem, according to Dibelius, was numerous school administrators in Brandenburg continued to prevent religious education from actually occurring.[53]

The response of the CDU in the Soviet zone to the question regarding religious education remained a prominent issue for Jakob Kaiser, but less so for his successor Otto Nuschke. During 1946 and 1947, when Kaiser led the CDU in the Soviet zone, the CDU newspaper *Neue Zeit* regularly emphasized the need for the party to maintain its support of church efforts to offer religious education to all German youths. In a front page article in the July 2, 1946, issue of *Neue Zeit*, the CDU proclaimed the compromise on religious education had been one of its most important accomplishments. Given the fact so many German youths had lost their spiritual and moral foundations during the Weimar era, which in turn paved the way for the horrors of Nazism, it was absolutely essential Christian morals be instilled in Germany's youth. The article concluded only the educational role of the Protestant and Catholic churches could accomplish this.[54]

Neue Zeit frequently noted the struggles both the Protestant and Catholic churches faced in offering religious education in the schools due to the various restrictions placed on their activity by the *Abteilung Volksbildung*. One notable article which appeared on Christmas Day 1946 proclaimed the Soviet authorities and especially the SED party members who controlled the *Abteilung Volksbildung* were very duplicitous regarding religious education policies, often dismissing teachers or severely restricting the times that religious instruction could be offered. Consequently, throughout the Soviet zone the churches had been unable to offer religious education to many German youths, despite the fact this went explicitly against the wishes of their parents.[55]

Following Kaiser's replacement by Nuschke in December 1947 at the orders of the SVAG authorities, the discussion of religious education gradually ceased to be a relevant issue in the pages of *Neue Zeit*, or, if it was mentioned, was quickly dismissed as nothing religious Germans should concern themselves about. An article written on May 6, 1948, by the noted left-wing Protestant minister in the Soviet zone Ludwig Kirsch clearly reflected this trend. Kirsch wrote the Soviet authorities and their allies in the SED and the "progressive" parts of the CDU had succeeded in democratizing Germany to a far greater extent than had occurred in the Western zones. Furthermore, Kirsch emphasized the German people should remain content with the new education system introduced in the Soviet zone, and reject the comparisons made between it and that of the Nazis, a comparison made largely by reactionary clergy and exiled CDU politicians.[56]

The need to protect the freedom of the Protestant and Catholic churches to offer religious education in the schools following the compromise of April 1946 was an essential element of CDU political agitation under Kaiser's leadership until his removal in December 1947. The difficulties faced by the churches throughout the Soviet zone in offering religious instruction after regular school hours was frequently discussed by the CDU executive leadership. Electoral materials and party newsletters distributed throughout this period stressed the CDU agreed in principle the education of children was the affair of the state and religious education was the affair of the churches. They insisted optional religious education should be provided in German schools as long as some parents desired it, without any unnecessary impediments by the state.[57]

The CDU under Kaiser made its role in defending religious education a major part of its electoral propaganda in 1946 and 1947. For Kaiser, the availability of religious education for German youths, even if it was not part of the school curriculum, was an essential aspect of the CDU's plan to restore Christian faith to its proper place at the center of Germany's culture. Once the CDU under Nuschke abandoned its attempt to promote Christian Socialism, it also abandoned mentioning the issue in *Neue Zeit* or in speeches made by CDU leaders such as Nuschke, Georg Dertinger, or Hugo Hickmann. The need to protect religious education from attacks by the SED and the SVAG was no longer a major priority for the CDU party leadership, and the essentially the churches were on their own with regard to this issue.

The experience regarding SED and SVAG violations of the religious education compromise served to further embitter the church leadership towards the Soviet and SED authorities. While the Catholic and Protestant authorities tried to deal with the issue of religious education much like they had with charitable work, that is, to continually petition authorities in order to hold them to their promises of allowing the churches a limited free space to continue its religious mission, these were often met with stark refusal regarding religious education. The tendency of SED education authorities in the *Abteilung Volksbildung* to quickly and continuously violate the religious education compromise after April 1946 served as one of the clearest examples to Protestant and Catholic clergy that their suspicions regarding the atheistic Soviets and their German allies were correct concerning their desire to create an atheistic society in Germany.

Dibelius, Zimmermann, von Arnim, and Preysing were quick to make comparisons between the education policies of the Nazis and the SVAG/SED, claiming the Communists merely substituted materialism and militant atheism for the Nazis' doctrine of racism and anti-Semitism. The struggles over religious education in the Soviet zone was an essential ingredient in pushing the leadership of the Catholic and Protestant church in a more openly confrontational policy towards the SVAG and SED authorities, which in turn motivated them to drop even the pretense of allowing the churches an independent role in educational, social, and political life in the Soviet zone.

It would be incorrect to state that the authorities in the SVAG-ONO and its leader Colonel A. D. Danilov were not involved in the dispute over religious education controversy. This was, however, an issue where the SED, through its control of the German organs of self-government, especially the *Abteilung Volksbildung*, took the lead in policy making. This is not say Danilov merely allowed the SED chief of the *Abteilung Volksbildung,* Paul Wandel, and his subordinates to pursue whatever policies they desired in the Soviet zone. The *Abteilung Volksbildung* in the Soviet zone reported directly to the SVAG-ONO. It is highly unlikely the SED education officials would have pursued such a policy if it had gone against the wishes of the Soviet military authorities, given the importance they attached to the educational process.[58]

Nevertheless, officials in the SVAG-ONO tended to be preoccupied with debates over the role of dialectical materialism in the school curriculum, the removal of "reactionary" professors and students from the universities, and most importantly, the broad Soviet cultural offensive designed to demonstrate the superiority of Stalinist culture to that of the Nazis and of the Western powers. Day to day issues involving the administration of the schools tended to be left to SED, as opposed to SVAG authorities.

THE NEBULOUS STATUS OF RELIGIOUS EDUCATION IN THE SOVIET SECTOR OF BERLIN, APRIL 1946 TO OCTOBER 1949

In the Soviet sector of Berlin both the SVAG-ONO authorities and those in the *Abteilung Volksbildung* were more limited in the policies they pursued due to the unique four-power administrative structure of the former German capital. For the first three years of the Soviet occupation, the issue of religious education in the schools was often left to the Berlin city government (*Berlin Magistrate*) to deal with this issue, especially its Advisory Council on Church Affairs. Furthermore, the *Abteilung Volksbildung* officials in the Soviet sector of the city, which was not entirely dominated by the SED, had to share power with the CDU from October 1946 to December 1947. In early 1948 the Soviet, American, British, and French authorities agreed to a modified version of the religious education compromise of April 1946 as the education policy for the entire city. This was greeted with strong protests from the Protestant and Catholic authorities, but barely had a chance to be implemented before the four-power structure in Berlin completely broke down during the Berlin Blockade of June 1948 to May 1949.

The division of Berlin into four Allied sectors also provided the churches and German parents greater freedom in providing religious education to German children, as even after the SVAG and SED authorities moved towards more restrictive education policies many students living in the Soviet sector attended schools in the Western sectors, where the American and British authorities did not interfere with attempts by the churches to offer optional religious education. Following the beginning of the Berlin Blockade, the three western authorities allowed the churches to establish religious schools, something they had been hesitant to allow before the break with the Soviet authorities in June 1948.

This did not mean KPD or SED authorities in the *Abteilung Volksbildung* in the Soviet sector of Berlin did not attempt to reduce the church's influence in the education process. For example, officials in the Berlin suburb of Pankow in March 1946 attempted to ban any efforts by the churches to offer religious education in any school buildings in the district, even if this was entirely optional.[59] Another notable example came from July and August of 1946, when the various SED education officials in the Soviet sector of Berlin banned thousands of war orphans in the city from attending religious education classes, since they had never received parental permission to attend the classes in the first place. The Catholic and Protestant churches were unsuccessful more often than not in reversing these decisions, but these policies enacted by the *Abteilung Volksbildung* under SED control usually proved to be the exception rather than the rule.[60]

The SED education authorities and the SVAG officials they answered to remained determined to eventually reverse the relatively free situation in the Soviet sector of Berlin regarding religious education in the German schools. Lieutenant Colonel Vsevolod Ermolaev, the head official for religious affairs in the SVAG Propaganda Administration revealed this to the Protestant Church General Secretary Dr. Kurt Krummacher in a meeting with him on August

26 1946. Ermolaev admitted while he could not predict what the Western authorities would do in their sectors of Berlin, the Soviets were determined to bring about the clean break between the churches and the school system in their sector of Berlin.[61]

The SVAG and SED authorities began to take steps in this direction in early 1948. On January 12, 1948, the Central Committee of the SED's department of Culture and Education, headed by Paul Wandel, issued a statement emphasizing the education of the youths was solely to be matter for the state. Thus, no private schools or home schooling would be allowed in the new anti-fascist and democratic Germany. It also restated religious instruction could be provided in school buildings, but only after regular school hours and only up to the age of 14. Wandel conceded during the instruction of certain subjects, such as literature, history, or art, teachers could mention religious issues, but they should not be allowed to dwell on religious topics inordinately.[62] Shortly thereafter leading SED theorist Anton Ackermann wrote to party members involved in educational work that they could expect sustained attacks by West German reactionaries, backed by the British and American authorities, over continued attempts by the SVAG and SED to reform the education system in the Soviet zone, including the promotion of a secular identity for the schools.[63]

The SVAG and SED party authorities in the Soviet sector of Berlin pushed for an adoption of the education compromise in Soviet zone of April 1946 to apply to all four Allied sectors of Berlin. This approach was unsurprising given the fact SVAG did not want to entirely write off a role influencing developments in the Western sectors of Berlin and consequently were willing to consider the same faux compromise for Berlin which they had agreed to for the Soviet zone two years before. A substantial majority of children in the Soviet sector were still able to participate in religious education, although less than in the Western sectors. A report from the Berlin *Magistrate* council on church Affairs dated January 12, 1948, revealed 71.7 percent (287,766) took part in Protestant religious education in Berlin, 7.4 percent (29,638) take part in Catholic religious education, and 20.9 percent (83,691) did not take part at all. In the Russian sector it was: 67.4 percent, 6.4 percent, and 26.2 percent, respectively. In the American sector, it was: 74.6 percent, 7.9 percent, and 17.5 percent. In the British sector it was: 78.6 percent, 9 percent, and 12.4 percent. In the French sector it was: 68.9 percent, 6.9 percent, and 24.2 percent.[64]

In one of the last major decisions made by the four Allied powers in Berlin, the education authorities approved the new *Schulgesetz* for the entire city of Berlin to go into effect on April 2, 1948. The law stated the same basic agreement in the Soviet zone of April 1946, two hours of optional religious education once a week if parents desired it, but it was not to be a part of the official curriculum and would be held after school hours. It was the responsibility of the schools, and of the local *Abteilung Volksbildung,* to provide adequate space in the school buildings for religious education classes and to ensure classrooms were properly heated and lighted during time periods allotted for religious education. Religious instructors had to be provided by the churches and were to be paid by them, not the schools. Any background in the Nazi party could disqualify a teacher from serving as a religious educator.[65]

Neither Dibelius nor Preysing were pleased with this decision. One month after the Allied Control Authority in Berlin had made their decision on religious education in the Berlin schools, they sent a joint letter to the Western authorities protesting the acquiesce of Western authorities with the Soviet demands for the secularization of school curriculum throughout Berlin. Dated May 29, 1948, the letter stated the Catholic and Protestant churches in Berlin strongly protested new school laws. Dibelius and Preysing claimed the removal of religious education from the official curriculum meant "parents are deprived of their right concerning their children's scholastic education, and the State is conceded total control over the schools." The letter noted "to their utter surprise and alarm" the churches, which represented over 90 percent of Berlin's parents, have been left out of a role in the education process since the School Law had been agreed to by all four commandants in Berlin.[66]

The threats by Dibelius and Preysing were not put to the test due to the final division between the Soviets and the Western allies in the spring of 1948. The breakdown of even of the resemblance of a unified approach to the governing of Berlin lead to considerably different educational policies in the Soviet sector as compared to those in the Western sectors. The SED authorities in the *Abteilung Volksbildung* in the Soviet sector of Berlin, with the encouragement of the military authorities in the SVAG-ONO, quickly turned to the same policies which had been implemented in Brandenburg during the past two years. This meant the exclusion of the churches from using school buildings for religious education classes, even after school hours, and dismissing teachers provided by the churches, on the grounds of their "reactionary" political and social background.

In July 1948, the *Abteilung Volksbildung* for the Treptow district of Berlin decided the Protestant Church would not be allowed to use any school buildings in the district for religious education. EKD General Secretary Kurt Krummacher, who had a much better relationship with the SVAG and SED authorities than Otto Dibelius or Hans von Arnim, wrote to the head of SVAG-ONO for Berlin Major V. P. Demidov to protest this decision. Demidov bluntly informed him "religious activities within the schools have recently taken on a more militaristic character, so now religious activities would no longer be allowed in school areas, even after school hours." As for Krummacher's concern there was not suitable instructional space in the district to offer religious education, that could not override SVAG concerns of the Western authorities using religious education to undermine the political transformation of the Soviet zone, including the Soviet sector of Berlin.[67]

For the last sixteen months of the Soviet occupation, Protestant and Catholic church officials would be frustrated in their attempts to offer optional religious education in school buildings, much like they had in Brandenburg since April 1946. Since the western sectors of the city remained under the control of the American, British, and French military authorities during the blockade, the churches were able to circumvent the SVAG and SED policies in the Soviet sector of the city. In September 1948, as the new school year began the Protestant and Catholic churches in the Western sections of the city opened confessional schools. SVAG-ONO commander Danilov promptly declared this to be a violation of the Berlin school law of April 1948 and, more importantly an obvious demonstration of the cooperation between the reactionary Western military authorities and the Evangelical and Catholic clergy in the Western sectors of Berlin.[68]

On September 20, 1948, Otto Dibelius sent a letter to all Protestant clergy and their assistants involved in education work in the four sectors of Berlin. Dibelius informed them they could continue to expect harassment from the SVAG and SED authorities concerning the church's attempt to maintain a presence in the educational process, as they are seen as the primary enemy by SVAG and SED education authorities. He concluded this bitter conflict was inevitable since the SED authorities were determined to dominate the education system in the Soviet sector of Berlin just as they had in Brandenburg and throughout the rest of the Soviet zone. In a similar letter sent four days later to all Evangelical laity in the city Dibelius urged parents in the Soviet sector to take advantage of the more tolerant attitudes of British and American authorities in the western sectors of Berlin, especially their permission for the construction of Protestant religious schools.[69]

The Protestant schools were to be located in the districts of Charlottenburg, Fronau, Neuköln, and Spandau, although they did not actually open until the following January. The one Catholic secondary school was in Neuköln, and it opened in September 1948. During the Blockade and afterwards, parents in the Soviet sector sent their children to these religious schools or even secular schools in the Western sectors to attend religious education classes, as they remained confident at least the British and American authorities would not attempt to interfere with the churches' use of the school buildings.[70]

This did not mean the arrangement entirely satisfied the leadership of the Protestant and Catholic churches in Berlin-Brandenburg. In a letter sent by Otto Dibelius on November 18, 1948 to the provisional Berlin *Magistrate*, Dibelius complained despite the fact the new *Schulgesetz* (School law) for the western sectors of Berlin provided for the creation of Protestant religious secondary schools, so far the Protestant church has not been allowed by city authorities to create any despite the fact that the Catholic Church has been successful in doing so in the district of Neuköln.[71]

On November 25, Dibelius received a letter from the Berlin city government's Council on church Affairs suggesting to him that he petition the American authorities in their sectors of Berlin in order to create a number of Protestant schools in their sectors. The officials also proposed he write to a number of officials in the *Abteilung Volksbildung* to discussion securing the appropriate facilities, supplies, and to obtaining teachers, particularly teachers of religious education. On December 15, 1948, the Berlin city government, the head office of the *Abteilung Volksbildung* in the western sectors of Berlin, and the leadership of the Catholic and Protestant churches issued a new joint statement regarding the status of religious schools in the Western sectors of Berlin. For the churches' part, they agreed to respect the integrity of the secular school system, and the city authorities promised not to discriminate against Christian educators in the school system. The churches could open one religious secondary school for every two secular schools in the districts of the Western sectors but their curriculum had to include mathematics, science, foreign languages (in addition to Greek and Latin), and studies of a "practical" use.[72]

The military authorities in the Western sectors also promised to work on a definitive plan regarding optional religious education in the school system, with no more than four hours per week dedicated to it and not to discriminate against the churches in terms of providing adequate space in the schools for religious education.[73] This arrangement allowed for the Protestant and Catholic churches in the Soviet sector of Berlin to effectively circumvent SVAG and SED religious education policies, although this did not mean they continued to attempt to provide religious education classes in schools located in the Soviet sector. Their difficulties with the Western authorities reveal the somewhat unbending positions of Dibelius and von Preysing did contribute to the impasse which existed in the Soviet zone.

At the same time, while SVAG and especially SED education authorities attempted to violate the agreement to allow optional religious instruction in the schools, they continued to claim this privilege extended to the churches would be protected in a new German state under the leadership of the SED.

The October 29, 1948, issue of *Tägliche Rundschau* announced the new constitution for an all-German state under the leadership of the *Volkscongress* would explicitly forbid the use of the Protestant and Catholic churches for political ends. In addition, voluntary religious education would be allowed in the schools areas after regular school hours, to be provided by the churches with instructors they selected.[74]

The SED and CDU newspapers in the Soviet zone, *Neues Deutschland* and *Neue Zeit*, also made similar claims during this time period. The June 17, 1948, issue of *Neue Zeit* reflected the accommodating stance of the CDU leadership under Otto Nuschke towards the question of religious education in the Soviet zone. The article explicitly rejected the comparison made by church leaders between SED and Nazi educational policies. It noted the churches should now be glad their role in providing optional religious education in the schools had been preserved, and they had to accommodate themselves to an antifascist and democratic Germany with a secular school system.[75]

A particularly vicious attack against the education policies in the Western sectors of Berlin, appeared in the November 17, 1948, issue of the SED newspaper *Neues Deutschland*. Written by SED education official Karl Mewis, the article accused the CDU and the churches in West Berlin, aided by the "Imperialist Occupation Powers" of attempting to sabotage the democratic school reforms in the Soviet sector of Berlin. Mewis stated the CDU's and the churches "religious motivations" were a key factor in why they continued to attack the school reforms implemented by the SVAG and the SED. Mewis concluded the schools in West Berlin continued to indoctrinate children with militarist and racist propaganda in addition to reactionary religious teachings specifically directed against dialectical materialism.[76]

The Berlin Blockade effectively ended joint administrative and political control of the city, so the SVAG and SED authorities had little ability to halt German children in the Soviet sector from attending religious schools or religious education classes in the Western sectors. As Paul Zimmermann admitted to the assembled bishops of the Protestant Church on March 3, 1949, the status of Western sectors of the city under American, British, and French control allowed children in the Soviet sector to continue to obtain religious instruction. Zimmermann noted this was especially valuable, given the fact the SVAG and the SED were increasing their campaign against religious education elsewhere in the Soviet zone, including in the Soviet sector of Berlin.[77] It would not be until the physical division of the city with the construction of the Berlin Wall in 1961 that Protestant and Catholic children in the Soviet sector were prevented from attending religious education classes in West Berlin.

CONCLUSION

Norman Naimark and David Pike are certainly correct in demonstrating, that SVAG and SED policies in the Soviet zone did not follow one set formula devised before the end of the war and strictly implemented in a series of carefully defined stages from 1945 to 1949. SVAG and SED educational policies, like so many other religious policies implemented during the history of the occupation, were dictated and limited by political and administrative realities on the ground. This explains the agreement on religious education in Soviet zone in April 1946, due to the political independence of the CDU, the newly formed SED's determination not to be characterized as an atheistic political party, and a preference to avoid a sustained conflict with the Catholic and Evangelical churches over the religious education issue.[78] As this chapter has demonstrated, education authorities in the SVAG and SED never viewed the religious education compromise as a serious impediment to their plans of preventing the churches from offering religious education, and they began to circumvent the agreement almost as soon as it was enacted.

The failure to implement similar restrictive policies towards religious education in the Soviet sector of Berlin during the first three years of the occupation was grounded in the unique four-power administration of the city. The SVAG push for a similar compromise on religious education in the spring of 1948 among the four occupying powers reflected the determination of Soviet officials to maintain the semblance of four-power control over Berlin and by extension, Germany. Yet the ability of children in the Soviet sector to continue to receive religious instruction in schools in the Western sectors, even during the tensest times of the Berlin Blockade, demonstrated the limits of the SVAG and SED authorities to enforce their religious education policies to the extent they wished.

It is false to believe that because of the opportunistic nature of SVAG and SED religious policies neither had any long term goals in the Soviet zone with regards to religious institutions. From the very beginning of the occupation, authorities in the SVAG-ONO and the KPD (later SED) officials in the various *Abteilung Volksbildung* made it quite clear only a thoroughly secular school system could be part of the new democratic and antifascist Germany. What this actually meant was the curriculum of schools in the Soviet zone would emphasize dialectical materialism in all subjects as part of the broader goal of the Stalinist indoctrination of the entire population. Religious institutions would have no role to play in the educational process, either in operating their own schools or by offering religious education to children whose parents desired it. This too was part of the broader plan by both the SVAG and SED to minimize the role the churches could play in the society of the Soviet zone, especially with regards to education.

What proved true of the rest of Eastern Europe was equally valid in the Soviet zone of Germany, namely, what was promised during the early "antifascist-democratic" period of 1945–1946 would be swiftly withdrawn when the construction of Stalinist-style socialism began in 1947. In the case of Brandenburg it did not even take that long, as the SED authorities began to violate the agreement almost immediately after April 1946. The SVAG and SED were careful not to resort to blatant tactics such as rescinding the religious education compromise, but rather they fulfilled it in a such a manner that the churches would be unable to comply with it, such as allowing religious education classes at the most inconvenient times of day. The search by the SED-controlled *Abteilung Volksbildung* for religious education teachers with Nazi backgrounds was done less in order to assist in the building of an antifascist Germany and more to prevent religious education from occurring at all in the schools. These policies were pursued in Brandenburg and later in the Soviet sector of Berlin in a piecemeal fashion, almost certainly in order to avoid widespread discontent among the religious population and the churches.

Recognizing the right of churches to offer religious education in school buildings in theory while denying it in reality, enabled the SVAG and SED authorities to work towards their goal of creating an atheistic German society in the Stalinist model. At the same time, by refusing to actually rescind the agreement and pushing for its implementation in all of Berlin in the spring of 1948, the SED could still claim a unified German state under SED leadership would pose no threat to religious freedom.

The SED played a more active role than the SVAG authorities in the day to day attempt to deny religious institutions the ability to offer religious education in the school buildings. Yet it would be incorrect to assume authorities in the SVAG-ONO, especially its leader Lieutenant Colonel A. D. Danilov, did not take an interest in these activities. Danilov's own history of the SVAG-ONO's activities noted the encouragement given to the SED in pursuing these restrictive policies on religious education, and even expressed disappointment when the SED did not go as far as the SVAG authorities wanted. These policies were unsurprising given the fact that the educational process was far too important for the SVAG's and SED's long term goals for anything less than complete state control to be tolerated.

The CDU in the Soviet zone under Jakob Kaiser protested these policies, as the unhindered ability of the churches to offer religious education was an essential element of Kaiser's theory of Christian Socialism as an alternative to the SED's ideology. Their use of it as an electoral issue was limited somewhat by the fact the CDU agreed to the religious education compromise of

April 1946. After Kaiser's removal in December 1947, the CDU in the Soviet zone gradually abandoned raising the issue, just as they had ceased striving for any implementation of Christian Socialism as an alternative to the Stalinist model offered by the SED.

For the Protestant and Catholic churches, especially leaders such as Preysing, Dibelius, Zimmermann, and von Arnim, the SVAG and SED policies concerning religious education only confirmed their worst suspicions about them. Already viewing the Soviets and their German "friends" as duplicitous, tyrannical, and determined to destroy religious belief, the violations of the religious education agreement of April 1946 did nothing to change this perspective. This in turn aided the increasingly open criticism of both Preysing and Dibelius to religious policies in the Soviet zone, which they readily compared to those of the Nazis.

Even Protestant leaders more inclined to compromise with the SVAG and SED authorities, such as Kurt Krummacher, were deeply disappointed with the difficulties placed before them by the state authorities in offering religious education. This was especially damaging given the fact that nearly all Catholic and Protestant leaders had looked forward to the period after the war as one that would be free of Nazi persecution of religious instruction of German youths. Unlike with the case of charitable relief, but just as with youth and women's organizations, the churches largely experienced frustration and disappointment that further embittered them against the Stalinist regime which was swiftly being constructed by the SVAG and the SED.

Notes

1. John Rodden, *Textbook Reds: Schoolbooks, Ideology, and Eastern German Identity*. University Park: The Pennsylvania State University Press, 2007. 6.

2. Much like other church-State conflicts which emerged during the Soviet occupation, the controversy over religious education continued during the history of the German Democratic Republic throughout the 1950s and early 1960s.

3. The bitter aspects of the struggle are touched on in most works concerning the Soviet occupation of Germany and/or the experience of the churches in East Germany, such as those by Naimark, Besier, and Goeckel, as one of the first examples of conflict between church and state authorities in East Germany after 1945. While the conflict over religious education in the German schools was certainly not the only conflict concerning religious issues, it was the most intense and longest-lasting during the history of the Soviet zone. It also mirrored Soviet and SED religious policies in other areas, as some initial concessions in 1945 and 1946 gave away to sustained efforts to block religious education in German schools during the last three years of the occupation.

4. Naimark, 465. Pike, 5.

5. As German religious historians Hörst Dahn and Gerhard Besier correctly point out, the SED's determination to have absolute control over the education system in the Soviet zone as an essential tool for the building of Stalinist socialism would inevitably lead to conflicts with the Catholic and Protestant churches. John Rodden ably demonstrates in his two excellent works on the history of the East German education system, from the very beginning of occupation both the SED and the Soviets desired that the education young Germans in the Soviet zone received would mold them into devout Marxist-Leninists. This meant that infusion of every topic with the ideology of Communist regime in East Germany, including its militant atheism. This chapter concurs with Rodden's broader argument in his two works that the education system constructed in the Soviet zone very closely resembled that which existed in the Soviet Union, and that this occurred due to close collaboration between the SED and the Soviet authorities. Benita Blessing's recent work on the reforms of the German school system during the Soviet occupation concurs with this central argument of Dahn and Besier regarding the initial inevitability of conflict between the SED and the churches, although she incorrectly argues that religious education compromise in April 1946 was implemented throughout the Soviet zone without incident. See Benita Blessing, *The Antifascist Classroom: Denazification in Soviet-Occupied Germany 1945–1949.* New York, NY: Palgrave, 2006. 168. Hörst Dahn, *Konfrontation oder Kooperation? Das Verhältnis von Staat und Kirche in der SBZ/DDR 1945–1980.* Düsseldorf: Westdeutscher Verlag, 1982. 31. Gerhard Besier, *Der SED-Staat und die Kirche.* Munich: C. Bertelsmann, 1993. 29. John Rodden, *Painting the Little Red Schoolhouse: A History of East German Education, 1945–1995.* Oxford: Oxford University Press, 2002. 14. *Textbook Reds: Schoolbooks, Ideology, and Eastern German Identity.* 7.

6. The sources for this chapter include the records of the Soviet military government in Berlin-Brandenburg, especially the Propaganda and People's Education departments. The People's Education Department (*Otdel narodnogo obrazovaniia,* SVAG-ONO) was headed by A. D. Danilov, who often coordinated his work with Colonel Sergei Tiul'panov, head of the Propaganda/Information Administration. Danilov's administration had an ambiguous relationship with Tiul'panov's department, which was in charge of all printing and publishing enterprises in the Soviet zone. The chapter also accesses sources from the state agencies in Berlin and Potsdam devoted to educational affairs, in particular the Department of the People's Education (*Abteilung Volksbildung*), and finally the official papers of SED party leaders who focused on educational issues, especially leading SED party theorist Anton Ackermann and the head of the *Abteilung Volksbildung* for the entire Soviet zone, Paul Wandel. In addition, this study uses the party documents of the CDU and the records of the Protestant and Catholic churches that focus on educational issues, including material from the private archives of the Evangelical and Catholic bishops of Berlin-Brandenburg, Otto Dibelius and Konrad von Preysing, respectively as well as the first three leaders of the Eastern CDU, Andreas Hermes, Jakob Kaiser, and Otto Nuschke.

7. Naimark, 453.

8. GARF, f.7317-SVAG, op. 54-Otdel narodnogo obrazovaniia, d.2-Istoriia SVAG narodnogo obrazovaniie II, l. 5.

9. GARF, f. 7317, op. 54, d. 2, l. 17. Danilov also noted that all four antifascist political parties desired offices on the German *Abteilung Volksbildung* at the zonal, provincial, and local levels, but SVAG authorities ensured the KPD would dominate these offices, from KPD education "expert" Paul Wandel on down.

10. SAPMO-DDR Abteilung, DY 30- SED Zentral Kommittee IV 2-ZK Secretariat, 9.05- Abteilung Volksbildung, 70-September-Dezember 1945.

11. SAPMO-DDR Abteilung, DY 30- SED Zentral Kommittee IV 2-ZK Secretariat, 9.05- Abteilung Volksbildung, 78-Juni-September 1945.

12. SAPMO-DDR Abteilung, DY/30/IV 2/9.05/78. 3–7.

13. SAPMO-DDR Abteilung, DY/30/IV 2/9.05/70. 15–17.

14. GARF, f.7077 (SVAG-Brandenburg), op.2 (Otdel narodnogo obrazovanniia), d. 52- (Correspondence June–December 1945), ll. 28–29.

15. "Neuer Schulgeist" *Neue Zeit.* 14 Aug 1945. 1.

16. SAPMO-DDR Abteilung, DY/30/IV 2/9.05/78. 1.

17. ACDP, *Signatur* 07–010-CDU-Ost, #672.

18. DAB, Abteilung V-Konrad von Preysing, Repositur 16–7-2.

19. Robert Goeckel, 43. Other prominent Protestant clergy in the Soviet zone, such as Kurt Krummacher and Heinrich Gruber, expressed similar concerns about preserving religious education in the schools, although they lacked Dibelius's stronger condemnation of state authorities. Krummacher and Gruber stated they would accept the new secular education system in the Soviet zone, as long as it allowed for optional religious instruction in the classrooms.

20. SAPMO-DDR Abteilung, DY/30/IV 2/9.05/70. 27–35.

21. *Tägliche Rundschau.* 23 Oct 1945. 4. Since the SED and SVAG education officials viewed religious belief as inherently reactionary, religious instruction in the schools would have an equally reactionary character. More importantly, the presence of religious instruction in the schools, even if it was voluntary, would challenge the dominance of dialectical materialism in the other aspects of curriculum.

22. Brandenburgisches Landeshauptarchiv (BLHA-Brandenburg Main Provincial Archive) Repositur 202A- Büro des Ministerpräsidents, Provinzial Verwaltung, #506- Kirchen Angelegenheiten, Juni 1945 bis October 1949, 4–6.

23. *Die Protokolle der Kirchlichen Ostkonferenz 1945–1949.* Eds, Michael Kuhne, Gottingen: Vandenhoeck & Ruprecht, 2005. 99. Krummacher, along with the Bishop of Thuringia Moritz Mitzenheim, was known as the leading Protestant figure most willing to compromise with the SVAG and SED authorities.

24. Landesarchiv Berlin (LAB- City Archive for Berlin) C Repositur 101–04-Rat für Kirchen Angelegenheiten, Berlin Stadt Regierung, #7, 3.

25. Naimark, 454.

26. *Neue Zeit.* May 22 1946.

27. DAB, Abteilung I- Bischöfliches Ordinariat Berlin, Repositur 8–12–1.

28. ACDP *Signatur* 07–010- CDU-Ost, Repositur 1846.

29. *Neues Deutschland.* 9 May 1945.

30. GARF, f. 7317-SVAG, op. 54 (Otdel narodnogo obrazovaniia), d.1 (Sbornik materialov po istorii otdela narodnogo obrazovaniia), I, l. 52.

31. GARF, f. 7077 (SVAG-Brandenburg), op.1 (Upravlenie propagandy), d. 203 (Correspondence January–May1946), ll.118–130.

32. SAPMO-DDR Abteilung DY 30/IV 2/9.05/78. 25–29.

33. GARF, f. 7317 (SVAG), op. 54 (Otdel narodnogo obrazovaniia), d.1-(Sbornik materialov po istorii otdela narodnogo obrazovaniia III), l. 20.

34. *Tägliche Rundschau.* 7 Aug 1946. 3. Werner was one of the most popular Evangelical clerics in the eyes of the Soviet authorities.

35. *Neues Deutschland.* 18 Oct 1946. 2.

36. BLHA, Repositur 202A, #506, 22.

37. BLHA, Repositur 202A , #505, 24. The Brandenburg civilian administration like the administrations in the other four provinces of the Soviet zone, was dominated by the SED. From June 1945 to January 1948 it was referred to as the *Provinzial Verlwaltung* (Provincial Administration) and afterwards as the *Landesregierung* (State Government).

38. BLHA, Rep. 202A, #505, 27.

39. BLHA, Rep. 202A, 506, 37–41.

40. BLHA, Rep, 202A, 506, 69.

41. BLHA, Rep. 202A, 506, 109–114.

42. Ibid., 115. Von Arnim's appeal to the head office of the Brandenburg *Abteilung Volksbildung* ultimately had little effect, as he never even received a response.

43. Ibid., 117–118.

44. Ibid., 134.

45. Ibid., 161–163.

46. Ibid., 170–175.

47. *Die Protokolle der Kirchlichen Ostkonferenz 1945–1949.* Eds, Michael Kuhne, Gottingen: Vandenhoeck & Ruprecht, 2005. 157–159.

48. BLHA, Rep.202A, 506, 190.

49. DAB, Abteilung V, Repositur 16–7-2.

50. *Die Protokolle der Kirchlichen Ostkonferenz 1945–1949.* Eds, Michael Kuhne, Gottingen: Vandenhoeck & Ruprecht, 2005. 254–255.

51. Ibid., 347.

52. Evangelisches Landeskirchliches Archiv Berlin (ELAB-Evangelical Provincial Archive for the church in Berlin-Brandenburg) Bestand 603-Otto Dibelius, A 7–1.1.

53. Ibid.

54. *Neue Zeit.* 2 Jul 1946. 1.

55. *Neue Zeit.* 25 Dec 1946. 2.

56. *Neue Zeit.* "Der Weg der CDU in der Ostzone." 6 May 1948. 3.

57. ACDP, *Signatur 07–010, Repositur 1848.*

58. Pike, 94.

59. LAB, C Rep, 101–04, #7, 3.

60. DAB, Abteilung I, Repositur 8–12–1.

61. EZA, Bestand 4-EKD Kirchenkanzlei, #313. It is important to emphasize that even when religious education was offered in schools in the Soviet zone, the churches did not press their luck by asking that it should be made an official part of the curriculum.

62. SAPMO-DDR Abteilung, . DY/30/IV 2/9.05/72. 1–7.

63. SAPMO-DDR Abteilung, . DY/30/IV 2/9.05/72. 46–54.

64. LAB, C. Rep 101–04, #7. 8. In the case of Brandenburg, the ability of students to attend religious education classes was much more limited, at thirty to forty percent.

65. LAB, C Rep. 101–04, #7, 4–5. The actual decision had been made in early March shortly before the complete collapse of the Allied Control Authority when SVAG Commander in Chief Vasilii Sokolovskii walked out of a meeting with his Western counterparts, due to plans by the Western authorities to introduce a new currency for the Western zone.

66. ELAB, Bestand 603, B 17.

67. LAB, C Rep. 101–04, #75, 7–10.

68. GARF, f. 7317, op. 54, d. 2, l. 71. Danilov recounted his statements made over the radio in the Soviet sector in his history of the SVAG-ONO's activities.

69. EZA, Bestand 4, *Repositur* 515.

70. Ibid. Danilov also noted leaders in the American, British, and French zones, with the aid of reactionary German clergymen, launched into a propaganda campaign against Soviet school reforms.

71. ELAB, Bestand 603, B 17. During this period, because of the Berlin Blockade, the Berlin city government exercised administrative authority only over the Western sectors of the city. The new school law of September 1948 allowed for the creation of religious schools, although religious education remained an optional class in public secondary schools.

72. Ibid.

73. Ibid.

74. *Tägliche Rundschau*. 29 Oct 1948. 3.

75. *Neue Zeit*. 17 Jun 1948. 1.

76. *Neues Deutschland*. 17 Nov 1948. 5.

77. *Die Protokolle der Kirchlichen Ostkonferenz 1945–1949*. 299–300. Zimmermann also noted it was unfortunate the rest of the children in the Soviet zone could not take advantage of the opportunities offered to those living in Berlin.

78. As Robert Goeckel points out in his work on the Protestant Church in East Germany, the SED and SVAG wanted to maintain the appearance of a non-confrontational approach towards religious institutions during the early years of the occupation, and policies such as allowing the churches to use school buildings after regular school hours for religious education lent themselves to this. Blessing's recent work on the reforms of the German secondary education during the Soviet occupation concurs with Goeckel's analysis of SVAG and SED intentions, but she incorrectly accepts at face value SED claims the religious education compromise was honored during the Soviet occupation.

Chapter Five

The Competition between Socialist and Religious Youth and Women's Organizations in Berlin-Brandenburg, 1945–1949

INTRODUCTION

In a letter dated February 25, 1948, Otto Dibelius, asked the head of religious affairs for the SVAG's Information Administration, Lieutenant Colonel Vsevolod Ermolaev, why certain religious youth leaders had been called to report to the NKVD and subsequently never returned. Dibelius reminded Ermolaev the Protestant Church in Germany bore no hatred towards the Soviets but their arbitrary arrests of Protestants engaged in youth work would certainly create it. He received little from Ermolaev besides a vague promise to look into the matter.[1]

The Catholic Archbishop of Berlin Konrad von Preysing also received dozens of requests in the late fall of 1947 and early spring of 1948 from Catholics in Berlin and Brandenburg asking him to intercede with SVAG authorities to release Catholic youths from the custody of either the Red Army or the NKVD. Many of these youths, according to the appeals Preysing received, had been leaders of local Catholic youth organizations before disappearing. The appeals also noted following their disappearance, the organizations they had led were dissolved. Preysing's appeals to SVAG Supreme Commander Sokolovskii nearly always went unanswered.[2]

These policies were the ultimate result of the frustration of the Soviet authorities at the inability of "their" antifascist youth and women's organizations, the Free German Youth (FDJ-*Freie Deutsche Jugend* and the Democratic Women's Federation (DFD- *Demokratischer Frauenbund Deutschlands*) to crush the influence of religious youth and women's organizations over the population of the Soviet occupation zone. While such harsh policies were not a foregone conclusion in 1945, the determination of the Soviet authorities and their allies in the Socialist Unity Party that only they could define what constituted an "antifascist-democratic transformation" in Germany and the equal determination of the churches to preserve their independent role in youth and women's work led to this state of events by early 1948.

Communist youth and women's organizations were pillars of the Soviet-constructed regimes in Eastern and Central Europe in the Cold War era. After the end of the "antifascist-democratic" transformation in 1947 they were often the only legal youth and women's organizations. Even by 1949 this was not yet the case in the westernmost "people's democracy" in the Soviet empire, the Soviet occupation zone of Germany. The policies of the Soviet Military Administration in Germany towards independent youth and women's organizations were determined by the fact the Soviet zone of Germany followed a slower trajectory in its emergence as a Soviet satellite than the rest of Eastern and Central Europe from 1945 to 1949. SVAG and SED authorities preferred a gradual approach that slowly limited the ability of the churches and the CDU to act independently as opposed to any violent and immediate suppression. As was the case with the churches' independent charitable activities, the SVAG's goal of suppressing activity by the churches was left unfinished. Throughout the 1950s, authorities in the GDR finished the process begun during the Soviet occupation, effectively forcing religious youth and women's organizations underground.

This chapter examines how the experience of religious youth and women's organizations and so to illuminate power realities in the Soviet zone of Germany, and how they affected long-term SVAG and SED plans for the Soviet zone. How did SVAG authorities react to religious youth and women's organizations which were theoretically beyond their control? How did the Protestant and Catholic churches respond? What did this reveal about church-state relations in the Soviet zone and in the future GDR?

SVAG and SED policies towards religious youth and women's organizations reflected the general trend of religious policies in the Soviet zone. Just as the SVAG allowed the creation of *Volkssolidarität,* an umbrella charitable organization to "unite" all elements of society in the Soviet zone under the Socialist Unity Party (SED) to alleviate the humanitarian disaster in the Soviet zone of Germany, it formed umbrella youth and women's organizations under SED leadership to prevent the other antifascist parties and the churches from operating fully independent youth and women's movements. Before the acceleration of Stalinist-style socialism in late 1947, the SED even allowed representatives from the Protestant and Catholic churches to serve on the executive committee of the FDJ, and female members of the CDU to serve on the executive committee of the DFD. These representatives exercised little influence on the activities of either organization and were marginalized and then removed once they became too outspoken about what they saw as the FDJ's and DFD's complete domination by the SED.

The SVAG and SED authorities' hopes to funnel religious youths and women into organizations they controlled were disappointed by the churches' refusal to comply with these plans. The youth and women's organizations not affiliated with the dominant Socialist Unity Party (SED), the CDU's *Junge Union* and the CDU's *Frauenausschuss* (The Women's Committee), and the various Protestant and Catholic youth and women's organizations engaged in an intense struggle with the DFD and FDJ for the hearts and minds in the Soviet zone. To the frustration of SED and SVAG officials, the DFD and the FDJ, despite having far more members, were unable to dominate youth and women's affairs in the Soviet zone.

In this case, the different religious background between Russia and Germany possibly played a significant role in this development. The organizational structure, ritualistic practices, and role of women and children in the Orthodox Church before the Russian Revolution were considerably different than what existed in the Protestant and Catholic churches in eastern Germany following the end of the Second World War. The Soviet officials, operating from a background influenced by the fight to destroy the Russian Orthodox Church in the 1920s and 1930s, were not always inclined or able to comprehend the differences between various religious institutions.[3] Many of their internal communications reveal a general assumption that the absorption or co-opting of church women's and children's organizations would be a relative easy and quick affair.

The SVAG's Propaganda/Information Administration, eventually abandoned this approach of the SED's attempt to co-opt religious youth and women's organizations during the first two years of the Soviet occupation. Following the banning of the CDU's *Junge Union* and the *Frauenausschuss* in January 1948, state authorities implemented policies designed to limit and eventually suppress the activities of religious youth and women's organizations. This was part of the great turn by SVAG and SED policies to a more anti-religious character following the end of the political independence of the CDU in December 1947. By the time of the founding of the GDR in October 1949, these policies had achieved considerable but by no means absolute success. These policies included a SED-led propaganda campaign in the Soviet zone, SVAG officials banning or dissolving religious youth and women's organizations, issuing decrees to prevent them from meeting in public places, and finally arresting and imprisoning their leaders.

The Protestant and Catholic churches responded to these policies just as they had to SVAG and SED policies towards charitable relief and religious education. They refused to allow their own youth and women's organizations

merely to join the DFD or the FDJ, but instead insisted they operate independently from them, and indeed actively compete with them in urban and rural
areas for membership and public support. They were so successful in regards
to this that rural areas in Brandenburg were often bereft of support for the FDJ
and the DFD, and even in urban areas the Catholic and Protestant youth and
women's organizations did quite well.

Only in working class districts of major cities did these organizations
face serious problems in recruiting new members and holding public events,
although many working-class youth who turned away from them tended to
join the CDU's youth and women's groups rather than the FDJ or the DFD.
For Catholic and Protestant leadership in Berlin- Brandenburg, women's and
especially youth organizations were a key element to their attempts to rebuild
Germany on Christian foundations following the disaster of Nazism. Most
Catholic and Protestant clergy, especially in senior positions, tended to view
SED-sponsored FDJ and DFD with extreme suspicion, viewing them as little
different from similar Nazi youth and women's organizations which had sup-
pressed those of the churches from 1933 to 1945.

Regional officials in the SVAG Propaganda/Information administration
frequently complained to their superiors of the "reactionary" activities of
religious organizations, and their ability to weaken the control of the FDJ and
the DFD over the majority of German youths and women. SED party officials
who led its youth work, including future GDR leader Erich Honecker, made
similar observations, and claimed the FDJ should be the only "legal" youth
organization in a Socialist Germany. During the early transitory period of
the Soviet occupation from 1945 to 1947, comparatively little was done by
SVAG or SED authorities to limit or control their activities. This occurred
for two other reasons. The first was both the SVAG and SED wished to keep
up appearances of tolerating "religious freedom" and avoiding an open feud
with the churches. The second was neither the SED nor the SVAG wanted to
pursue policies that would abandon hopes to control all of Germany, since
the Americans and British in their zones were quite willing to allow religious
youth and women's organizations to operate freely.

Once the building of Stalinism in the Soviet zone had accelerated in
mid-1947 and hopes of Soviet control over a united German state faded,
this brought about a sharp reversal in policies towards religious youth and
women's organizations. Unlike religious charitable activity, which was tolerated by the SVAG throughout the history of the occupation despite the failure
of the SED-dominated *Volkssolidarität* to control it, religious youth and
women's organizations were soon subject to harsh persecution, including the
arrest of their leaders and the banning of their meetings. By October 1949,

while religious youth and women's organizations had not been suppressed entirely, their activities had been effectively curtailed and their membership had dropped significantly, a clear result of the SVAG and SED's determination to create an atheist German state on the Stalinist model.

SVAG and SED policies towards religious organizations demonstrate, as historians such as Norman Naimark, David Pike, and Wilfried Loth have pointed out, the process of the transformation of the Soviet zone of Germany into the German Democratic Republic from 1945 to 1949 did not follow one set pattern or a plan with clearly defined stages.[4] The relative freedom of religious youth and women's organizations in the early years of the Soviet occupation was based on political and social realities in Germany that neither the SVAG nor SED authorities could simply bend to their will. However, as Vladislav Zubok and Gary Bruce argued, the emergence of a Stalinist German state in 1949 was no accident, and from the very beginning the SVAG and their German "friends" were determined to maintain all crucial levers of political power in their hands. They were equally determined in their belief only they knew what constituted a "democratic-antifascist transformation" of Germany.[5] Neither group intended for independent youth or women's organizations of any kind to exist once the conditions for the creation of Stalinist-style socialism had been established. The efforts to repress religious organizations after the CDU's political independence had been crippled in January 1948 were the natural outcome of these beliefs.[6]

THE LIMITED TOLERATION OF RELIGIOUS YOUTH AND WOMEN'S ORGANIZATIONS AT THE BEGINNING OF THE OCCUPATION TO THE CREATION OF THE SED JUNE 1945 TO APRIL 1946

The SVAG authorities were not immediately willing to allow youth and women's organizations to form in the Soviet zone, believing those involved in Nazi youth and women's work would attempt to dominate antifascist women's and youth organizations. On August 3, 1945, Major General V. A. Sharov, commander of the Soviet military government in Brandenburg, issued orders explicitly banning the formation of any youth organizations in the Soviet zone of Germany. Sharov justified his decision by stating since so many German children had been involved in the Hitler Youth, involving them in youth activities again would violate the SVAG's denazification policies.[7] On September 19, 1945, the SVAG Supreme Commander, Marshal Georgii Zhukov, issued a similar order banning all youth sports organizations,

including those administered by the churches. Zhukov included church athletic organizations in this ban, and that control over athletic activities would
be placed under the control of local SVAG authorities.[8]

In the fall of 1945, SVAG authorities began to consider the revival of youth
and women's organizations. On October 17, Major General Sharov met with
the KPD's (*Kommunistische Partei Deutschlands*) leader for youth work,
Erich Honecker, to discuss the possibility of reviving youth organizations.
Honecker was open to the idea, and stated the KPD had to take the lead role
in youth work in the Soviet zone, since the SPD would be unable to because
of its ideological weaknesses and the CDU and the churches were hopelessly
reactionary. Sharov agreed to this and informed Honecker the KPD needed
to prevent the SPD, the CDU, and the churches from coordinating their own
youth activities against those of the KPD. Sharov stated this had already hap-
pened clandestinely in Brandenburg as well as openly in the Western zones of
Germany and the Western sectors of Berlin, often with the active assistance
of British and American military authorities.[9]

In a report sent on October 25, 1945, Zhukov informed Sharov women's
and youth organizations would soon be officially formed with SVAG permission. While Sharov's response expressed worries that the churches could
use these organizations for "reactionary" activities, he also noted they could
prove potentially useful under the influence of the SVAG and especially the
KPD.[10] Three weeks later, Zhukov issued an official SVAG order allowing
the creation of antifascist women's committees. Antifascist women's committees were assigned three central tasks. The first was "the fulfillment of
political, educational and cultural Enlightenment of Women as part of their
antifascist-democratic foundations. The second was the preparation of German women to participate fully in the political and social life of Germany,
and to help make possible the democratic recovery of Germany. The third
was the expectation the antifascist women's committees would assist mothers
in raising their children in a democratic spirit. Zhukov explicitly stated
women who had been members of the Nazi Party or part of fascist women's
organizations would not be allowed to participate, nor would women's antifascist organizations be allowed to merge directly with German antifascist
political parties.[11]

In actuality, while the Soviet authorities had not legally allowed the formation of women's antifascist committees, they had done little to halt German
women from organizing them. All four of the antifascist parties that emerged
in June 1945 had encouraged their members to create local women's committees to assist the victims of the war. By November 1945, there were already
hundreds of women's committees in the Soviet zone, although most dedicated

themselves to assisting German women left homeless and destitute by the war as opposed to political education.[12]

Zhukov also authorized the creation on November 9, 1945, of a "lead" Antifascist Women's Committee located in the Soviet sector of Berlin to supervise the work of women's committees throughout the Soviet zone. Serving on the committee were representatives of each of the antifascist political parties. Its leaders were Kathe Kern of the SPD and Elli Schmidt of KPD, who later became the leading female officials in the Socialist Unity Party after April 1946. The three other representatives on the executive committee were Helene Beer of the LPD, Martha Arendsee of the FDGB (*Freier Deutscher Gewerkschaftsbund*-The Free German Trade Union), and Margarete Ehlert of the CDU. Equivalent antifascist women's committees were also formed at the provincial and city levels throughout the Soviet zone with executive committees drawn from all four of the antifascist parties.[13]

By the fall of 1946, there were over six thousand women's antifascist committees in the Soviet zone. The new SVAG Supreme Commander, Vasilii Sokolovskii, was frustrated with the extensive involvement of representatives from the "bourgeois" CDU in day to day administration of the antifascist women's committees, especially in rural areas. This was a particular concern due to the fact that representatives of the KPD and SPD outnumbered those of the LPD and the CDU on the executive leadership of the antifascist women's committees by a ratio of three to one. Therefore, this dominance of the women's committees by the KPD and the SPD at the executive level should have also extended to the base, but it had not.[14]

SVAG officials began to push the leadership of the SED to form umbrella women's organizations that would contain representatives from the antifascist women's committees, as well as religious and "non-political" women's organizations. On September 14, 1946, Kern and Schmidt informed SED leaders Wilhelm Pieck, Walter Ulbricht, and Otto Grotewohl they had begun to form a broad-based women's organization due to repeated requests from SVAG leaders, especially Supreme Commander Sokolovskii, to create one. They informed them it would be called "the Democratic Women's Federation of Germany" and by September 25 they would have met with leading representatives of the FDGB, LPD, and CDU to begin its creation. They promised the DFD would serve the same function as the umbrella charity organization, *Volkssolidarität*, as it would ensure the SED would control the activity of the antifascist women's committees rather than the CDU or the churches.[15]

On October 31, 1945, the DFD issued its founding proclamation, written by Kathe Kern. It stated the DFD had five central tasks in rebuilding an antifascist Germany. The first was to maintain a visible part in the struggle for the complete destruction of fascism. The second was to eliminate fascist ideas and reactionary elements in German society. The third was to support the collaboration of all antifascist, democratic, and peace-loving women for the democratic reconstruction of Germany, the securing of peace, and to win the trust of women from all of Europe in the achievement of these goals. The fourth was to strive for the political, economic, legal, and social equality of women. The fifth and final task was to secure the education of children in the spirit of democracy and humanism, and to push them to strive for social achievement and economic productivity.[16]

In the social sphere the declaration also called for equal pay for equal work, legal and financial protection for women and children, the provision of adequate kindergartens for mothers with young children, and the legal establishment of representation of women on housing boards. The notable absence of religious concerns in this proclamation was unsurprising; given the fact the leaders of the Protestant and Catholic women's organizations showed little interest in joining the DFD, since the leadership of these organizations correctly believed their independence would be compromised if they did so.[17]

The formation of the Free German Youth (FDJ) followed a largely similar pattern. In February 1946, SVAG authorities allowed the antifascist parties to form their own youth branches and the Catholic and Protestant churches to form youth organizations. The SVAG authorities did not immediately push for the creation of an umbrella youth organization under the leadership of the KPD following its legalization in June 1945. Once the SED had been formed in April 1946, the SVAG authorities did put considerable pressure on it to form an SED equivalent to the Soviet Komsomol, which, like its equivalent in the USSR, would eventually become the only legally recognized youth organization in the Soviet zone of Germany. The formation of the SED-sponsored Free German Youth was officially proclaimed on June 1, 1946.[18]

The FDJ's founding proclamation had five official goals. The first was the preservation of German unity. The second was winning over German youths to the ideals of freedom, humanism, and the struggle for democracy and peace between nations. The third was the active participation of German boys and girls in the reconstruction of their country. The fourth was the securing of a renewed antifascist educational system, and the right to equal pay for equal work. The fifth and final was the provision of cultural, educational, and sporting activities for all German youths. The fact that most of these goals had a non-political nature was no accident; at this point the explicit identification of the FDJ with the SED was something the SED and SVAG authorities wished to avoid in order to appeal to the largest cross-section of German youths.[19]

When the Central Council of the FDJ met for the first time on October 1, 1946, it included representatives of the Protestant and Catholic churches.

Robert Hanisch was the representative for the Protestant Church and Fritz Lange for the Catholic Church. Their specific position on the Council was to offer advice to the FDJ's chairman, Erich Honecker, concerning ways in which the FDJ could appeal to religious German youths.[20]

The Protestant and Catholic churches in Berlin and Brandenburg never seriously considered having their own youth organizations absorbed into the FDJ. A major speech given by Otto Dibelius in the British sector of Berlin to assembled Protestant clergy from all of Berlin and Brandenburg on April 28, 1946, made this quite clear with regards to religious youth organizations. Dibelius affirmed that work with religious German youths was among the most important tasks facing the Protestant Church in the years to come, and while he would not rule out a limited level of cooperation with antifascist youth organizations, the church had to administer its own youth activities without any external interference.[21] Konrad von Preysing was even more unyielding on this issue than Dibelius. In a letter sent to the Allied Control Council headquarters on July 7, 1946, he made clear that the Catholic Church under his leadership would continue its work among youths independent of advice from authorities in the Soviet zone. Preysing also claimed the church would resist efforts "to use the energy and enthusiasm of Germany's youth towards violent political ends, as has been the case in the past."[22]

SVAG and SED officials were equally suspicious of church intentions with regards to both youth and women's organizations, as they considered both groups to be particularly susceptible to "reactionary" religious beliefs. In addition, these organizations were supposed to be subordinated to state-run youth and women's organizations, and when church groups resisted this it only served to increase the suspicion of SVAG and SED officials. On December 12, 1945, the head of SVAG Propaganda Administration for Brandenburg Lieutenant Colonel I. I. Mil'khiker wrote to his superior Colonel Tiul'panov concerning the activities of the women's antifascist committees. Mil'khiker complained KPD members in the antifascist committees were failing in their task of integrating German youth into political life in the Soviet zone. In addition, they had been unable to win over German women to support the Soviet military authorities, and consequently the churches and the CDU had taken advantage of their failures to influence a growing section of the female population in Brandenburg towards "reactionary" political beliefs.[23]

Officials in the Propaganda Administration often viewed religious youth organizations as mere fronts for the CDU, especially for those German youths who did not want to expose their political views openly. Major V. A. Koloss, head of the Propaganda Administration for the Soviet sector of Berlin, reported to Mil'khiker on February 23, 1946, that the CDU and the churches were working together to draw German youths to religious and

CDU organizations. Koloss noted the KPD had not done an adequate job in resisting these activities, and its strength among the population had suffered accordingly. He also claimed the CDU's *Junge Union* was a much greater political threat than either Protestant or Catholic youth organizations.[24]

Mil'khiker reported to Tiul'panov on March 8, 1946, concerning the ability of the Protestant and Catholic churches to offer material assistance to poor families if they sent their sons and daughters to join religious youth organizations as well as gifts such as chocolates, candies, bibles or crucifixes. He claimed this was used to extract promises not to join any youth organizations sponsored by the KPD or the SVAG. Mil'khiker noted that these tactics were particularly successful in the cities of Königs-Wusterhausen and Blankenfeld. He assured Tiul'panov any protests by the churches that this financial assistance was only given out of belief in Christian charity were nonsense, because the churches specifically pursued these policies to recruit new members for the CDU. Mil'khiker suggested two solutions. The first was to put more pressure on their German allies to offer greater material benefits to their youth members. The second was to close meetings of religious youth organizations where bribes were offered to German youths. In his response to Mil'khiker, Tiul'panov encouraged the implementation of the first tactic but not the second, maintaining the sense of restraint which characterized early SVAG religious policies.[25]

Among the groups viewed as a particular threat by the SVAG was the *Evangelischer Frauenbund*; formed in 1899, it had been forced underground during the Nazi period and only began to re-emerge in open activity in late 1945. A bulletin distributed by the Protestant church throughout Brandenburg in March 1946 stated its purpose was to assist German women from all walks of life in their roles both as Christian wives and mothers and as contributors to the spiritual and economic reconstruction of Germany. The bulletin also claimed the leadership of the *Evangelischer Frauenbund* believed women's issues to be deeply connected to the social, political, cultural, and religious life of Germany. Much like the DFD or the antifascist women's committees, the bulletin argued. The Protestant women's organizations supported the full integration of women into the workforce and also equal opportunities for the education of German girls.[26]

Thus, at the end of the first eleven months of the Soviet occupation, the SVAG authorities had allowed the formation of antifascist youth and women's organizations by their own allies as well as the churches and the CDU. However, it was clear even at this early point the only "true antifascists" were those who served on the FDJ and the DFD. Their rival organizations created by the CDU and the churches were already living on borrowed time.

THE COMPETITION OF BETWEEN RELIGIOUS AND SOCIALIST YOUTH AND WOMEN'S ORGANIZATIONS DURING THE PERIOD OF THE "ANTIFASCIST TRANSFORMATION" APRIL 1946 TO DECEMBER 1947

Following the formation of the SED in April and the FDJ in June, Propaganda Administration officials were more confident in the ability of their German allies in countering the churches' youth and women's work. On August 8, 1946, two months after the formation of the FDJ and two months before the zonal elections, Major Koloss gave a positive evaluation of the work of the FDJ in the Soviet sector of Berlin to Mil'khiker. Koloss admitted that a large number of both Protestant and Catholic clerics were specifically engaged in work designed to attract German youths to religious youth organizations. The real purpose behind this, according to Koloss, was to encourage youths to join the CDU and work against the SED in the upcoming zonal elections. Despite this, the FDJ in the city had been able to limit the success of the churches in drawing youths away from the SED in favor of the CDU. Koloss confidently predicted if the FDJ continued this similar pattern of work, by October "only priests and ministers would remain in the CDU."[27]

This enthusiasm on the part of Soviet military authorities in Germany was not shared by their counterparts in Moscow. A report from a special commission of the Central Committee Secretariat's Administration for Agitation and Propaganda to the head of the CC Secretariat for International Affairs, Andrei Zhdanov, on October 11, 1946, found a great deal of fault with the work of SVAG's Propaganda Administration and the SED with regards to youth and women's issues in Germany. The report complained the DFD's influence over German women paled in comparison to the churches', and that both it and the numerous antifascist women's committees were far too concerned with cultural as opposed to political activities. The report made similar complaints regarding the FDJ, claiming it was not "politically-minded" enough and it, too, wasted too much time on cultural and athletic events as opposed to political education. The end result of this had been the Protestant and Catholic churches had been largely successful in winning over large numbers of youths and women in the Soviet zone towards the side of the CDU and its masters, the Anglo-Americans.[28]

The records of the CDU in the Soviet zone do not reveal any intent to coordinate activities with religious youth organizations in order to increase their electoral strength. CDU leader Jakob Kaiser and his deputy Ernst Lemmer frequently emphasized the need for the churches to operate their own youth organizations freely without state interference. At the CDU party conference in Berlin on June 12–15 1946, the party's leadership issued an official proc-lamation restating the CDU's commitment to protect religious freedom in the Soviet zone, which specifically mentioned legal protections for religious youth groups.[29]

In the meetings of the CDU's executive committee during the summer and fall preceding the October 1946 elections in the Soviet zone, the idea of using CDU youth organizations to funnel religious youth support towards the CDU was mentioned as a possible electoral tactic. At the meetings of the CDU executive committee on July 3 and September 15, 1946, Kaiser and Lemmer frequently mentioned the need to appeal to religious German youths in order to improve the CDU's electoral fortunes. Throughout this period, the CDU leadership refused to coordinate any activities of *Junge Union* with the FDJ, which Kaiser viewed solely as an SED front. At the first meeting of the CDU leadership after their success in the zonal elections on November 11, they reaffirmed these tactics. They continued to apply them until Kaiser's and Lemmer's removal on SVAG orders in December 1947.[30]

During this period the Protestant and Catholic representatives on the Cen-tral Council of the FDJ, the Protestant minister Hanisch and the Catholic priest Lange, were more open to some coordination of youth activities with the FDJ than the leadership of the CDU. Hanisch tended to take a more active part in debates in the FDJ Central Council than did Lange. At the meeting of the FDJ Central Council on November 28, 1946, Hanisch admitted to the other members of the Council that he agreed with limited collaboration between religious youth organizations and the FDJ in the construction of antifascism and democracy in the Soviet zone through sponsoring cultural and athletic activities. Hanisch concluded this was possible even though he did not share the philosophical views of those on Central Council, especially Erich Honecker.

Yet, the reason this had not occurred to any great extent in Berlin-Brandenburg Hanisch laid squarely at the policies of the SVAG and their SED allies who served on the German PVs. Hanisch noted the exclusion of religious education from the curriculum of the secondary schools and its replacement with dialectical materialism would only increase the pressure on religious youths to avoid joining the FDJ, due to its close affiliation with the atheistic SED.[31] Hanisch also noted the majority of Protestant and Catholic youths viewed the FDJ with skepticism, although this was rooted in the actions of Soviet authorities in the past year and not because of any conspira-torial acts of the churches or the CDU. Hanisch denied the Protestant youth groups were recruiting new members for *Junge Union*, which Lange also seconded. Honecker responded by claiming he did not believe them, and that collaboration between the churches and the CDU in recruiting new CDU party members was an established fact.[32]

At the next meeting of the FDJ Central Council on January 14 1947, Hanisch claimed the churches could not abandon their own youth work or simply merge it with the FDJ, as this meant the churches would have abandoned the spiritual needs of Germany's youth at their most desperate hour. He also claimed the FDJ and SED had created a dichotomy by which German youths interested in politics joined the FDJ, and those who were personally religious joined Protestant or Catholic youth organizations. Hanisch and Lange both claimed that there was no reason German youths could not be both religious believers and politically engaged, but the SED party propaganda, the rhetoric of its leaders, and anti-religious SVAG policies had effectively made this impossible. Hanisch reminded others on the council the churches were far older institutions than any of the antifascist political parties in the Soviet zone, and they tried to stay above political issues in the Soviet zone.[33]

Hanisch and Lange made similar comments over the next six months, although their complaints were ignored by the other members of the FDJ Central Council. At the meeting on June 12, 1947, Hanisch claimed the use of Marxist-Leninist propaganda by FDJ members as a recruiting tool had effectively crippled it as an organization which could claim to represent all German youths in the Soviet zone. It also kept it from effectively cooperating with youth organizations in the Western zones of Germany. Since the SED policies had forced the churches to compete openly with the FDJ for the allegiance of German youth, according to Hanisch, this situation would only damage the interests of Germany's young people and further isolate the Soviet zone.[34]

Hanisch returned to this critique at the meeting of the FDJ Central Council on September 7, 1947. He argued that the FDJ had to try to appeal to a broader base than just youths who were members of the SED, and that many religious German youths still felt there was a strong dichotomy between the churches and the FDJ. He urged the other members on the Central Council of the FDJ to stand above party identification; for that was the only way religious youths and the church leaders themselves would not view the FDJ with suspicion. Lange concurred with this point, and Hanisch stated the FDJ and the SED members who composed most of its leadership at the zonal and local levels were somewhat responsible for this by excluding the churches from any meaningful cooperation. Hanisch and Lange then pointed to a number of cases where FDJ leadership in different cities throughout Brandenburg had simply excluded religious youths from membership and vetoed the idea of joint athletic, cultural, or social activities with religious organizations. Both clerics argued that these tactics were symptomatic of the SED's belief only they could sufficiently instruct German youths in the concepts of antifascism and democracy. As a consequence, the FDJ had grown more isolated from religious youths even though it still theoretically allowed them to join and had pledged to cooperate with religious youth organizations.[35]

This situation was unsurprising given the true goals of the SVAG and the SED towards religious youth organizations, which Tiul'panov summarized in a report sent to the head of the SVAG Information Administration for Brandenburg I. I. Mil'khiker on May 22, 1947. Tiul'panov stated the plans of the churches to revive Christian culture in Germany meant they would invest a great deal of time and resources into youth work. Since the Soviet authorities and their German allies believed that increasing their influence over German youths was an essential part of their goal of building Stalinism in Germany, conflict with the churches was inevitable. It would soon be necessary to decrease the role the churches in the lives of German youths and eventually eliminate religious youth organizations entirely once the FDJ had reached a position of sufficient strength.[36]

The implication of Tiul'panov's statement reveals the policy of the SVAG and SED allowing Protestant and Catholic clergy to serve on the leadership councils of the FDJ at the zonal, provincial, and local levels was nothing more than a temporary tactic to convince religious youths that the FDJ was a genuinely broad-based youth organization rather than a mere front for the SED.

During much of 1947, SVAG officials did not feel the FDJ was strong enough yet to implement the policies which Tiul'panov had mentioned in his report to Mil'khiker, as religious youth organizations remained successful in recruiting new members. Because of this fact, the churches and the CDU had been successful in preventing a significant number of German youths from joining the FDJ. Tiul'panov admitted as much to Major General S. I. Ivanov, a member of the Political Council of SVAG on June 17 1947. He claimed the churches, through their charitable and educational work, now exercised a powerful influence over youths in the Soviet zone, including many who did not come from religious families. Tiul'panov further argued the churches used this influence to encourage youths to join the CDU and reject notions of working with FDJ members in any joint activities. He noted this situation existed regarding women's organizations as well, and if the FDJ and DFD were not able to combat it effectively the SVAG would have to take more stringent measures against religious youth and women's organizations.[37]

The status of women's organizations, especially the women's antifascist committees, posed a number of difficult questions for the SVAG and the

KPD/SED, as did the status and role of women in the "antifascist democratic transformation" of Germany. *Tägliche Rundschau, Deutsche Volkszeitung,* and *Neues Deutschland* frequently contained articles that discussed the political, social, and economic progress German women had made since the end of the war. An article in *Tägliche Rundschau* on June 21, 1945, commended German women for their role during the first month of the occupation, especially in providing charitable relief for those left destitute or crippled by the war. It argued such efforts, under the guidance of the KPD and the SPD, would point the way towards a greater role for women in the political life of Germany.[38] The SVAG newspaper was also quick to point to economic progress made by Soviet women, and to hint that if Germany followed the same path German women could rapidly advance in society just as Soviet women had. The July 29 issue of *Tägliche Rundschau* contained a front page article on Zinaida Troitzkaia, the director of the Moscow Metro, as an example of the equality of women in the Soviet Union; the article also claimed in its first paragraph women in the USSR received equal pay for equal work.[39]

At the same time, the SVAG authorities attempted to appeal not only to "liberated" women but also to more traditionally minded women. An article "Die Frau und die demokratische Erneuerung" (The Woman and the Democratic Renewal) which appeared in the October 5, 1945, issue, attempted to do this. The unnamed author wrote that a central part of the ideology of the Nazis had been the exclusion of women from all participation in public life. In the new democratic and antifascist Germany women would be able to participate in all forms of economic, political, and especially cultural life of the Soviet zone. The author encouraged women in the Soviet zone to join cultural organizations, labor unions, and especially the antifascist women's committees which were the backbone of the struggle to rebuild democracy in Germany.

Since Germany faced severe material deprivations which would likely continue to for some time, the work of the German housewife and mother was just as important as the obligations of those who worked directly in the political and economic reconstruction of the state. The author concluded by arguing even if their immediate concerns with their families kept many German women from participating in the antifascist committees they should at least vote in the future elections and shuns reactionary political sentiments. There also, of course, in all these articles a strict avoidance of one of the most immediate topics for German women, the constant threat of rape by marauding Red Army soldiers.[40]

The KPD's newspaper, *Deutsche Volkszeitung,* followed a similar pattern during the first year of the Soviet occupation. Its June 24, 1945, issue included an article that promised the KPD would strive with its Soviet allies to provide women with greater political and economic rights. The article asserted the repression of women during the Nazi era would never return and German women would no longer be expected solely to perform roles as mothers and wives.[41] The KPD leadership continued these promises into the next year. The February 16, 1946, issue of the newspaper contained a declaration for the upcoming KPD conference in March, signed by KPD leaders Wilhelm Pieck and Walter Ulbricht. It stated the KPD was determined to crush all forces of German reaction, and one of the main tools in accomplishing this would be the creation of full legal equality for all women in Germany. The article ended with a call for German women to join the KPD and the women's antifascist committees. In addition, it stressed the era when German women were expected to stay at home and leave political and economic affairs to men was over.[42]

Neues Deutschland, in a fashion similar to the SVAG and the former KPD newspaper, published numerous articles promising the rapid expansion of political, social, and economic rights for women and/or extolling their attainment in the Soviet Union. Unlike *Tägliche Rundschau* but much like *Deutsche Volkszeitung*, the SED newspaper did not try craft a message to the *Hausfrau*, but rather targeted women who had already joined the antifascist committees and the labor unions and were supposedly encumbered by bourgeois attitudes towards the place of women in society. For example, the July 24, 1946, issue noted the recent implementation of equal pay for equal work for women in the Soviet zone. The article's unnamed author noted this was the result of the efforts by women who joined the antifascist political parties and antifascist committees, with assistance of the SED and the Soviet authorities. Hopefully, these economic reforms would lead more German women to leave their traditional places in the home and take a more substantial role in the political and economic development of the Soviet zone.[43]

These tactics were not surprising due to two substantial fears of the SVAG and SED leadership during the first two years of the occupation. The first was that German women, much like German youths, were particularly susceptible to the forces of "reaction", especially the churches and the CDU. The second was the belief that the antifascist committees, and later the DFD, were not doing an adequate job of gaining female support for the SED but were allowing the CDU and the Protestant and Catholic churches to recruit the majority of German women to support their reactionary political goals.

The leadership of the DFD in the Soviet sector of Berlin, SED party members Kathe Kern and Eli Schmidt, received a series of complaints from SED members throughout the spring of 1947 regarding these concerns. For example, Kern and Schmidt received a letter from a SED party member named Mina Amann on January 26, 1947, complaining how the CDU in the Soviet sector of Berlin, with active assistance of the CDU and military authorities in the Western sectors, were engaged in a successful propaganda campaign to discourage women from joining the DFD. More importantly, they had been successful in engineering the election of female CDU party members to head the antifascist committees in the Soviet sector.[44] Another report, sent from a SED party member named Emma Czernitzki on March 8, 1947, claimed the tension between the CDU and SED representatives on the women's antifascist committees and the DFD had broken out into open conflict, and it appeared as if the CDU would gain the upper hand.[45]

Despite the considerable financial support given to it by the SVAG authorities, the SED leadership was reluctant to help the female SED members who belonged to the DFD or the women's antifascist committees in the spring and summer of 1947, because the SEDs own financial resources were severely strained at the time despite extensive SVAG material support. SVAG supreme commander Sokolovskii "solved" the problem of CDU domination of many antifascist committees by formally dissolving them in November 1947, leaving the DFD and religious women's organizations as the only alternatives.[46]

Even after the women's antifascist committees were abolished, the DFD continued to face competition in acquiring new members from the CDU and increasingly, Protestant and Catholic women's organizations. A report sent from Mil'khiker to Tiul'panov on June 12, 1947, admitted the SED held a huge advantage in local youth and women's organizations in Brandenburg, with 390 branches of the FDJ and DFD totaling 56,000 members, while the CDU had only 12 branches of *Junge Union* and the *Frauenausschuss* with 2,300 members from both groups. Mil'khiker noted organizations such as a joint CDU/Protestant women's organization named the Society of Female Christians, formed under the direction of British military authorities in the district of Wilmersdorf, posed a clear threat because of their role in spreading "antidemocratic and anti-Soviet" propaganda in the Soviet sector of Berlin. In his response, Tiul'panov concurred that such independent women's organizations would eventually need to be suppressed once the construction of socialism in the Soviet zone had entered into its decisive phase.[47]

During the first two and a half years of the Soviet occupation, SVAG and SED policies towards youth and women's organizations were marked by a sense of caution. Yet the SVAG and SED authorities had no doubt concerning the long-term fate of religious and CDU youth and women's organizations, which were basically interchangeable in their eyes. During the early period of the occupation, the SVAG authorities hoped to weaken the independent religious youth and women's organizations by incorporating their membership in the antifascist women's committees, the DFD and the FDJ, which, in the case of the last two, were firmly in the hands of the SED. The Protestant and Catholic churches in Berlin-Brandenburg refused to abandon their own independence but also tried successfully to use their representation in the FDJ to protect church work with youths. In this sense, the policies of the churches resembled those towards the SED umbrella organization for charitable work, *Volkssolidarität*, in that they agreed to work with it but would never abandon the independence of religious organizations.

The SVAG authorities soon realized the SED youth and women's organizations were simply not up to the task of eliminating the independence of their equivalents in the CDU or the churches. This was unlike the case with religious charitable activity, which continued to perform a vital service in alleviating the material deprivation in the Soviet zone and thus continued without excessive interference by state authorities. By contrast, religious youth and women's organizations, which performed no valuable function in the eyes of the SVAG and the SED, were soon subject to state policies designed to limit their ability to operate independently. The churches responded by continuing clandestinely to operate youth and women's organizations, but they made no great efforts to petition SVAG authorities for moderation of repressive policies.

THE END OF THE INDEPENDENCE OF RELIGIOUS YOUTH AND WOMEN'S ORGANIZATIONS WITH THE BUILDING OF STALINISM IN THE SOVIET ZONE JANUARY 1948 TO OCTOBER 1949

The end of the political independence of the CDU in December 1947 was the clearest indicator of the more repressive SVAG and SED policies towards the Protestant and Catholic churches, which continued to the end of the Soviet occupation and throughout the 1950s. Once Kaiser was removed by the SVAG's Information Administration on the orders of SVAG Supreme Commander Sokolovskii, the end of CDU youth and women's organizations was inevitable. Nuschke's policies were dictated by his belief the CDU could only survive in the Soviet zone if it was subservient to the SVAG and to SED leadership of the antifascist bloc. This meant the CDU leadership would urge its youth and women's organizations to abandon their own independent activity and instead continue their work as members of the FDJ or the DFD. As Nuschke stated in a letter to SED leader Wilhelm Pieck on March 3, 1948, the CDU in the Soviet zone would redouble its efforts in coordination with the SED to prevent the "Adenauer clique" of the CDU in western zones and the American, British, and French authorities from achieving their separatist political goals. Nuschke noted this was a particularly urgent task since both Adenauer and SPD leader in the West, Kurt Schumacher, had rejected any possible cooperation with the "democratic-progressive" forces in the Soviet zone.[48]

The new CDU leadership was fairly successful in gradually dismantling the *Frauenausschuss*, but the main CDU youth organization, *Junge Union*, presented a larger problem. During the CDU party crisis of the fall of 1947, when Kaiser refused to recognize the legitimacy of the SVAG-supported *Volkscongress* as a genuine representative government for all of Germany, the *Junge Union* pledged their support for Kaiser's position. Later, when Kaiser and his deputy Ernst Lemmer were removed and replaced by Nuschke and Georg Dertinger, the *Junge Union* membership strenuously protested and refused to participate in the *Volkscongress* movement. Because of these actions, Sokolovskii banned *Junge Union* on February 1, 1948, driving it underground. Swift arrests of its leaders who remained in the Soviet zone brought an end to much of its resistance work, often done in coordination with SPD youth groups as opposed to religious youth organizations.[49]

This left religious youth and women's organizations as the only legal alternatives to the FDJ and DFD by the spring of 1948. The Protestant and Catholic church leadership in Berlin-Brandenburg, clearly sensing the direction of SVAG and SED policies in the Soviet zone, continued to urge German youths and women to continue their work in religious organizations. In an open letter sent by Dibelius to Protestant youths in Berlin-Brandenburg in January 1948 entitled "Wir Warten auf Euch" (We await You), Dibelius called on them to join religious youth organizations and dedicate themselves to expanding their membership. Dibelius wrote that this would be absolutely necessary to revive religious life in Germany, to maintain unity with the Protestant churches in the Western zones, and ominously, to strengthen their religious faith in preparation for "the challenges which will soon come."[50]

Preysing made statements very similar to those of Dibelius. On January 18, 1948, he sent out a pastoral letter to all Catholics living in the diocese of Berlin concerning the church's work with youths and encouraged Catholic parents to enroll their children in church youth organizations. More explicitly than Dibelius, Preysing informed them the SED and their SVAG allies were swiftly constructing a new Communist dictatorship in the Soviet zone of Germany, and would continue to create obstacles to prevent the church from continuing its youth work, just as they had done with religious education. Only if the Catholic youth organizations had strength in numbers could they hope to withstand pressure from state authorities.[51]

The remarks by the Catholic and Protestant representatives on the Central Council of the FDJ also reflected the more belligerent tone of the churches in defending their independence. At the meeting of the Central Council on January 29, 1948, the Catholic representative Lange noted while the FDJ strove to stand above party identification in its propaganda rhetoric, it was not perceived as an independent youth league in the Soviet zone, especially by former members of *Junge Union* who had largely refused to join the FDJ. He stated it was increasingly difficult for religious believers in the FDJ to maintain their membership, due to the prevalence of atheistic beliefs among its leadership. Hanisch supported these comments, stating Protestant and Catholic youths could not be expected to maintain their membership in the FDJ when SVAG and SED policies continued to drive the Soviet zone towards the Soviet model.[52]

At the next meeting, on March 16, 1948, Erich Honecker and his deputy for SED youth affairs Otto Weissner noted members of *Junge Union* were not joining the FDJ but continued to work clandestinely with religious youth organizations to undermine the FDJ. Hanisch and Lange admitted that some members of *Junge Union* had joined religious youth organizations but restated their claim that neither church desired to harm the FDJ. Honecker angrily rejected this claim. This meeting marked the last time during the history of the occupation that either Hanisch or Lange made any major contributions to a meeting of the FDJ's Central Council. In fact, although records throughout 1948 list both clergy as in attendance, beginning in January 1949 members of their staffs usually sat in for them. They too ceased to attend by the summer of 1949.[53]

By this time, the SVAG authorities began to take more active steps to prevent the churches from continuing their work with youth organizations. Both Dibelius and Preysing wrote to high-ranking SVAG officials to express concern over waves of arrests of Protestant and Catholic youths engaged in religious youth activity.

Once the CDU's political independence had been destroyed with the removal of Kaiser and his replacement by Nuschke, the SVAG and the SED turned their attention to the churches as the most prominent symbols of political resistance to their goals. This meant that once the CDU's youth and women's organizations had been dealt with, those operated by the churches would be next. This became more prominent as neither the FDJ nor the DFD were able to absorb religious organizations voluntarily, and SVAG officials began to take more active measures to suppress them, including arresting those involved in youth work.

Authorities in the SVAG's Information Administration in the spring of 1948 were still unsatisfied with the progress of the FDJ in asserting its dominance in the Soviet zone, despite efforts by the SVAG to cripple the competition they faced from *Junge Union* and religious youth organizations. In a report he sent from to the Central Committee of the Communist Party of the Soviet Union on July 26 1948, Tiul'panov admitted once the CDU's independence ended with the removal of Kaiser, the churches would no longer be able to use the CDU as to tool to pursue their reactionary political goals. Now it was time to work towards suppressing religious youth and women's organizations as the final obstacles to the dominance of the FDJ and the DFD.[54]

A report sent by the new head of the Information Administration for Brandenburg, Lieutenant Colonel K. V. Martem'ianov, to Tiul'panov on June 15, 1948, noted both the FDJ and the DFD had grown considerably in the previous six months. The FDJ in Brandenburg had added 700 sport clubs with 30,000 members, although the DFD had grown at a slower rate, since many former members of the women's antifascist committees were reluctant to join the organization, due to its status as an SED front, one which never complained about the negative actions of their Soviet "friends." He admitted, the "reactionary propaganda" of the churches had kept a significant number of German youths and women from joining the FDJ or the DFD. Their most successful tactic had been their comparisons of the FDJ to the *Hitlerjugend* and convincing religious parents that the SED-dominated FDJ would cultivate atheist beliefs in their children.[55]

In a report sent a month later, on July 6, 1948, Martem'ianov admitted to Tiul'panov that his previous analysis of the situation regarding the FDJ and the DFD had been overly optimistic. He stated both organizations were much stronger in the cities in Brandenburg than in rural areas. Martem'ianov concluded in his report that the culprit for these failures was the SED leadership in Brandenburg, which had failed to recruit dependable party members to lead the SED's youth and women's organizations. This in turn allowed the churches to make significant inroads with German youth and women. The situation was particularly unacceptable because the CDU's removal from political significance should have made the DFD and FDJ's tasks easier, not harder.[56]

The SED leadership also noted these problems. SED party leader Wilhelm Pieck, in a report to the SED division for the Press and Radio on August 8, 1948, informed them the SED, working with the Soviet authorities, needed to be more aggressive in preventing church interference with the FDJ's work among German youth. He noted that religious youth organizations were particularly aggressive in these tactics in Potsdam and in the Soviet sector of Berlin. Pieck also wrote the situation was even worse elsewhere in Brandenburg, such as in the cities of Cottbus and Frankfurt an der Oder, and also in rural areas, where the "conservative mentality" of much of the population and the active undermining of the work of the FDJ and the DFD by the churches had accelerated since the suppression of the CDU's youth and women's organizations. Pieck reluctantly concluded the Protestant and Catholic churches had been successful in demonizing the FDJ as an atheistic organization, which, combined with their demagoguery concerning the new German-Polish border, meant the FDJ would not have the upper hand in the struggle for some time.[57]

Throughout the spring and summer of 1948, the SVAG and SED continued the propaganda offensive against religious youth organizations on behalf of the FDJ, despite its disappointing results. One example comes from the April 13, 1948, issue of *Tägliche Rundschau*, which reprinted a speech by Tiul'panov to the assembled provincial and local leaders of the FDJ. Tiul'panov informed them the FDJ would be at the forefront of resistance against the British and Americans who wished turn Germany into a colony of Western imperialism. Tiul'panov concluded the FDJ was the only youth organization operating openly in the Soviet zone that was not tainted by the stain of cultural and political reaction.[58]

In the early months of 1948, the SED members who controlled the DFD, Eli Schmidt and Kathe Kern, were still attempting to co-opt religious women's organizations while at the same time working against them. In January 1948, the leaders of the DFD in all five provinces of the Soviet zone met with representatives of Protestant women's organizations in order to coordinate charitable activities for war widows. While there had been some progress with regards to cooperation between the DFD and religious women's organizations, it was soon undermined by the DFD's insistence on disseminating scientific-materialist Marxist propaganda among German women in rural areas. After reviewing the work of the DFD in March 1948, Tiul'panov noted while it had been useful in propagandizing against the Anglo-Americans and their reactionary supporters in the Soviet zone, it was still unable to overcome its religious rivals in women's work.[59]

These examples demonstrate during the last two years of the Soviet occupation, religious youth and women's organizations proved harder to suppress than those of the CDU. There were numerous reasons for this. The first was the simple fact that the SVAG could not simply remove the leadership of the Protestant and Catholic churches and replace them with leaders who would be more compliant, as was the case with the CDU. As chapter seven will show, the SVAG and the SED were actively engaged in cultivating religious "progressives," especially in the Protestant Church, during the occupation, but this process had not reached the point in 1948 where they could dictate which policies towards youth and women's organizations the churches could pursue. The second was the SVAG authorities preferred to pressure religious youth and women's organizations to coordinate their activities with the FDJ and the DFD, with the goal of eventually merging with the SED organizations. This resembled similar policies the SVAG pursued with regards to religious charitable activities through its umbrella organization *Volkssolidarität*, which were equally unsuccessful to achieving the results desired by the SVAG.

Rather than blaming SVAG policies that had alienated the population of the Soviet zone, especially the vicious behavior of Red Army soldiers towards German women, officials in the SVAG's Information Administration blamed the leaders of the FDJ and DFD for showing insufficient vigilance in combating the influence of religious youth and women's organizations. In response to these failures, the SVAG was not averse to more direct tactics such as arresting and imprisoning Germans involved with youth work. As the occupation entered its final eighteen months, both the SVAG and the SED made a greater push to drive religious organizations underground if not suppress them entirely, despite the considerable resilience of religious leaders in continuing youth work.

The leadership of the churches was well aware of long-term SVAG and SED intentions for youth and women's work. Otto Dibelius, in a letter sent to all parishes in Berlin-Brandenburg in October 1948, noted that exceedingly difficult times were ahead for the churches. Writing at the height of the Berlin Blockade, Dibelius stated "two camps" had staked a position in Berlin and throughout Germany. One represented political and spiritual freedom, the other the harshest tyranny which hoped to expand its power all the way to the Atlantic Ocean. The Bishop noted that while the inhabitants of the western sectors of Berlin lived "without potatoes and without coal," those in the Soviet sector and in the Soviet zone faced something far worse, the loss of their spiritual and political freedom. Dibelius concluded all youths and women involved in religious work could fall under the influence of "materialism" as articulated by the SED and its front organizations, for they were there the strongest reservoir for the preservation of religious life in Germany.[60]

Protestant officials were quick to compare new restrictions on youth and women's organizations, such as decrees forbidding their assembly, the arrest of their leaders, and the sustained propaganda offensive directed against them, to similar policies pursued by the National Socialists. The head of the Protestant Church's charitable organization, the *Innere Mission*, Dr. Paul Wenzel, wrote to the Protestant Church administration in Brandenburg on September 26, 1948, concerning this problem. Wenzel claimed that the assault on religious youth and women's organizations in 1948 had been accompanied by new restrictions regarding religious education in the Soviet sector of Berlin, efforts to discourage the Protestant Church from pursuing charitable activity independently of *Volkssolidarität*, and a press and radio offensive against religious belief. Wenzel acknowledged these were the products of the political division of Germany between the Soviets and the West, and predicted that once the division was enshrined with the creation of two German states, repression would only become worse.[61]

Preysing issued a number of similar letters at the same time to Catholic parishes in the diocese of Berlin, stating as long as the SVAG and SED authorities continued in their policies of establishing a new Communist dictatorship, youth and women's work by the Catholic Church would be subject to continual interference. He warned they might be even suppressed entirely if German Catholics showed any weakness in the face of atheist state authorities.[62]

The SVAG authorities showed an increasing apprehension concerning the more aggressive tactics used by the Protestant and Catholic churches against the FDJ and the DFD in late 1948 and into 1949. Martem'ianov reported to Tiul'panov on December 18, 1948, and claimed supporters of exiled CDU leader Jakob Kaiser and Western SPD leader Kurt Schumacher were actively working with Protestant and Catholic youth organizations against the FDJ. He argued the building of socialism in the Soviet zone of Germany meant greater resistance on the part of reactionaries was inevitable: "The increasing class struggle in the Soviet zone of occupation has also brought about the significant strengthening of the activities of the churches among the youths."[63]

He pointed out a number of tactics used by the churches to gain greater influence over German youths and to fatally weaken the FDJ. He noted the churches, both Protestant and Catholic, provided material assistance to the families of youths who join religious youth organizations instead of the FDJ. In addition, Protestant and Catholic clergy sponsored meetings of religious youth, supposedly to study the bible or sing hymns, but in actuality to engage in propaganda against the FDJ. He mentioned to Tiul'panov a meeting of Protestant youths in Potsdam on November 8 to discuss the use of atomic energy and its relation to God. In reality, the meeting was used to condemn the FDJ as an agent of the materialist and atheistic ideology of the SED and their Soviet masters. Martem'ianov concluded the FDJ leadership in Brandenburg had done an inadequate job of realizing the reactionary nature of the churches and had allowed them to increase their "political" work among religious youths. He suggested to Tiul'panov while SVAG authorities would have to take more active legal measures against religious youth organizations, the FDJ leadership had to be forced to combat the religious threat.[64]

Martem'ianov received similar reports from his own subordinates concerning failures of the DFD in Brandenburg. A report from Lieutenant E. I. Stroilov, head of the Information Administration for Potsdam, sent on January 19, 1949, asserted the overall influence of the Protestant churches over the German population had decreased since the Soviet zone had moved decisively along the socialist path. Yet the DFD, despite its attractiveness to greater numbers of German women, had been unable to bring about a significant decrease in membership of the Protestant women's organizations. Stroilov argued the continued resiliency of the Protestant women's groups was based on their ability to provide significant material support in terms of shelter, clothing, and even employment to new members. This was a particular problem, according to Stroilov, because of the huge number of German refugees in the Soviet zone, many of whom remained in a desperate financial situation four years after the war.[65]

Losing patience with the inability of the DFD to force a merger between itself and the Protestant and Catholic women's organizations, Tiul'panov sent a directive to all regional heads of the SVAG's Information Administration on January 18, 1949, expressing his displeasure. Tiul'panov reminded them the DFD, like the antifascist women's committees created before it, was not designed to integrate women into the political and social life of the Soviet zone but to increase the political control of the SED over German women. Yet four years after the "antifascist democratic transformation" had begun in the Soviet zone, the reactionary bourgeoisie who dominated religious women's organizations were still far too strong and influential. Much as with religious youth groups, meetings were occasionally banned by SVAG authorities, often because of claims religious women's organizations were working for Western intelligence organs.[66]

In February 1949, Tiul'panov informed all provincial leaders of the Information Administration their policies towards the churches should be guided by strengthening control over the social activities of the churches and the scientific-educational propaganda. The Information Administration could not allow any type of independent church youth organizations of any kind and every cleric, Protestant and Catholic, had to be made aware of this. Tiul'panov emphasized further work had to be done by the Information Administration to isolate in every way possible reactionary clergy, especially from working with the youths, women, and refugees from formerly German territories now in the hands of Poland and the Soviet Union. While he made an explicit point that clergy should not be allowed to criticize the SVAG or the SED, Tiul'panov did not mention any need to keep them from collaborating with the CDU in the Soviet zone.[67]

Martem'ianov responded a few days later to Tiul'panov's complaints, stating the leadership of the DFD had recently begun a new campaign of political propagandizing in Brandenburg, distributing educational pamphlets to other German women with titles such as "What is Democracy?" and "The Political Divide in Germany." He did acknowledge the DFD still suffered from a number of glaring weaknesses. The most important was the fact the SED had not chosen dependable party members to lead the DFD, especially in rural areas.

Consequently, the DFD at the local level had failed to engage in sufficient educational work and had not even recruited enough working-class women as new members of the DFD, to say nothing about those from the peasantry or the bourgeoisie. This meant "reactionaries" who led religious women's organizations continued to exert a great deal of influence over a significant percentage of German women, many of whom remained indifferent to the goals and political message of the DFD.[68]

Clearly, the SVAG authorities were still unwilling to abandon entirely their approach towards youth and women's organizations, which consisted of three central tactics. The first was an aggressive propaganda campaign on behalf of the FDJ and the DFD as the only organizations that could guide German youths and women on the "antifascist-democratic path." The second were the extra-legal attempts by SVAG officials to suppress religious youth and women's organizations, such as revoking legal permission for their assembly and arresting of their leaders. The third, which in many ways resembled SVAG policies towards religious charitable activities, was to pressure the churches into merging their own religious organizations with those sponsored by the SED. The inclusion of Lange and Hanisch on the Central Council of the FDJ and of Protestant and Catholic women on the antifascist women's committees and later the DFD was clearly intended to accomplish this.

These tactics reflected the SVAG's and to a lesser extent the SED' shifting impulses with regards to religious organizations, moving between suppressing them outright as reactionary organizations and co-opting them as institutions that could allow them to influence developments in the western zones of Germany. At the same time, moving swiftly towards repressing religious youth and women's organizations could have jeopardized the propaganda claims of SVAG and SED leaders concerning the importance of "religious freedom" in a future socialist Germany. Protestant and Catholic organizations did not represent the same threat as the women's branches of the CDU or *Junge Union*, because they simply did not present the same political threat as did CDU members who remained loyal to Jakob Kaiser following his expulsion from the Soviet zone in December 1947. This was why the SVAG never took the same step they did with *Junge Union* and simply banned religious youth and women's organizations outright.

By the spring of 1949, internal reports from the SVAG's Information Administration revealed the Soviet military authorities, the DFD and the FDJ had made some progress against religious women's and youth organizations. A report from Martem'ianov to Tiul'panov from May 25, 1949, noted that the DFD, through its twin recruitment campaigns emphasizing the dedication of the DFD to the peaceful unification of Germany and the advancement of German women in all levels of society in the Soviet zone, had attracted thousands of new members and weakened the standing of religious organizations in the community. Martem'ianov did not claim Protestant and Catholic women's organizations were no longer a threat, but thanks to the DFD's propaganda campaign and "extra-legal measures" directed against leaders of religious women's organizations by SVAG authorities, the situation had improved considerably in four months.[69]

The analysis of the FDJ's activities provided by SVAG Information Administration reports was not quite as optimistic but still noted substantial improvement in its strength in comparison to religious youth organizations. In a report sent by Martem'ianov to Tiul'panov on March 24, 1949, Martem'ianov admitted the "reactionary" elements of the bourgeoisie in the Soviet zone were still using Catholic and Protestant youth organizations against the FDJ, often scheduling competing athletic or cultural events or attempting to demonize the FDJ as an atheistic organization dedicated to the destruction of religious faith. However, the churches were gradually losing the battle against the FDJ, and in one to two more years the influence of the FDJ over the youth in the Soviet zone would be completely dominant.[70]

In response to Martem'ianov's report, Tiul'panov wrote to Pieck and Grotewohl, insisting they place greater material resources in the work of the FDJ so that they could compete more effectively with Catholic and Protestant churches, which had made youth work a top priority and continued to receive considerable financial support from the churches in the Western zones of Germany and from abroad. Pieck and Grotewohl agreed with this assessment concerning the success of the FDJ, and promised that since the Soviet zone had been placed irrevocably on the road to socialism, the SED leadership would ensure that the FDJ would suppress its religious rivals in a few years.[71]

Following the formal end of the Soviet occupation and the founding of the GDR in the fall of 1949, the SED leadership was true to its word regarding efforts to suppress religious youth and women's organizations. The East German secret police, the *Staatssicherheistdienst* (State Security) or the Stasi, arrested hundreds of leaders involved in religious youth or women's work, claiming religious organizations were illegally being used by Western intelligence services to undermine the social and political order in the GDR. In addition, the FDJ, now under the leadership of Erich Honecker, often physically disrupted meetings, events, and religious services associated with religious youth organizations. While repressions in the GDR still did not match those in Hungary or Czechoslovakia, religious youth and women's work had been effectively forced underground by the 1950s, a process that had begun in the late 1940s during the Soviet occupation.[72]

CONCLUSION

Regarding the question of religion, this chapter has argued that the policies of the Soviet authorities often served as a test case for the harsher policies subsequently adapted against the churches in the GDR, especially during the Ulbricht era. As with religious education, SVAG and SED efforts towards religious youth and women's organizations were designed not to crush the activities of the churches immediately and completely, but to reduce them gradually to complete irrelevance in German society while continuing to proclaim their support for religious freedom.

These actions by the SVAG and the SED represented an odd mix of the policies pursued towards religious charitable work and religious education in the secondary schools. Leaders of the SVAG and SED frequently complained religious organizations were being used by bourgeois Germans to undermine the work of the FDJ and DFD, especially after CDU youth and women's organizations were suppressed. However, the SVAG preferred to push the religious organizations to merge with the FDJ and the DFD, much as they requested the Protestant and Catholic churches join their charitable work with the umbrella organization *Volkssolidarität*. Once *Junge Union* and the CDU's women's branches had been suppressed, the SVAG reverted to more aggressive tactics which limited the ability of religious youth and women's organizations to operate freely, but were not successful in suppressing them entirely during the 1948 to 1949 period.

The inclusion of representatives from the Protestant and Catholic churches on the Central Council of the FDJ was a key element in SVAG and SED tactics in pressuring the churches to abandon independent youth work. Also important was the constant barrage of propaganda articles in the SVAG and SED newspapers which proclaimed the FDJ as the only genuine antifascist and democratic youth organization. This was never supposed to be an equal partnership, as any advice or requests concerning cooperation between religious youth organizations and the FDJ which were offered by Hanisch or Lange at the meetings of the Central Council of the FDJ were ignored or derided. Given the refusal of Dibelius and Preysing even to consider merging the churches' youth organizations with the FDJ and the FDJ's leadership's own refusal to abandon the materialistic and atheistic ideology of the SED, such an agreement on permanent cooperation was probably impossible.

Interestingly, neither Dibelius nor Preysing appeared very interested in petitioning the Soviet authorities for greater freedom to conduct religious youth work, unlike the case with religious education and charitable work. This can likely be attributed to the fact that SVAG policies regarding religious youth and women's work were not particularly harsh before December

1947, however, during the last two years of the occupation the general trend of SVAG religious policies made it obvious to both Bishops that appeals to SVAG authorities on the issue of religious youth work would be useless.

The situation regarding the DFD was more complicated, given its nebulous status with regards to the antifascist women's committees until their suppression in 1947, and since the SED leadership did not provide the DFD leaders, Eli Schmidt and Kathe Kern, with sufficient resources to compete effectively with religious women's organizations. Given the unfortunate association of the DFD with the SED, and by extension, with the Red Army, religious women's organizations were even less likely to consider merging their own organizations with the DFD.

In both cases, the *Junge Union* and the CDU *Frauenausschuss* were always perceived by the SVAG and SED from June 1945 until December 1947 as the primary threat to their efforts, not religious youth and women's organizations. This was largely because the CDU represented a political challenge to the SED, in theory if not in reality, while religious organizations, especially those for Protestant and Catholic women that were largely engaged in charitable work, did not pose the same type of threat. The danger of the CDU, especially *Junge Union,* was mentioned far more by the SED and SVAG authorities than any religious organization during Andreas Hermes's and Jakob Kaiser's tenures as the CDU's leaders.

The decision by SED and especially SVAG authorities to engage in more aggressive tactics against religious organizations in 1948 and 1949, including arresting those involved in religious youth work, was part of a broader policy designed to accelerate the transformation of the Soviet zone into a German state on the Soviet model. Both believed that only the FDJ and the DFD should be allowed to represent Germany's youth and women once socialism had been constructed. Perhaps the best evidence of this is that neither the SVAG nor the SED appeared interested in recruiting "progressive" elements in religious youth and women's organizations, as they did for CDU members and those of the Protestant and Catholic clergy. While the SED authorities who led the FDJ and the DFD tended to deal with religious youth and women's organizations during the first three years of the occupation, it would be the SVAG authorities after 1947 who instituted the policies designed to weaken religious organizations, such as arresting their leaders and banning their meetings

The fact that religious youth and women's organizations were not banned as were their CDU counterparts can be explained by the SVAG's and SED's decision to pursue repressive but not extreme policies towards religious institutions during the last two years of the occupation. These policies were intended to marginalize and gradually eliminate the churches from the social life of the Soviet zone. They were also intended not to alienate the clerical "progressives" whom the SVAG and SED were trying to recruit, while at the same time maintaining the illusion of SVAG support for "religious freedom" despite the construction of an atheistic political and social order in the Soviet zone of Germany.

Notes

1. ELAB, Bestand 603- Nachlässe Otto Dibelius B 13. The NKVD by this point had been re-named the MGB (Ministry of State Security), although Dibelius was unaware of this.

2. DAB, Abteilung V- Nachlässe Konrad von Preysing, Repositur 16–5.

3. Martin Georg Goerner, *Die Kirche als Problem der SED: Strukturen kommunistischer Herrschaftsausübung gegenüber der evangelischen Kirche 1945 bis 1958.* Berlin: Akademie Verlag, 1997. 23.

4. Naimark, 465. Pike, 5. Loth, 10. This chapter focuses largely on the institutional policies of the Soviet and East German authorities regarding religious youth and women's organizations, it is not a social history of these organizations.

5. Zubok, 62. Bruce, 5.

6. The sources for this essay include the records of the SVAG's Propaganda/ Information Administration, which was the main department within the Soviet military government that dealt with religious issues; the city authorities in Berlin and provincial authorities for Brandenburg in Potsdam; and the records from the SED's branch for Women's and Youth Affairs, which contain the minutes of the meetings of the Central Council of the FDJ. These records were particularly useful, as they contained dozens of interactions between SED party leaders and Protestant and Catholic clergy in defining the role youth organizations would play in the Soviet zone. Also important were the records from the Catholic and Evangelical church administrations for Berlin-Brandenburg and those of the CDU in the Soviet zone. In the Protestant archives, the records from the church Chancellery for Berlin-Brandenburg were particularly useful, as were the official papers from the office of the Catholic Bishop in Berlin.

7. GARF, f.7077 (SVAG Brandenburg), op.1 (Upravlenie propagandy), d. 179 (Correspondence August–November 1945), l. 5. The other SVAG commanders in the four other provinces of the Soviet zone issued similar orders during the month of August.

8. GARF, f. 7077, op. 1, d. 179, l. 6.

9. *Die UdSSR und die Deutsche Frage 1941–1948: Dokumente aus dem Archiv für Aussenpolitik der Russischen Föderation Volume 2*: 9 Mai 1945 bis 3. October 1946. Eds, Jochen Laufer, Georgii Kynin and Viktor Knoll. Berlin: Duncker & Humbolt, 2004, 149–152.

10. GARF, f.7077, op.1, d. 179, ll. 22–23.

11. SAPMO-DDR Abteilung, DY 31/IV 2-Zentral Kommitee Demokratischer Frauenbund Deutschlands, 1639-Jahre 1945.

12. Naimark, 132. Assisting women who had been raped and assaulted by Red Army soldiers was also a common concern for German women's committees, much to the chagrin of the KPD leadership.

13. SAPMO-DDR Abteilung, DY 31/IV 2/1639.

14. Naimark, 132.

15. SAPMO-DDR Abteilung DY 30- SED Zentral Kommittee IV 2-ZK Secretariat 17-SED Central Secretariat:Abteilung Frauen, 80-Jahre 1945, 25–26.

16. SAPMO-DDR Abteilung DY 30/IV 2/17/80, 61–65.

17. Ibid.

18. SAPMO-DDR Abteilung DY 30- SED Zentral Kommittee IV 2-ZK Secretariat 16- Abteilung Jugend, 4-Jahre 1946.

19. Ibid.

20. SAPMO-DDR Abteilung, DY 24-FDJ Zentral Rat, 2100-August–September 1946.

21. ELAB, Bestand 38-Abteilung Kurt Scharf, Repositur 722 Both the Protestant and Catholic leadership looked towards the end of the war as an opportunity to revive religious youth and women's work which had been attacked constantly by the Nazi regime.

22. DAB, Abteilung I- Bischöfliches Ordinariat Berlin Repositur 4–3.

23. GARF, f. 7077 (SVAG-Brandenburg), op.1 (Upravlenie propagandy), d. 187 (Correspondence September–December 1945), ll. 15–20.

24. GARF, f.7077 (SVAG-Brandenburg), op.1-Upravlenie informatsii), d. 197 (Correspondence January–August 1948), ll.82–89.

25. GARF, f. 7077, op.1, d. 197, ll.112–113.

26. EZA,Bestand 4-EKD Kirchenkanzlei, Repositur 373.

27. GARF, f. 7077, op. 1, d. 197, ll.147–152. Mil'khiker received similar optimistic reports from his subordinates throughout Brandenburg concerning the success of the FDJ in limiting the clerical offensive it.

28. Rossiiskii gosudarstvennyi arkhiv v sotsial'no-politicheskoi istorii (RGASPI-Russian State Archive for Social and Political History). f. 17 (Tsentral'nyi Komitet CPSU), op. 117-(Sekretariat), d. 674- (Correspondence September to October 1946), l. 80. The special commission was composed of A. Panushkin, K. Kuzakov, and M. Burtsev, specially selected by Zhdanov and his ally A. A. Kuznetsov to report on conditions in the Soviet zone on the eve of the October 1946 elections. Officials in the SVAG's Propaganda Administration made similar complaints about the SED's work regarding the DFD and the FDJ but exempted themselves from any criticism.

29. ACDP, *Signatur* 07–010-CDU Ost, Repositur 1846.

30. ACDP, *Signatur* 07–010-CDU Ost, Repositur 2179.

31. SAPMO-DDR Abteilung DY 24-FDJ Zentral Rat, 2102.

32. Ibid.

33. Ibid.

34. SAPMO-DDR Abteilung, DY 24-Zentral Rat FDJ, 2105-Juni-Juli 1947.

35. SAPMO-DDR Abteilung, DY 24-Zentral Rat FDJ, 2108.

36. GARF, f. 7077 (SVAG-Brandenburg), op.1 (Upravlenie propagandy), d. 220 (Correspondence April–May 1947), ll. 55–59. The Propaganda Administration changed its name to the Information after the SED's disappointing electoral showing in October 1946.

37. Die UdSSR und die Deutsche Frage 1941–1948: Dokumente aus dem Archiv für Aussenpolitik der Russischen Föderation Volume 3: 6 Oktober 1946 bis 15 Juni 1948. Eds, Jochen Laufer, Georgii Kynin and Viktor Knoll. Berlin: Duncker & Humbolt 2004, 244–253.

38. *Tägliche Rundschau* 21 Jun 1945. 2.

39. *Tägliche Rundschau*. 29 Jul 1945. 1.

40. *Tägliche Rundschau*. 5 Oct 1945. 2.

41. *Deutsche Volkszeitung*. 24 Jun 1945. 2

42. *Deutsche Volkszeitung*. 16 Feb 1946. 1.

43. *Neues Deutschland*. 24 Jul 1946. 4.

44. SAPMO-DDR Abteilung DY 30/IV 2/17/80. 97.

45. SAPMO-DDR Abteilung DY 30/IV 2/17/80. 228.

46. Naimark, 132.

47. GARF, f.7077 (SVAG Brandenburg), op.1 (Upravlenie informatsii), d. 213 (Correspondence January–June 1947), ll.121–127.

48. ACDP, *Signatur* 07–010-CDU-Ost, Repositur 1843.

49. Bruce, 81.

50. ELAB, Bestand 603-Otto Dibelius, A 7, 1.1.

51. DAB, Abteilung V, Repositur 16-7-2

52. SAPMO-DDR Abteilung, DY 24- FDJ Zentral Rat, 2109

53. SAPMO-DDR Abteilung, DY 30/IV 2/16- DY 30- SED Zentral Kommittee IV 2-ZK Secretariat 16-Abteilung Jugend 20-Januar-März 1948.

54. GARF, f. 7077 (SVAG-Brandenburg), op.1 (Upravlenie informatsii), d. 238 (Correspondence January–June 1948), ll.123–156.

55. GARF, f. 7077 (SVAG Brandenburg), op.1 (Upravlenie informatsii), d. 226 (Correspondence July 1948), ll. 13–48.

56. GARF, f. 7077, op. 1, d. 226, ll. 325–344.

57. SAPMO-SED Abteilung, NY 4036/756- Nachlässe Wilhelm Pieck, 13–15.

58. *Tägliche Rundschau*. 13 Apr 1948. 1.

59. GARF, f. 7077 (SVAG-Brandenburg), op.1 (Upravlenie informatsii), d. 241 (Correspondence January–March 1948), ll. 40–43, 91–93.

60. ELAB, Bestand 603, A7, 1.1

61. EZA, Bestand 4, Repositur 350.

62. DAB, Abteilung V Repositur 16-7-2.

63. GARF, f.7077 (SVAG-Brandenburg), op.1 (Upravlenie informatsii), d. 242 (Correspondence January–November 1948), l. 216.

64. Ibid., ll. 216–222. Tiul'panov concurred with Martem'ianov in his response to the report, but expressed a distinct lack of faith in the FDJ's abilities to combat the religious youth organization without sufficient help from SVAG.

65. GARF, f. 7077 (SVAG-Brandenburg), op.1 (Upravlenie informatsii), d. 254 (Correspondence January–May 1949), ll. 28–29.

66. GARF, f.7077 (SVAG-Brandenburg), op.1 (Upravlenie informatsii), d. 254 (Correspondence January–June 1949), ll. 2–3.

67. GARF, f. 7077 (SVAG Brandenburg), op.1 (Upravlenie informatsii)., d. 254 (Correspondence January–June 1949), ll. 39–43.

68. GARF, f. 7077, op.1, d. 259, ll. 70–78.

69. GARF, f. 7077, op.1, d. 259, ll. 104–113.

70. GARF, f.7077 (SVAG-Brandenburg), op.1 (Upravlenie informatsii), d. 260 (Correspondence March–May 1949), ll. 14–23.

71. Ibid.

72. Goeckel, 46.

Chapter Six

The Conflict over Charitable Activity by the Protestant and Catholic Churches in Berlin-Brandenburg, 1945–1949

"Postwar Berlin was a city of debris. Although the first substantial air raids to target the city struck only in November 1943, Berlin had endured 363 attacks and absorbed 45,517 tons of bombs by the time the war ended. These air raids and the devastating bombardment of the final Soviet attack on the city produced some 70 million cubic meters of rubble, 17.5 percent of the wartime total within the boundaries of the 1938 German Reich. Wartime destruction cost Greater Berlin 612,000 apartments, and lost no less than 50 percent of its total housing space."

—Paul Steege[1]

INTRODUCTION

The Second World War had left much of the Soviet zone of Germany in ruins, as it was the site of the most intense fighting between the Wehrmacht and the Red Army in the spring of 1945 as well as sustained bombing since 1943. This humanitarian disaster worsened throughout 1945 and into 1946 with the expulsion of millions of ethnic Germans from territory that had passed from German to Polish, Czech, and Soviet rule. Most of these refugees ended up in the Soviet zone of Germany, putting severe strain on the already crippled infrastructure. The Soviet authorities and their allies in the SED who controlled the German organs of self-government found providing humanitarian assistance to the refugees, the impoverished, and the orphans created by the war beyond their means, especially during the early years of occupation.[2]

135

It was here the Protestant and Catholic churches played a substantial role in providing humanitarian relief for the inhabitants of the Soviet zone, especially the refugees from the former territories of East Prussia and Silesia. The SVAG authorities grudgingly allowed the churches to continue their charitable activities in the zone. They acquiesced because no other organizations in the Soviet zone provided the extensive variety of charitable relief as did the churches. Throughout the history of the Soviet zone, both the SVAG and the SED remained deeply suspicions of Protestant and Catholic intentions behind charitable activities. They believed clerical "reactionaries" used charitable relief either to win supporters to oppose the policies of the SVAG and the SED or to swing electoral support over to the Christian Democratic Union.

The tolerance of the SVAG for the continuation of religious charitable work in the Soviet zone marks an interesting contrast with general Soviet policies in Europe during the immediate post-Second World War period. Soviet difficulty on the question of reparations from the Western zones of Germany was directly tied to a desire by Stalin to see Western Europe, including the Western occupation zones of Germany, mired in impoverishment. This in turn would cause the desperate populations to eventually turn to the Communists for political and economic solutions. In the Soviet zone of Germany, the SVAG authorities did not desire a similar humanitarian disaster, as the political destiny of its inhabitants was already sealed. Furthermore, the Soviet authorities simply did not have the capacity to handle the humanitarian crisis on their own, given the considerable problem of a lack of adequate personnel and resources at all levels of the Soviet administration.[3]

This did not mean the SVAG intended to allow the churches to play a dominant role in proving charitable relief indefinitely. To limit the charitable role of the churches, the SVAG created an umbrella organization called *Volkssolidarität* (National Solidarity) wherein all the antifascist political parties, the churches, and organizations such as the Free German Youth and the Free German Trade Union (*Freie Deutsche Gewerkschaft Bund*-FDGB) were supposed to coordinate charitable relief into one massive effort.

The churches remained a part of *Volkssolidarität* until the end of the occupation. While they occasionally did work with the other members in providing charitable relief, none of the clerics in charge of charitable activity in either the Catholic or Protestant churches seriously believed their charitable activities should merely be limited to cooperation with *Volkssolidarität*. Realizing this, the SVAG encouraged the SED to use the organizations it dominated, such as the FDJ and the FDGB, to surpass the churches in providing charitable relief. This too, failed, as SED organizations never challenged religious dominance of charitable activity in the Soviet zone. On other occasions the SVAG seized certain buildings or estates used by the churches for charitable activity and refused under a variety of pretexts to give it back.

SVAG officials feared "external" influences on church charitable activity, such as the Vatican in the case of the Catholic Church and Lutheran communities in the United States in the case of the Protestant Church. Their fears were not entirely unfounded. Relief efforts by both the Catholic and Protestant churches were heavily dependent on aid from abroad, and the leadership of both churches hoped charitable relief could draw new believers into the fold. Among the leaders of the churches, plans for using charitable relief to support the political goals of the CDU or as a weapon against the SVAG or the SED were never seriously discussed. Religious leaders justified their efforts by pointing to the Christian commandments to provide for the needy and downtrodden.

While the educational efforts of the churches immediately came under attack by the SVAG and the KPD/SED, and religious youth and women's organizations came under continuous assault during the end of the Soviet occupation, charitable relief was the one area where the churches remained generally free from state harassment. There were a few notable exceptions to this, especially the SVAG attack on religious hospitals in 1948 and 1949 and the extreme reluctance of Soviet authorities to release German POWs or political prisoners from internment camps at the request of Protestant and Catholic leaders. This in turn mirrored later developments in the GDR, where the state authorities came to appreciate religious charitable activities as removing a considerable burden from the state.

The churches directed much of their charitable relief through two different agencies in the church administrative structure. The Protestant Church's charitable agency was named the *Innere Mission* while the Catholic charitable body took its name from the Latin word for charity, *Caritas*. Most of the efforts of *Innere Mission* and *Caritas* were divided into three distinct fields. The first was to provide housing, food, and clothing for impoverished German citizens, especially those who had been expelled from former German territories in Eastern Europe. The second was to work for the improvement of the spiritual conditions of German POWs still held in Soviet custody in Germany, as well as for those held at the Soviet "special camps" for political enemies of the SVAG and SED authorities. The third was to administer aid to orphans, the elderly, and war invalids through religious orphanages, rest homes, and hospitals.[4]

PROTESTANT AND CATHOLIC CHURCH EFFORTS TO ADDRESS THE REFUGEE CRISES AND THE MATERIAL CATASTROPHE IN THE SOVIET ZONE

At the first meeting of the leadership of the Protestant Church in Soviet zone on September 15, 1945, bishops Dibelius (of Berlin-Brandenburg), Beste (Mecklenburg), Mueller (Sachsen-Anhalt), and Mitzenheim (Thuringia) agreed that, while the Protestant Church could work with other political and economic organizations in order to address the massive humanitarian crisis facing the Soviet zone, it could never compromise its own independence with regards to charitable relief.[5] Otto Dibelius argued not only should all the regional Protestant churches coordinate their charitable work, but they should also cooperate with the Catholic Church in the Soviet zone.[6] Two weeks before, Konrad von Preysing, in a speech given to the assembled Catholic bishops of Germany at Fuldaer in the British zone, stated the Catholic Church in the Soviet zone was determined to continue charitable work that had been restricted by the Nazi regime. Preysing said that given the scale of the humanitarian crisis facing the population of the zone, Caritas would begin its work immediately in providing humanitarian aid for the victims of the war.[7]

In a letter to the Mayor (*Burgermeister)* of the Soviet sector of Berlin, Ferdinand Friedensburg, the central office for the *Innere Mission* detailed their various charitable activities, including the distribution of food and clothing to the elderly, orphans, impoverished refugees and war veterans in the Soviet Zone, as well as establishing new rest homes and orphanages. Some of the material aid the *Innere Mission* distributed came from food and clothing drives conducted in the regions of Brandenburg which had not been hit as hard by the effects of war. Most, as the Protestant Church officials freely admitted to Soviet and German authorities, came from abroad, especially the United States, Scandinavia, and Switzerland. In fall of 1945 Lutheran churches and organizations in the United States donated 3,643,567 kg. of food and 1,202,038 kg. of shoes and clothes; churches in Sweden donated 1,775,737 kg. of food and 163,015 kg. of shoes and clothes, while religious institutions in Switzerland donated 216,583 kg and 155,008 kg respectively, most of which had been transported to Germany by the International Red Cross. The letter concluded with promises the *Innere Mission* had no intention behind its charitable mission besides following the example of Christ in providing assistance to the victims of war, and did not discriminate in offering charitable aid based on the religious background of those receiving it.[8]

Two months later, as winter quickly approached and the material conditions in the Soviet zone remained extremely dire, the SVAG's Supreme Commander Marshal Georgii Zhukov ordered the formation of *Volkssolidarität*, wherein all antifascist political parties, organizations, and the churches would coordinate charitable relief in the Soviet zone. Among the first major activities of all of *Volkssolidarität*'s members was a clothing drive directed towards children and the elderly which occurred throughout the Soviet zone during the third week of November in 1945. The SVAG's newspaper *Tägliche Rundschau* proudly reported on the success of the Soviet initiative and forthrightly stated this should be the pattern for all forms of charitable relief in the Soviet zone. The article concluded that no organizations should strike out to provide charitable relief on their own.[9]

Neither the Protestant nor Catholic churches followed this directive. On December 14, 1945, the head of the Propaganda Administration of SVAG in the Soviet sector of Berlin, Major L. L. Koloss, reported to Lieutenant Colonel I. I. Mil'khiker, that the *Innere Mission* and *Caritas* dominated charitable activity throughout the city. Koloss stated he had already pushed the antifascist organizations under the control of the German Communist Party (KPD-*Kommunistische Partei Deutschlands*, the predecessor of the SED), such as the Free German Youth and the Democratic Women's Federation to commit themselves to charitable work, in order to minimize the religious dominance in this area. Koloss pointed to a recent drive led by the DFD to obtain shoes for impoverished German youths as evidence of the ability of the antifascist political organizations to supplant the role of the churches in providing material relief.[10]

Mil'khiker responded to reports by Koloss and other subordinates by informing his commander, Tiul'panov, on January 9, 1946, of the numerous charitable activities conducted by the Protestant and Catholic churches in Brandenburg. Mil'khiker noted many clergy took little interest in combining their activities with those of secular antifascist organizations and asked Tiul'panov if he needed take steps to restrict religious charitable activities. Mil'khiker admitted that the relief work by the churches served a valuable function, but this did not erase the fact that religious reactionaries who opposed the political goals of the Soviet authorities often directed it. Tiul'panov replied a few days later, stating religious charitable activities were useful and should not be immediately restricted. Tiul'panov noted a similar policy would be administered in all of the provinces in the Soviet zone.[11]

Other leaders of the Propaganda Administration in the different provinces were not content to let KPD-fronts such as the FDJ or DFD attempt to counter the advantage of the churches in the field of charitable relief. Lieutenant Colonel V. M. Demidov, head of the Propaganda Administration in Sachsen-Anhalt, informed Tiul'panov on January 5, 1946, he had directed officers on his staff to work with a few members of the KPD to distribute potatoes and clothes to the homeless and to needy children. Demidov noted these activities, when combined with SVAG support of public Christmas celebrations, had improved the image of the Soviet authorities among the population, especially in larger cities where the bulk of charitable activity was concentrated.[12]

By the spring of 1946, Tiul'panov articulated a different position to the heads of the regional Propaganda Administration than he had three months earlier. Demidov informed Tiul'panov in April 1946 about the revival of an Protestant society named "Christliche Gemeinschaft" (Christian Community) in Sachsen-Anhalt, which was dedicated to fighting alcoholism and caring for the families of alcoholics while at the same time distributing religious literature, especially Bibles, to those who had requested their assistance. Tiul'panov instructed Demidov to keep the organization under strict surveillance with the aim of ultimately replacing them with a secular organization under SVAG and SED control that could pursue the same goal of providing charitable relief without corrupting the German people with reactionary religious literature.[13]

The members of the KPD/SED who controlled the German organs of self-government in Brandenburg also shared Tiul'panov's concerns. In April 1946, the Provincial Administration for Brandenburg (PV-*Provinzial Verwaltung Brandenburg*), received a series of complaints from the SED party members in the various cities throughout the province, claiming SED leaders were not providing adequate material assistance to impoverished German women, which caused them to turn to the churches and not to the SED for assistance. Some letters also acknowledged the huge advantage of churches in providing charitable relief was not likely to change in the near future.[14]

The newspapers of the SVAG and the KPD, *Tägliche Rundschau* and *Deutsche Volkszeitung*, trumpeted the success of secular charitable initiatives through the cooperation of all antifascist organizations in *Volkssolidarität*. An article in *Tägliche Rundschau* on March 21 described how *Volkssolidarität*, led by representatives of the KPD, had spearheaded the opening of new factories, schools, and businesses in all of the provinces since the beginning of 1946.[15]

Deutsche Volkszeitung also followed this line, although it printed far fewer articles concerning charitable relief in the Soviet zone, probably due to the fact that while KPD leaders were quick to mention the humanitarian disasters in the Western occupation zones, where the Christian Democratic Union (CDU) and Social Democratic Party (SPD) dominated, they were more reluctant to discuss material problems in the Soviet zone. For example, a front-page article in the January 8, 1946, edition of *Deutsche Volkszeitung* mentioned while *Volkssolidaritat* had performed an admirable good in administering charitable relief under the leadership of the KPD, the problems of material impoverishment in the Soviet zone were minimal and were largely caused by "German bandits in Russian uniforms."[16]

According to their own internal communications with the leadership of the churches, both *Innere Mission* and *Caritas* described the results of charitable relief as far less satisfactory. In a report to Preysing concerning material conditions within the Soviet zone dated March 23, 1946, the office of *Caritas* responsible for Berlin-Brandenburg offered a highly pessimistic view of the situation. The report stated the condition of inhabitants of the Soviet zone was far worse than conditions in the Western zones, and only assistance from Catholic churches in the Western zones as well as help from abroad could enable the Church in the Soviet zone provide adequate charitable relief. The report claimed over 5.5 million refugees from East Prussia and Silesia had arrived in the Soviet zone since the spring of 1945, twenty-five percent of which were Catholic, and their desperate condition was "hard to describe."[17]

The report emphasized that only about ten percent of ethnic German refugees had died in the transfer to Germany, while a far greater number had all types of medical problems or illnesses. Hunger remained the biggest problem, but illness and the effects of the brutal winter of 1945–1946 were not far behind. While Soviet authorities had usually not hindered charitable activities, the KPD did try to discourage them, especially charitable work directed towards children. An even greater problem, the report concluded, was the fact Soviet authorities refused to allow newspapers or radio broadcasts to reveal the truth about the terrible humanitarian crisis in the Soviet zone, and thus European and North American sources needed by the German churches for material assistance were often not aware how bad the situation truly was.[18]

The officials in the Protestant Church were similarly discouraged throughout the first winter of the Soviet occupation. Hans von Arnim, the head of the Protestant Church Chancellery for the province of Brandenburg, sent instructions to all of the parish church leaders on March 29 1946, which stated providing food, clothing and housing for the enormous number of Protestant refugees who had fled to the Soviet zone was largely the responsibility of the Protestant Church. Neither Protestant laity nor clergy could expect any form of assistance from Soviet or German authorities to alleviate the problem.[19]

The Protestant Church was also faced with the considerable problem of a lack of space to house for German refugees, as some church buildings had been destroyed during the war or were currently occupied by the Soviet authorities.[20] There was little the Protestant Church could do about this matter but use the resources they had, Dibelius and the other bishops in the Soviet zone admitted at their meeting on February 5 in Berlin they lacked the funds to repair the buildings that had been damaged during the war, and Soviet authorities were not forthcoming in returning many of them to the Protestant church.[21]

In other cases, estates and monasteries used by the Protestant Church as refugee shelters were seized as part of the process of the land reform implemented by the SVAG in the fall of 1945, despite the fact church lands and monasteries were supposed to be exempted from the plan of the Soviet authorities to redistribute the large estates to the German "new farmers."[22] One example involved the refugee shelters administered by the Protestant church on the monastic lands of Heiligengrab and Kenkendorf in Brandenburg. Once the land was redistributed to the "new farmers" in November 1945 Soviet authorities closed down the refugee shelters. When the leadership of the *Innere Mission* protested these actions in the spring and summer of 1946, the SVAG's commanding officer in Brandenburg, Major General V. M. Sharov, stated simply that once the land had been redistributed the decision could not be rescinded. Sharov made some vague promises for financial compensation for the Protestant Church in Brandenburg, which were predictably not followed through. In his private correspondence with a member of the military council of SVAG, F. E. Bokov, Sharov admitted the loss of the refugee shelters was regrettable but the SVAG could not make any exemptions with regards to land reform, especially once it had been completed in a particular area.[23]

It is obvious while the SVAG authorities had some appreciation for the magnitude of the humanitarian calamity which faced the Soviet zone in the early years of the occupation, this would have to take a back seat to the broader goal of preparing the economic groundwork for the "antifascist democratic transformation," of which land reform played an essential part. The Protestant and Catholic churches certainly had greater liberty to administer charitable aid than to conduct their educational endeavors or work with German women and youths, but this did not mean they were able to use all of their resources to combat the problem if it clashed with Soviet long-term plans.

Nor had officials in the SVAG's Propaganda Administration, which dealt with religious issues more than any other branch of the Soviet military occupation, overcome their suspicions that the aid provided by the churches to the impoverished and refugees was merely a method to increase the electoral support of the Christian Democratic Union.

With the October 1946 zonal elections five months away, Mil'khiker informed Tiul'panov both the Protestant and Catholic churches in Brandenburg were deeply engaged in providing charitable relief for the refugees from former eastern German territories as well as those who had been left homeless by the war. Since many Protestant and Catholic clergy in charge of charitable relief were also secretly members of the CDU, Mil'khiker claimed, this could only mean the churches used material aid to demonstrate to the German people only the Christian Socialism of the CDU could provide for them, as opposed to the Marxist-Leninist-Stalinist socialism of the SED. Mil'khiker did not desire to directly restrict the charitable activities of the churches, but he revealed to Tiul'panov a plan for a concentrated effort by the SED to counter the religious dominance in this field.[24]

Mil'khiker's caution in this matter was unsurprising, given that the fact Tiul'panov consistently instructed his subordinates at all levels of the Propaganda Administration during the first few years of the Soviet occupation to closely supervise religious charitable work but not to restrict it, with the long-term goal of replacing it with secular charitable initiatives by the SED and the antifascist organizations it controlled.[25]

This did not mean the churches did not occasionally hope Soviet authorities would assist them in providing charitable relief. Throughout 1946 the Protestant and Catholic churches faced the nearly overwhelming problem of providing adequate transportation for ethnic Germans fleeing the Sudetenland, East Prussia, and Silesia. In December 1946 Dibelius asked both the Allied Control Council and the SVAG authorities for assistance in transporting German civilians from new Polish or Czech territories to Germany, where the Protestant Church could provide for their material assistance. In both cases Dibelius's request was refused; SVAG Supreme Commander Sokolovskii wrote back to him stating such assistance was simply beyond the means of the Soviet authorities.[26]

The Catholic charitable organization *Caritas* also attempted to arrange transportation for German refugees from Polish and Czech territories, but Preysing informed them they should not even ask Soviet authorities for assistance with this task.[27] Clearly, while Soviet authorities did not want to destroy the charitable initiatives of the churches, as they relieved a considerable burden for the Soviet occupation, they did not want the dominant role of the churches in providing charitable relief to continue indefinitely.

Soviet officials also continued to express displeasure at the inability of *Volkssolidarität* to do more to provide for the relief of refugees and impoverished Germans. In a report sent to Mil'khiker from the head of SVAG's Information Administration in Eberswald, Lieutenant Colonel V. A. Rosenzweig on April 5, 1946, Rosenzweig expressed severe disappointment with the ability of *Volkssolidarität* to force the Protestant and Catholic churches to abandon independent charitable initiatives. Rosenzweig concluded if *Volkssolidarität* continued to fail in this mission the SVAG should consider restricting charitable activities of the churches.[28]

In his subsequent report to Tiul'panov, on April 15, Mil'khiker passed on the concerns of his subordinates regarding *Volkssolidarität*, and claimed the SVAG should take the step of exercising direct control over religious charitable activities or suppressing them. He argued the Protestant and Catholic churches remained "deeply engaged" in charitable activities, especially providing food, clothing, shelter and even employment, especially for the massive number of German refugees in the Soviet Zone. Tiul'panov, rather than giving permission to implement this policy, continued to urge restraint.[29]

The newly formed Socialist Unity Party also expressed ambivalence about the charitable initiatives of the churches. Dr. Naas Weiman, deputy head of the SED's Department for Cultural and Educational Affairs, sent out a directive on July 15, 1946, to all regional and provincial SED party organizations. Weiman wrote that rather than complain about the advantages the churches had in providing charitable relief, SED party members and leaders of antifascist organizations such as the FDJ and the FDGB should attempt to match their every activity. In addition, Weiman ordered them to publicly support clergy who worked with the SED in providing material relief, as opposed to those who pursued these activities independently of *Volkssolidarität*.[30]

The appeal of religious charitable initiatives for German refugees as the material situation failed to improve in the fall of 1946 was a frequent topic among Soviet authorities as the zonal elections approached in October 1946. The local and provincial heads of the Propaganda Administration throughout Brandenburg reported to Mil'khiker numerous times the success of the Protestant and Catholic churches in aiding impoverished Germans, particularly refugees, could have a beneficial effect for the CDU, especially as material conditions had not substantially improved despite the land reform the year before. One example of this was a report sent to Mil'khiker on June 21, 1946, from Major V. I. Lerner, head of the Propaganda Administration for the city of Frankfurt am Oder. Lerner complained that the CDU had capitalized on religious charitable work among refugees and those left destitute and homeless by the war. He specifically referenced CDU claims that only an economic and political order built on Christian foundations could help Germany recover from the war. The failure of the SED to administer its own charitable relief efforts through *Volkssolidaritat* meant the SVAG's German allies had no effective response to this charge.[31]

One month later, Mil'khiker informed his subordinates that Tiul'panov had instructed him the Protestant and Catholic churches in the Soviet Zone should encourage religious Germans to participate in the political process, although attempts by clergy to agitate for the CDU had to be immediately stopped. However, unless a definite link could be proven between religious charitable and political agitation for the CDU, such as having political speeches at soup kitchens or the distribution of clothing, religious charitable activities for impoverished Germans could continue unimpeded.[32]

Tiul'panov's decision to allow charitable work to continue among German refugees, probably the most embittered of all elements of the German population outside of former Nazi party members was due to a number of the factors. The first, as numerous SVAG documents reveal, was that providing for millions of displaced and impoverished Germans was often beyond the means of the SVAG, and the Protestant and Catholic churches provided a temporary but necessary service that relieved the burden on the Soviet authorities. The second reason was the overwhelming confidence held by both SVAG and SED authorities concerning the electoral fortunes of the SED. As Norman Naimark and David Pike have pointed out, both the Soviets and their German allies fully expected an electoral sweep that would provide public validation for the Soviet "antifascist democratic transformation" of Germany and provide the SED a platform to compete in the Western occupation zones. Consequently, any political advantage the CDU could gain from religious charitable initiatives was unimportant.

This did not mean the SVAG or the SED had given up their attempt to present *Volkssolidarität* was the prime method by which charitable aid was provided. On Wednesday, September 24, *Tägliche Rundschau* published a front page article on the activities of *Volkssolidarität*, stating only if all German antifascist institutions worked with this organization could enough aid be provided to German refugees and the impoverished, and asked for volunteers to assist these efforts.[33] *Neues Deutschland* published a similar article a few weeks later; announcing over 60,000 German children from former German territories in the East had received clothes and shoes for the winter due to the combined antifascist efforts of *Volkssolidarität*.[34]

As discussed in chapter one, the results of the zonal elections in October 1946 did not go the way the SVAG and SED planned. In a report sent one month later to the Soviet Deputy Foreign Minister Andrei Vyshinsky and the head of the Military Council for SVAG, A. M. Bokov, Tiul'panov admitted that those who had benefited from religious charitable activities, especially German refugees, were drawn to the CDU because of the close link between it and the churches. He noted this was a secondary concern compared to the CDU's demagogic treatment of the question of Germany's former eastern borders and the general success of the CDU under Jakob Kaiser in assembling the forces of German reaction.[35] Nor did Tiul'panov issue any orders to Mil'khiker or any of his other subordinates in the five provinces of the Soviet Zone in the aftermath of the zonal elections to take any steps to restrict religious charitable activities. This applied even to charitable activities directed towards such "susceptible" groups such as refugees and disabled war veterans.

According to the records of the CDU in the Soviet Zone and the Protestant and Catholic churches, there does not appear to any effort to coordinate charitable aid to German refugees or those left impoverished by to improve the electoral fortunes of the CDU. At the meeting of the executive committee of the CDU on September 16 1946, CDU leaders Kaiser and Ernst Lemmer admitted the only group they believed would provide reliable support would be religious German women, not refugees. While everyone assembled at the meeting expressed hope the CDU's guiding ideology of Christian Socialism would assist the party's fortunes, there was no discussion concerning how religious charitable initiatives would benefit them. In fact, party leader Robert Tillmann mentioned the CDU youth and women's organizations should urge the churches to work in *Volkssolidarität* as opposed to acting independently of it.[36] In the case of the Protestant church, at the meetings of bishops before and after the zonal elections, none of the assembled leaders mentioned the political implications of charitable relief.[37]

At the meeting of the Central Council of *Caritas* for all four zones of Germany a week before the zonal elections, the director of the *Caritas* branch of the Soviet Zone, Heinrich Solbach, noted that the majority of refugees were currently located in the Soviet Zone. Solbach expressed gratitude that SVAG had not placed too many obstacles in the path of the Catholic Church in providing charitable relief. He concluded his Protestant counterparts in the *Innere Mission* felt the same way, and their efforts in providing charitable relief would remain heavily dependent on aid provided from the Western zones. At no time did Solbach mention how Catholic charitable relief would aid the CDU.[38] A few months later, in April 1947, at the next meeting of the leaders of *Caritas*, Solbach admitted the lack of a cooperative relationship between the leaders of *Caritas* and the Soviet authorities meant the Eastern branch of *Caritas* was dependent on supplies of food and clothing from the Western zones, especially from the American zone, where the Catholic authorities had an excellent relationship with the military commander-in-chief, General Lucius Clay.[39]

The records of both the Protestant and the Catholic churches during the first two years of the occupation largely conform to the descriptions in the Propaganda Administration's records. While the Soviet authorities did little to prevent the churches from administering aid to German refugees and to those left destitute by the war, it also did little to assist them. SVAG's overall goal of ending the independent role of the churches in providing charitable relief in favor of integrating them within the SED-led *Volkssolidaritat* meant

Soviet authorities would do as little as possible to assist the churches in any fashion.

SVAG policy towards Catholic and Protestant relief work to German refugees remained consistent in 1947 and 1948. In a report from April 24, 1947, Mil'khiker informed Tiul'panov that *Volkssolidaritat* employed over 2,000 volunteers from all of the major antifascist organizations, and the majority of their charitable initiatives were directed towards providing food, clothing, shelter and employment for refugees and those left homeless or impoverished by the war. Mil'khiker admitted the charitable activities of the Protestant and Catholic churches still overshadowed those of *Volkssolidarität* but the population remained grateful for the charitable initiatives under the SED's leadership, and this reflected positively on the SVAG as well. Mil'khiker acknowledged the long-term goal was to ensure that *Volkssolidarität* was the only organization which provided charitable relief in Brandenburg, but there was no reason to rush this development. Tiul'panov noted his agreement to this policy, and assured Mil'khiker a similar policy would be implemented in the other four provinces of the Soviet zone.[40]

By the last year of the Soviet occupation, as the immediate humanitarian threat had subsided slightly, officials in the renamed Information Administration took a much more negative view of religious charitable aid. In January and early February of 1949, Lieutenant Colonel K. V. Martem'ianov, who had replaced Mil'khiker in late 1947 as the new commander of the Information Administration for Brandenburg, received a number of complaints from his subordinates in Potsdam, Seelow, Guben, Beeskow, and Prentzlau concerning the "political" use of religious charitable directed towards German refugees.

Major V. M. Stroilov, head of the Information Administration for Potsdam, informed Martem'ianov the *Innere Mission* ran fourteen refugee shelters in the city, with over five hundred people living in them, as well as five refugee shelters for over 200 children. Stroilov admitted the inability of *Volkssolidarität* to administer anywhere near a comparable number was a serious problem, as many of the Protestant church leaders remained opposed to the SVAG's and SED's "democraticization" policies. Stroilov admitted while he was not in favor of closing down the shelters, measures had to be enacted to ensure that "progressive" religious elements administered them.[41]

First Lieutenant P. I. Gevorkian, head of the Information Administration in Beeskow, also called for increased SVAG efforts to end the independent administration of charitable relief by the Protestant and Catholic churches for refugees, although for different reasons than those of Stroilov. Gevorkian wrote during religious services in refugee shelters and soup kitchens, Protestant and Catholic clergy made political speeches in support of the deposed

CDU leader in the Soviet Zone Jakob Kaiser as well as the leader of the CDU in the West, Konrad Adenauer. He claimed these clergy proclaimed only that the CDU offered a future that provided the alleviation of poverty and the preservation of political freedom. Even worse, some speakers even agitated for the American government. Gevorkian pointed to a statement given by an Protestant cleric at a religious service for refugees that the American possession of the atomic bomb was a good thing, as the United States was the world's best hope against Soviet atheism.[42]

Even more disturbing for Martem'ianov was the fact all five reports mentioned that, in addition to administering their own efforts at charitable relief, Catholic and Protestant clergy were also attempting to seize control of refugee relief operations within *Volkssolidaritat*. Deeply concerned over these developments, Martem'ianov informed Tiul'panov of them in early February 1949. Martem'ianov claimed the Protestant and Catholic churches exercised a great deal of influence over the population of Brandenburg through their charitable activities. He noted they welded particular influence among German refugees, many of whom still had not been able to obtain proper employment or regular housing. He concluded since the SED and its front organizations such as the DFD and the FDJ had failed for over three years to break the religious dominance in providing charitable relief to refugees, it was time for harsher "antireligious" measures to reduce the Protestant and Catholic involvement in charitable relief to an almost nonexistent level. Only this could preserve *Volkssolidarität*'s role as the dominant and "progressive" charitable agency in the Soviet Zone.[43]

Tiul'panov responded shortly thereafter, stating since the churches exercised such as pernicious influence over the German population, especially among the refugees, it was necessary to take greater steps to reduce the "social activities" of the churches. Tiul'panov recommended the Information Administration in Brandenburg work with SED officials who controlled the Brandenburg PVs to transfer control over most charitable initiatives to *Volkssolidarität*.[44] A few weeks later, on February 15, 1949, Martem'ianov passed on Tiul'panov's orders to his subordinates throughout Brandenburg. He ordered them to choose the most qualified members of their staffs to work with "antireligious specialists" from the SED in this assignment, and to explicitly weaken religious charitable work among the "resettled."[45]

The decision by the SVAG officials to finally move to restrict the charitable activities of churches towards German refugees following four years of relative inaction can be explained by two factors. The first was the inability of the SED and its youth and women's organizations to break the dominant position of the churches in providing charitable relief to German refugees, who were commonly viewed as potentially disruptive and dangerous social elements in the Soviet Zone. The second was a part of the broader SVAG and SED initiative to restrict all activities of religious organizations was part of the process of creating a Stalinist German state, a process near completion by the beginning of 1949.

Despite Tiul'panov's and Martem'ianov's commands, during the last seven months of the Soviet occupation, no concentrated campaign on the part of the German PVs to restrict religious charitable activities emerged to any great extent in Berlin or in Brandenburg. Although the assembled Protestant bishops voiced a number of concerns about Soviet policies throughout 1949, the issue of restrictions towards the charitable relief for refugees was not even mentioned.[46] The leaders of the *Caritas* branch in Brandenburg did not report to Bishop Preysing any major problems with SVAG or SED authorities in preventing charitable assistance to refugees, according to their own reports cooperation with the *Innere Mission* in providing aid outside of the confines of *Volkssolidarität* actually increased during the end of the occupation.[47]

Martem'ianov and Tiul'panov seemed to have lost interest in this specific policy after February 1949, as it was not mentioned again in any internal reports of the Information Administration in Brandenburg, nor did the SED through the provincial administrative bodies attempt to enforce this policy. Even *Neues Deutschland* and *Tägliche Rundschau* largely abandoned emphasizing the work of *Volkssolidarität,* with the exception of an article published in *Tägliche Rundschau* on February 9, 1949, which stated nearly all charitable activity in the Soviet Zone would soon be controlled by *Volkssolidarität*.[48] This contrasted sharply with SVAG and SED policies elsewhere towards religious education, the dissemination of atheistic propaganda, and the role of religious youth and women's organizations.

THE DISPUTES OVER THE ADMINISTRATION OF RELIGIOUS ORPHANAGES AND HOSPITALS IN THE SOVIET ZONE

This restraint on the part of the SVAG and SED towards charitable relief for German refugees was similar with their policies towards religious orphanages. However, SVAG and SED authorities took a much harsher line towards hospitals run by the Protestant and Catholic churches, especially in the last two years of the occupation.

While SVAG officials occasionally expressed concern about the administration of so many orphanages in the Soviet Zone by the Protestant and Catholic churches, they rarely if ever recommended transferring control over the orphanages to secular authorities. Nor did the SED officials who controlled the German organs of self-government press the SVAG authorities on this question. Mil'khiker's comments to Tiul'panov in his April 15, 1946, report on church activities in Brandenburg were typical of this attitude. Mil'khiker acknowledged the administration of orphanages by reactionary clergy was a considerable problem, as they had every opportunity to indoctrinate German youths against the Soviet authorities, although he admitted that there was little the SVAG or SED officials in the German organs of self-government could do about the situation at the present time.[49]

Towards the end of the occupation in early 1949, certain officials in the SVAG's Information Administration in Brandenburg began to express a deeper dissatisfaction with the continuing dominance of the churches in administering orphanages, but they made reserved criticisms and were informed by their superior Martem'ianov little could done to immediately alter the situation. Representative of this was a report sent to Martem'ianov by Major V. I. Vasil'ev on February 28, 1949. Vasil'ev, commander of the Information Administration for the city of Guben, stated the Protestant church administered three orphanages whose inhabitants totaled 240 children, while the Catholic church administered two orphanages inhabited by 112 children. Vasil'ev admitted the orphanages had done an effective job in fighting *"bez-prizornost"* (roughly, "street-urchin hood") and, while children received a great deal of religious education, the administration of the orphanages by Protestant and Catholic clergy appeared non-political, the children were even allowed to read *Tägliche Rundschau*.[50]

Nevertheless, Vasil'ev expressed a concern the complete lack of the involvement of *Volkssolidarität* in the administration of orphanages meant the religious dominance in this area was likely to continue indefinitely. He recommended that he be allowed to meet with the SED members who lead *Volkssolidarität* in Guben to rectify this situation. Martem'ianov told him that he could look into this matter but to take no immediate action, as there was likely no readily available alternative to the churches.[51]

This did not mean there were not occasional conflicts regarding the Protestant and Catholic administration of orphanages and states authorities, although this tended to involve SED officials in the Brandenburg PVs as opposed to SVAG authorities. SVAG order number 225 mandated all religious orphanages be placed under the control of the German Department of the People's Education (*Abteilung Volksbildung)* and all staff and administration would have to register with the local representatives of *Abteilung Volksbildung,* who were nearly always members of the SED. In a number of cases, the *Abteilung Volksbildung* removed from leadership positions in the orphanages Protestant clerics who had protested this new policy, or who had issued any criticisms of SVAG and SED educational policies.[52]

In other cases, Protestant and Catholic authorities struggled with SVAG and SED authorities to retain use of buildings seized by the Nazis before 1945, buildings the churches intended to transform into orphanages. Many of these buildings were seized for the use of the SVAG or the KPD immediately after the end of the war, and it often took years before they were finally returned to the churches, the struggles often lasted much longer if the churches intended to term them into multi-function facilities, such as orphanages attached to a hospital or a refugee shelter.[53]

SVAG policies towards religious orphanages were largely similar to their policies towards charitable relief to refugees, deeply suspicious of the intentions of "reactionary" institutions such as the Catholic and Protestant churches, but unwilling to take any drastic steps to stop them. In addition, the existence of religious orphanages, much like religious charitable relief, removed a considerable burden on SVAG and SED authorities, as their own internal reports attested.

With regards to religious hospitals, SVAG and SED policies were very different. While SVAG and SED authorities were generally willing to tolerate their existence for the first three years of the Soviet occupation, by late 1948 the SVAG and SED took a decidedly different approach. During the last year of the occupation, SVAG's Administration of Public Health and the German PVs tried to exclude the Protestant and Catholic churches from any role in medical treatment in the Soviet sector of Berlin and in Brandenburg. These policies were designed against religious hospitals which were controlled by Protestant or Catholic authorities in the western sectors of Berlin, which was the case with nearly all religious hospitals in Berlin and many in Brandenburg. Ultimately, SVAG and SED policies towards religious hospitals mirrored their policies towards religious education, namely, to exclude them from any public role whatsoever.

Before 1948, there had been a number of conflicts regarding church hospitals. Often, if the SVAG took control over a church hospital formerly seized by the Nazi government, then the new KPD or later SED authorities in the German PVs and LRs would simply take over buildings used by the church. In a report to the Brandenburg provincial administration from the city government of Frankfurt am Oder, the city government acknowledged that they simply took over the Protestant hospital in city after the SVAG converted the state hospital in the city into a medical facility for the use of the Red Army. The Frankfurt city government admitted this had caused some problems with religious leaders in the city but it was a necessary measure to weaken the Protestant Church's role in medical care.[54] On other occasional Protestant Church buildings were taken over directly by the SED for entirely different activities than they were intended. In the city of Rathenow, the main house used by the Protestant Church's *Innere Mission* for training new hospital staffs had been taken over by the SED to conduct political speeches and rallies in June 1946, attempts by the officials in the *Innere Mission* and later by Hans von Arnim to redress the situation had little effect.[55]

These policies continued into the spring of 1948, since SVAG authorities or SED officials in the Department for Reconstruction (*Wiederaufbau*) in the Soviet sector of Berlin and in Brandenburg often refused to allow for the release of funds to pay for repairs in hospitals run by the Protestant Church. One such example was the Protestant hospital named Saint Hedwig in the Soviet sector of Berlin. The hospital had not undergone any repairs or maintenance since 1939. The hospital requested from both Soviet authorities and the German Department for Reconstruction 38,000 RM in 1945 for repairs and new medical supplies. By April 1947, after these requests had been repeatedly turned down, the hospital administration had been reduced to asking officials in the Western sectors of Berlin for financial assistance, and from the all-Berlin Advisory Council for Church Affairs, both which were unable to provide assistance.[56]

However, these policies were quite restrained compared to what was to come in late 1948, when the SVAG and to a lesser extent the SED began a sustained effort against the independence of religious hospitals in Berlin and Brandenburg. This was unique due to the fact that this was one of the few anti-religious policies implemented by SVAG that Tiul'panov and the Propaganda/Information Administration did not take the leading role in.

This campaign began with a report dated October 28, 1948, from the head of the SVAG department of Public Health A. E. Sokolov to the deputy chairman of the Main Administration of SVAG for Civil Affairs A. F. Kabanov, the chairman of the Main Administration of SVAG for Political Affairs A. G. Russkikh, and the Political Council to the Supreme Commander of SVAG Vladimir Semenov. Sokolov stated a survey conducted by the Department of Public Health revealed the Protestant and Catholic churches administered ninety-six hospitals in the Soviet Zone, with the Protestant Church running fifty-five and the Catholic Church thirty-nine. In the Soviet sector of Berlin the Catholic Church administered four hospitals and the Protestant Church eight, while in the province of Brandenburg the Protestant Church had ten hospitals while the Catholic Church had five. Sokolov claimed none of these hospitals operated under the control of the German organs of self-government, and criticized the SED authorities for not having already ended this situation. In addition, actual doctors in leadership positions did not properly staff them; but they instead were staffed by Protestant or Catholic clergy, many of whom had no medical knowledge. The Catholic hospitals in particular were heavily dependent on the aid of nuns who had some medical training, and had been known to expel lay staff who did not agree with the beliefs or political aims of the churches.[57]

Sokolov stated the Protestant and Catholic churches used the hospitals to exert an ever-increasing influence over the German population for their "reactionary and imperialist masters" in the western occupation zones of Germany. Therefore, the supervision of church-run hospitals in the Soviet zone had to be transferred out of the hands of the church charitable bodies and directly under the command of the German organs of self-government and the SVAG. The hospitals must be "nationalized" to accomplish such a plan, but, Sokolov concluded, it was absolutely necessary.[58]

Two weeks later, Tiul'panov's deputy commander of the Information Administration A. A. Abramov reported to the deputy head of SVAG's Civil Affairs Branch A. F. Kabanov that Sokolov's proposal concerning the ending of religious control of hospitals in the Soviet Zone had merit. Abramov emphasized it was necessary for the process to be carried out by the German LRs, as opposed to SVAG organs themselves, and the process must involve all antifascist organizations under the control of the SED. Abramov wrote this process should appear to be under the control of the German authorities, as it would make it harder for the churches to gain public support to resist the nationalization of religious hospitals. Kabanov concurred with Abramov and stated the SVAG branch for Public Health should obtain as much information as possible about religious hospitals and pass it along to the SED before beginning the process.[59]

In early December, Kabanov and Sokolov passed on a directive to the heads of SVAG for all five provinces of the Soviet Zone and the Soviet sector of Berlin. They stated SVAG could no longer tolerate the continued existence of religious hospitals in the Soviet Zone, since they were not under SVAG and SED control this meant they were used by reactionary clergy for "anti-democratic" activities and to disseminate anti-Soviet propaganda. Therefore, over the next few months, the SED-dominated assemblies of the Soviet Zone, the *Landtags,* would pass laws nationalizing religious hospitals, and the German organs of self-government would implement them. SVAG and SED newspapers would also print negative stories about the administration of religious hospitals and emphasize the need to transfer them over to secular control.[60]

In the following months, many of the Catholic and Protestant hospitals in Berlin and Brandenburg were placed under the German Ministry of Public Health by orders of the Ministry of the Interior of the Soviet sector of Berlin and Brandenburg. This followed decrees passed by the Berlin city assembly and the Brandenburg *Landtag* which effectively instituted secular control over religious hospitals and instituted new state exams for the doctors, nurses, and staff. Dr. Theodore Wenzel, the head of the *Innere Mission* for Berlin and Brandenburg, reported to all provincial leaders on September 29, 1949, that most Protestant hospitals were now under state control, and much of their staff were excluded from working at the "new" hospitals for various manufactured political reasons. Wenzel pessimistically concluded the situation was likely to get worse after the occupation ended, although he expressed little doubt that both the SED and SVAG were trying to squeeze the Protestant Church out of any role in providing medical care in the Soviet Zone.[61]

The leaders of *Caritas* reported the same information to their superiors, stating few independent Catholic hospitals remained free from the nationalization orders of the German organs of self-government. The *Caritas* report, dated May 5 1949, concluded the remaining hospitals still under the control of the Protestant and Catholic churches would be heavily dependent on financial aid and medical supplies from the Western occupation zones, although these had been very difficult to acquire during the Berlin Blockade.[62]

This undoubtedly provided "proof" to SVAG suspicions that hospitals in the Soviet zone under the control of authorities in the western sectors of Berlin were used for espionage activities. This factor, combined with the completion of the transformation of the Soviet Zone into a German state on the Stalinist model in 1949, meant that religious hospitals could not and would not be allowed to exist unless under new management by SED authorities.

THE QUESTION OF POWS AND THE "SPECIAL INTERNMENT CAMPS" FOR THE CATHOLIC AND PROTESTANT CHURCHES IN THE SOVIET ZONE.

The Catholic and Protestants churches also faced considerable difficulty in another main area of charitable relief, regarding the status of German POWs and prisoners in the internment camps. Dibelius and Preysing possessed a two-fold goal, to obtain the release of as many prisoners as possible, and failing that, to provide for the spiritual needs of POWs through the distribution of religious literature and the allowance of religious services in the Soviet internment camps. At the meeting of the Protestant bishops of the Soviet zone in Berlin on July 3, 1946, Dibelius admitted the church had not been successful in petitioning the Soviet authorities to allow for religious services in the internment camps, even at the camp where Dibelius had concentrated most of his own personal efforts, the Soviet "Special Camp Number One" in the Berlin suburb of Sachsenhausen. Sachsenhausen had been a Nazi concentration camp and served as the main training facility for individuals who

later served in an administrative capacity at other Nazi camps throughout
Europe. Following the end of the war the SVAG transformed numerous Nazi
camps in Germany into concentration camps for their own use, including
Sachsenhausen.

D. D. Asmussen, the lay official in charge of religious work in the internment and POW camps in the Soviet zone, stated to the assembled Bishops
of the Protestant Church in the Soviet zone on July 1946 the situation with
regards to providing for the spiritual needs of the prisoners would not improve
at any time in near future. Dibelius expressed a general agreement with
Asmussen, although he noted continual requests towards Soviet authorities to
allow for the release of German POWs and those interned in Sachsenhausen
and elsewhere could eventually lead to an improvement of the situation.[63]

One reason that the Soviet authorities flatly refused to consider requests to
provide religious services or distribute religious literature in the Internment or
POW camps during the first two years of the occupation was due to the fact
that the CDU in the Soviet zone and in the Western zones made the return of
German POWs a main point of their party propaganda. For example, on June
26, 1945, the CDU executive committee issued a public statement promising
all inhabitants of the Soviet Zone the CDU would never forget the Germans
POWs still held in the Soviet captivity and would work towards their spiritual needs, although it also honored the memory of the dead on all sides of
the conflict.[64] This continued to be the party line well into 1947, as a CDU
party recruitment brochure distributed in April 1947 stated the CDU would
continue to work for the release of German POWs, as well as those still held
in Soviet internment camps throughout the Soviet Zone, or at very least for
an improvement of their physical and spiritual conditions.[65]

Given the fact the SVAG authorities, especially those directly involved
with religious policies in the Propaganda/Information Administration, viewed
the CDU with intense suspicion as a "reactionary" political party, they were
unlikely to do anything that might improve CDU electoral fortunes. At the
same time, the Soviet newspaper *Tägliche Rundschau* continually informed
its readers of when and where German POWs would return; articles on this
subject appeared at least a few times each month, usually with a listing of the
number of POWs released on the upper-right hand corner of the newspaper's
front page. Thus, only SVAG and possibly its German "friends" in the SED
would receive any propaganda value for the release of German POWs.

Dibelius and Preysing wrote numerous letters over the course of the occupation to both Tiul'panov as well as the supreme commanders of SVAG,
Marshals Georgii Zhukov and Vasilii Sokolovskii, asking for the release of
German POWs, as well as prominent laity and clergy who had disappeared in
the camps. Dibelius's efforts were somewhat successful according to letters

he sent to various parishes throughout Brandenburg from October 1947 to April 1948, which stated he had been able to secure the release of some prisoners held in the Soviet internment camps, although the progress had been slow and likely would continue to be throughout the next year.[66] Dibelius also repeatedly requested from Tiul'panov and Ermolaev in the spring of 1948 to allow for the resumption of religious services in the camps of Sachsenhausen, Buchenwald, and Neubrandenburg, although the immediate SVAG responses were non-committal.[67]

Like Dibelius, Preysing also wrote letters to the SVAG authorities asking for the release of military chaplains and parish priests who were held in Soviet custody, such as a letter sent to Marshal Sokolovskii on February 7, 1947. He called for the release of "non-political" prisoners (especially women and the elderly) from the internment camp at Oranienberg-Sachsenhausen. He mentioned in his letter to Sokolovskii the high number of those who have already died at Sachsenhausen and that this would only serve to further comparisons between the order created in the Soviet zone and that of the Nazis. The next day Preysing wrote similar letters to commanders Lucius Clay, Brian Robertson (UK) and Henri Koenig (France) asking them to appeal to Sokolovskii to release at least some of the prisoners in Sachsenhausen. Koenig and Clay later wrote back to him (on March 8 and March 12, 1947, respectively), promising to do whatever they could to get civilians released from Sachsenhausen if they had been unjustly imprisoned, although Preysing did not receive a response from Sokolovskii or from any his subordinates.[68]

Preysing likely undermined his ability to influence SVAG officials in charge of the Internment camps with his letter circulated to Catholic clergy in the Soviet and Western sectors of Berlin on September 12, 1947. In this letter, Preysing, among other criticisms of SVAG and SED policies, stated the Soviet authorities had taken over former Nazi concentration camps for the sole reason to imprison enemies of the Communists. Preysing and Dibelius also informed the heads of the military governments in the Western occupation zones about these issues, and asked them to intercede for them with the Soviet authorities.[69]

D. D. Asmussen was even more actively involved in petitioning Soviet authorities. In August 1947 Ermolaev received a letter from Asmussen requesting his assistance in the release from special Soviet internment camp at Sachsenhausen of a particular Protestant cleric named Dirksen from the city of Rothenberg. Ermolaev promised to do what he could, although he could offer no timetable as to when Dirksen might be released.[70]

By early 1948, the Soviet policies towards the distribution of religious literature and religious services in the internment camps began to change slightly. On January 7, Dibelius informed the other Protestant bishops in the

Soviet Zone that thanks their combined interventions with SVAG Supreme Commander Sokolovskii, the SVAG authorities would permit the distribution of religious literature in the internment camps, and would allow for occasional religious services as well. Dibelius stated this was a very positive development but all Protestant clergy would have to continually monitor the situation to make sure the SVAG authorities did not abruptly reverse course.[71]

This did not mean, however SVAG policy towards releasing prisoners from the internment camps or German POWs had the request of Protestant or Catholic clergy had changed. A few months later on March 10, 1948, Asmussen sent another letter to the Soviet military headquarters at Karlshorst asking for the widespread release of Protestant military chaplains attached to Wehrmacht officer staffs who were still held by the Red Army, as they were desperately needed to engage in spiritual work for the German population in the Soviet zone. Asmussen received an answer from the SVAG Information Administration (unsigned, but probably written by Ermolaev) five days later, which stated while the SVAG could not release the Protestant clerics at this point, the Protestant Church could send packages to more than 500 chaplains in Soviet custody in Germany; an extension of a policy allowed the previous Christmas, in order to better provide for the spiritual needs of the German POWs in the Soviet zone.[72]

By the end of 1948, the SVAG authorities had moved to restrict some of the privileges they had given prisoners at the internment camps with regards to religious services and receiving religious literature. In a letter dated September 14, 1948 and sent to Protestant leaders in Brandenburg, Dibelius, Kurt Krummacher, and Heinrich Gruber, a minister named Heinrich Mehrhahn, who had recently been released from Sachsenhausen, expressed dissatisfaction with religious life in the internment camps. He noted religious services in the camps tended to be sporadic and depended on whims of the Soviet camp commandant. While Catholic prisoners could receive religious literature, it could not be in German but in French. He did acknowledge since the beginning of 1948 Soviet camp authorities were more open for allowing religious ceremonies as time went on, although there continued to be sharp reversals in these policies, such as religious services canceled at the last minute.[73]

Appeals by Protest authorities such as Dibelius, Asmussen, and Krummacher towards the SVAG authorities continued into 1949. These were usually sent to SVAG supreme commanders Sokolovskii and later Marshal Vasilii Chuikov, although they alwantys began with thanks for allowing religious services and the distribution of religious literature in the internment camps. The agreement by SVAG authorities to allow Protestant clergy to receive packages of religious literature to distribute was viewed by the church as a particularly important concession. On the other hand, appeals for the specific release of clergy imprisoned in the camps as well as army chaplains held in the Soviet Union proved to be similarly unsuccessful in 1949 as it was in 1945.[74]

Unlike in the areas of providing charitable relief for German refugees and administering religious hospitals and orphanages, SVAG policies towards the questions of religious services and the distribution of religious literature in the Soviet internment camps was more conciliatory at the end of the Soviet occupation. However, the SVAG was unbending from the beginning of the occupation to the end with regards to providing certain political prisoners or POWs an early release at the request of Protestant or Catholic clergy in Berlin and Brandenburg. Occasionally allowing prisoners to receive bibles or hymnals or conduct religious services had an obvious propaganda value for the SVAG authorities, while their refusal to release prisoners at the request of religious authorities demonstrated the continuing weakness of the churches in comparison to the Soviet authorities.

Had the Protestant and Catholic clergy not brought this to the attention not only to SVAG authorities but also on repeated occasions to American, British, and French officials then no change in the status quo would have occurred. The SVAG concessions on early 1948 with regards to spiritual life in the internment camps was connected to the wave of Soviet "concessions" on the verge of the Berlin Blockade to both the German public in the Soviet Zone and in an attempt to shift blame to the Western Allies for emerging economic and political division of Germany.

CONCLUSION

SVAG and SED policies towards religious charitable activities during the Soviet occupation were, in the words of Norman Naimark to describe Soviet policies in Germany from 1945–1949, inconsistent and opportunistic. SVAG tolerated the Protestant and Catholic churches providing material aid for German refugees and victims of the war as well as the administration of refugee shelters and orphanages, although they hoped the SED-led *Volkssolidarität* would eventually replace the church in this role. This was done not because the SVAG anticipated a long-term role played by the churches in providing charitable relief but because religious efforts removed a burden on the Soviet and SED authorities they were unable to handle on their own.

Likewise, allowing the distribution of religious literature and allowing for religious services in the internment camps allowed the SVAG authorities to use this concession for propaganda offensive that the Soviet authorities were supporters of "religious freedom", which will be examined in more detail in chapter seven. On other matters regarded POW or internment camps, SVAG remained completely unbending on requests by Protestant or Catholic clergy to release certain prisoners, especially former military chaplains.

SVAG and SED (through their control of the German organs of self-government) policies towards religious hospitals demonstrate the limits that they were willing to tolerate independent charitable work by the churches. On this issue the SVAG authorities were not even willing to consider their gradual replacement by *Volkssolidarität,* but instead simply placed them under state control. Like the schools, the hospitals were simply too important for Soviet ideological goals in Germany to allow them to maintain their independence. The end of religious administration of the hospitals was a part of a series of final steps taken by SVAG and SED in 1948 and 1949 to create the foundations for a German state on the Stalinist model before the end of the Soviet occupation.

The Catholic and Protestant churches treated charitable activity much as they did educational, youth, and women's issues. This meant they pushed the Soviet authorities for as great of a role as they could publicly perform. This put them in conflict with SVAG authorities on occasion, although far less so than other major issues facing the churches during the Soviet occupation. Charitable relief was the one field where the churches were allowed the greatest amount of freedom by the Soviet authorities, and they capitalized on this to the fullest extent. While the SVAG and SED still placed restrictions on some of their activities, the experience of the churches in providing charitable aid was generally free of the bitter conflicts surrounding religious education or the operation of religious youth and women's organizations.

Notes

1. Paul Steege, *Black Market, Cold War: Everyday Life in Berlin 1946–1949.* Cambridge: Cambridge University Press, 2007. 20–21.

2. Most historical works about the Soviet zone, such as those by Norman Naimark, Gary Bruce, Paul Steege, and David Pike, mention the desperate material situation of the Soviet zone, especially among the enormous numbers of refugees from East Prussia and Silesia. These works emphasize how the failure to improve the economic situation in the Soviet zone during the first few years of the occupation contributed to the unpopularity of the Soviet authorities and their German "friends" in the Socialist Unity Party. Yet none of these historians address which organizations played an active role in providing charitable relief for the German population, something the Soviet military authorities were unable to provide.

3. Norman Naimark, 40. The Soviets, for the most part, allowed for Catholic and Protestant churches to engage in charitable relief elsewhere in Eastern Europe during

the immediate post war era. The exception was with the Greek Catholic Church in Western Ukraine, Romania, and Western Byelorussia, where the Soviets worked to suppress all activities by these particular churches.

4. The sources used for this chapter largely consist of records from the *Innere Mission* and *Caritas*, as well as the records of Catholic and Protestant church leaders in Berlin-Brandenburg they reported to, namely Otto Dibelius, Hans von Arnim and Konrad von Preysing. The materials from the SED-controlled German organs of self-government, which frequently dealt with and occasionally attempted to restrict religious charitable work, were also an important source. The official records of the Soviet military government for Berlin-Brandenburg, especially the Propaganda/Information and Public Health administrations and the office of the Supreme Commander, as well as the German-language newspapers of the SVAG and SED, demonstrate how both Soviet and German authorities viewed charitable work by conducted by the Evangelical and Catholic churches, and what significance they attached to it.

5. *Die Protokolle der Kirchlichen Ostkonferenz 1945–1949.* Eds, Michael Kuhne. Gottingen: Vandenhoeck & Ruprecht, 2005. 69.

6. Ibid, 72.

7. *Neue Zeit*. 4 Sept 1945. 2. Caritas, much like its Protestant equivalent, the *Innere Mission* had operated in Berlin-Brandenburg since the late nineteenth century, its lay administrative staff was rather small, but its work was aided by hundreds of volunteers.

8. LAB, C Rep. 101–04 Abteilung 66, 16–26-Rat für Kirchen Angelegenheiten, Berlin Regierung). Ferdinand Friedensburg, a CDU member, was unlikely to be suspicions of religious charitable activity, until his removal at the behest of Walter Ulbricht, Freidensburg had been broadly supportive a visible public role for the Protestant and Catholic churches.

9. *Tägliche Rundschau*. 22 Nov 1945. 1.

10. GARF f. 7077 (SVAG Brandenburg), op 1 (Upravlenie propagandy), d. 187 (Correspondence October 1945–January 1946), l. 103. The shoe drive obtained over 2,800 pairs for impoverished children in the Soviet sector of Berlin.

11. GARF, f. 7077, op. 1, d. 187, ll. 4–5.

12. *SVAG i religioznye konfessii Sovetskoi zony okkupatsii Germanii 1945–1949: Sbornik dokumentov*. Eds, V. V. Zakharov, O. V. Lavinskaia, D. N. Nokhotovich, and E. V. Poltoratskoi. Moscow: Rosspen 2006. 141–147.

13. GARF, f. 7133 (SVAG-Sachsen-Anhalt), op.1 (Upravlenie informatsii), d. 273 (Correspondence January–April 1946), ll. 301–303.

14. BLHA, Repositor 202A-Präsident Brandenburg Provinzial Verwaltung, Abteilung 502, 82.

15. *Tägliche Rundschau*. 21 Mar 1946. 3.

16. *Deutsche Volkszeitung*. 8 Jan 1946. 1. Like many of the other newspapers within the Soviet zone, *Deutsche Volkszeitung* often did not name the authors of certain articles.

17. DAB, Abteilung I- Bischöfliches Ordinariat Berlin, Repositur 4–15–1.

18. Ibid.

19. ELAB, Bestand 405- Brandenburg Evangelische Kirchenkanzlei, #465.

20. EZA, Bestand 4- EKD Kirchenkanzlei, #351. Letter sent to Otto Dibelius, on February 22 1946 from the parish of Schloss Meiersdorf begging him to use his influence with Soviet authorities to return more buildings for church use.

21. *Die Protokolle der Kirchlichen Ostkonferenz 1945–1949.* Eds, Michael Kuhne. Gottingen: Vandenhoeck & Ruprecht, 2005. 96. Dibelius did acknowledge that the church should be grateful that the Soviet authorities and the KPD had not tried to excessively hinder Evangelical charitable relief.

22. Goeckel, 43. Most of the "new farmers" were former Wehrmacht soldiers released from Soviet captivity or industrial workers whose factories had been destroyed as well as the poorer members of the German peasantry. Many had little experience with large-scale farming and lacked the proper equipment.

23. *SVAG i religioznye konfessii Sovetskoi zony okkupatsii Germanii: Sbornik dokumentov 1945–1949.* Eds, V. V. Zakharov, O. V. Lavinskaia, D. N. Nokhotovich, and E. V. Poltoratskoi. Moscow: Rosspen 2006. 353–354.

24. GARF, f. 7077 (SVAG Brandenburg), op. 1- (Upravlenie propagandy), d. 203 (Correspondence August-December 1946), ll. 118–130.

25. *SVAG i religioznye konfessii Sovetskoi zony okkupatsii Germanii: Sbornik dokumentov 1945–1949.* Eds, V. V. Zakharov, O. V. Lavinskaia, D. N. Nokhotovich, and E. V. Poltoratskoi. Moscow: Rosspen 2006. 241–246. One year later, in his discussion of the Propaganda Administration's religious policies to his superiors on the Central Committee of the Communist Party of the Soviet Union, Tiul'panov continued to say nothing about restricting religious charitable work in the zone. He took decidedly different tone with regards to religious involvement in educational activity or work with German youths or women, constantly urging officials within the Propaganda Administration to restrict church involvement.

26. EZA, Bestand 4, #473. Dibelius's request is especially surprising given the fact internal church documents reveal that integrating refugee clergy and laity into the churches in the Soviet zone was an exceedingly difficult task.

27. DAB, Abteilung I, Repositur 7–24–13.

28. GARF, f. 7077, op.1, d. 203, ll. 109–114.

29. GARF, f. 7077, op.1 d. 203, ll. 118–130. Mil'khiker wrote that the primary beneficiary of the generosity of the churches would be the CDU and Kaiser's doctrine of "Christian Socialism."

30. SAPMO-DDR Abteilung, DY 30-SED Zentral Committee, IV 2- ZK Secretariat 14-Abteilung Volksbildung 1- Juni-Dezember.

31. GARF, f. 7077, op. 1, d. 204, ll. 39–42. Mil'khiker received similar complaints from his other subordinates.

32. GARF, f. 7077, op. 1, d. 204, l, 83.

33. *Tägliche Rundschau.* 24 Sept 1946.

34. *Neues Deutschland.* 6 Oct 1946. Both articles used the euphemism "the resettled" as opposed to refugees.

35. *Die UdSSR und die Deutsche Frage 1941–1948: Dokumente aus dem Archiv für Aussenpolitik der Russischen Föderation* Volume 3: 6 Oktober 1946 bis 15 Juni

1948. Eds, Jochen Laufer, Georgii Kynin and Viktor Knoll. Berlin: Duncker & Humbolt 2004. 52–60.

36. ACDP, *Signatur* 07–010-CDU-Ost, #2179, 282–285. Tillmann's proposal, which received broad approval from the other party leaders Kaiser, Lemmer, Otto Nuschke, and Georg Dertinger, agreed to this recommendation, as all still hoped for board cooperation with all antifascist organizations, including the SED.

37. *Die Protokolle der Kirchlichen Ostkonferenz 1945–1949.* Eds, Michael Kuhne, Gottingen: Vandenhoeck & Ruprecht, 2005. 122–136, 137–152.

38. DAB, Abteilung I, Repositur 7–24–1

39. Ibid. Many of the subsequent meetings of the leaders of *Caritas* continued to emphasize these issues, although often Solbach and other representatives from the Soviet Zone were unable to attend.

40. GARF, f. 7077 (SVAG Brandenburg), op.1 (Upravlenie informatsii), d.220 (Correspondence January–April 1947), ll.47–50.

41. GARF, f. 7077 (SVAG Brandenburg), op.1(Upravlenie informatsii), d. 254 (Correspondence January–June 1949), ll. 25–26.

42. GARF, f. 7077, op.1, d. 254, ll. 23–24.

43. GARF, f. 7077, op. 1, d. 254, ll. 34–38.

44. GARF, f. 7077, op.1, d. 254, ll.39–43. Tiul'panov issued similar directives concerning the religious youth and women's organizations as well as the dissemination of "scientific-atheistic propaganda" which will be discussed in greater detail in chapters four and five.

45. GARF, f. 7077, op.1, d. 254, ll. 44–45.

46. *Die Protokolle der Kirchlichen Ostkonferenz 1945–1949.* Eds, Michael Kuhne, Gottingen: Vandenhoeck & Ruprecht, 2005. 298–319, 320–338, 339–350.

47. DAB, Abteilung I, Repositur 7–24–1.

48. *Tägliche Rundschau.* 9 Feb 1949. 3. This may have been due to the fact that, four years after the "antifascist-democratic transformation" began, charitable relief was still necessary for many Germans in the Soviet Zone.

49. GARF, f. 7077, op. 1, d. 203, ll. 118–130.

50. GARF, f. 7077, op. 1, d. 254, ll. 45–46. Vasil'ev also noted, on a somewhat less enthusiastic note, that the children were also able to read the CDU newspaper *Neue Zeit.*

51. Ibid.

52. EZA, Bestand 4, Abteilung 791.

53. BLHA, Rep. 202A- Büro des Ministerpräsidents, Provinzial Verwaltung, Abt. 502-Soziale Angelegenheiten, Januar 1948-Juni 1949, 141–144. Potsdam and Frankfurt am Oder were particular locations where the Evangelical and Catholic churches did not finally receive permission to open new orphanages until 1947.

54. BLHA, Rep. 202A-Brandenburg Provinzial Verwaltung, Abt. 498-Soziale Angelegenheiten, Januar 1947-Dezember 1947, 253. This foreshadowed policies by SVAG and SED authorities in 1948 and 1949 to seize all Evangelical and Catholic hospitals in East Berlin, since they were convinced that the hospitals were used by church leaders in West Berlin for espionage against the Soviet zone.

55. BLHA, Rep. 202A, Abt. 498, 265.

56. LAB, C Rep 101–04, Abt. 63, 144.

57. GARF, f. 7317 (SVAG), op. 56 (Otdel zhdravookraneniia), d. 29 (Correspondence June–December 1948), ll.316–330.

58. Ibid. Despite Sokolov's use of the term "nationalization", the religious hospitals were not actually seized by the Soviet or German administrations of Public Health. However, religious leadership of the hospitals was ended and much of religious staff would be dismissed in the following year.

59. GARF, f. 7317, op.56, d. 29, l. 354.

60. GARF, f. 7317, op. 56, d. 29, ll 372–373

61. EZA, Bestand 4- EKD Kirchen Kanzlei, Abteilung 350-Innere Mission

62. DAB, Abteilung I, Repositur 7–24–13. The author also noted Konrad von Preysing's protests ultimately came to little avail.

63. *Die Protokolle der Kirchlichen Ostkonferenz 1945–1949.* 127.

64. ACDP, *Signatur* 07–011- CDU Ost, Rep 2376. This statement was signed by at the time party leader Andreas Hermes, as well as future leader Jakob Kaiser.

65. ACDP, *Signatur* 07–010-CDU Ost, Rep 1846. Records of the SVAG Propaganda/Information Administration referent refer to the CDU's "demagogic" use of the issue of German POWs.

66. ELAB, Bestand 603- Nachlässe Otto Dibelius, B 13.

67. Ibid.

68. DAB, Abteilung. V, Repositur 16–5. Preysing was correct in his claim of the number of victims in Sachsenhausen, over 12,000 out of 60,000 held in the camp died between 1945 and 1950.

69. DAB, Abt. I, Repositur 4–15–1.

70. EZA, Bestand 4, 473. Asmussen had written a letter to Dirksen's wife the day before he wrote to Ermolaev and promised to secure his release. This particular file also contains a number of letters written to military authorities in the Western zones (usually Americans or British) to intercede with the Soviet authorities on behalf of the Protestant Church.

71. *Die Protokolle der Kirchlichen Ostkonferenz 1945–1949*, 232. Dibelius made this admission at the Berlin meeting of the Protestant bishops in the Soviet Zone on January 7 1948.

72. EZA, Bestand 4, 474. Compromises such as this were fairly rare during the Soviet occupation, although the SVAG often demonstrated a greater willingness to offer concessions with regards to spiritual work in the internment and POW camps than on most other issues.

73. Ibid.

74. *Die Protokolle der Kirchlichen Ostkonferenz 1945–1949*, 330. The experience of Catholic authorities such as Preysing were largely similar, successful in convincing SVAG authorities to allow for religious services in the internment camps, but unable to obtain the release of specific POWs or political prisoners in the internment camps.

Chapter Seven

"Christianity and Marxism Are Not in Opposition"

The Propaganda Offensive Concerning "Religious Freedom" under Communism

INTRODUCTION

The "religious freedom" propaganda campaign served to illustrate the complexity of the religious policies of the SVAG and SED authorities. This policy demonstrated the numerous contradictions between SVAG and SED designs towards the churches as opposed to what they proclaimed in their propaganda. The SVAG and the SED moved to restrict the activities of the Protestant and Catholic churches in the areas of religious education and collaboration with the CDU, and to a lesser extent with religious charitable work. At the same time they proclaimed when socialism was created in Germany under SED leadership full religious freedom would be honored. This chapter will examine how effective the propaganda campaign was at winning over Protestant and Catholic clergy to the support of, or at least non-opposition to, the SVAG and SED authorities. It will also address how the actual reality of SVAG and SED religious policies contrasted with their propaganda claims.

This chapter will examine these issues more extensively than in the previous historiography during the period of the Soviet occupation, when the first cases of attempts at accommodation between the Protestant Church and SED were attempted. Later, following the building of the Berlin Wall in 1961 and the growing distance between the Western and Eastern German churches, a substantial accommodation, known as *Kirche im Sozialismus* (the church in Socialism) was established in 1967. Although these later events were more important for the emergence of the *Kirche im Sozialismus* movement, the "religious freedom" propaganda campaign demonstrates this process did began long before the Berlin Wall came up.

The propaganda of the SVAG and SED to prove complete religious free-dom was possible under Stalinist-style socialism was false, despite the lim-ited compromise made between Stalin and the Russian Orthodox Church in 1943. The vicious persecutions of churches in the Soviet Union and through-out Eastern Europe after the Second World War proved these claims were fraudulent from the beginning. The propaganda campaign in the Soviet zone, just as everywhere else in Eastern Europe, was initially formed to dupe gull-ible elements of Eastern Europe's population during the delicate period in the first few years after 1945 when the Communist parties had not yet assembled sufficient strength to seize power.

There was also a second, more important reason for this propaganda cam-paign. The SVAG and the SED did not print articles in *Tägliche Rundschau* or *Neues Deutschland* attesting to religious liberty in the Soviet Union or invite Protestant and Catholic clerics to visit Orthodox churches in Soviet Russia merely to convince them to drop any opposition to the creation of Stalinist-style socialism in the Soviet zone. It was also part of a long-term project begun by the Soviet authorities and continued by SED's political police, the Stasi, after the founding of the GDR to recruit clergy and clerical staff from the Protestant and (to a far lesser extent) the Catholic churches with the intention of undermining them from within, as well as to prevent collaboration between the two churches in resisting the GDR's policies. This propaganda offensive began almost immediately after the beginning of the Soviet occupation. The SVAG's Propaganda/Information administration and, in particular, Sergei Tiul'panov, played the central role in this process. The SED would not engage in this propaganda offensive until shortly before the zonal elections of October 1946, largely due to controversies among the SED leadership concerning exactly what its religious policies should be. It would not be until the end of the Soviet occupation that the SED would finally take the lead role in this process in Berlin-Brandenburg. By this time, SVAG had turned to producing anti-religious propaganda of a "scientific-atheistic" char-acter, while both it and the SED had turned to portraying the "progressive" Protestant Church as a partner in rebuilding German democracy as opposed to the "reactionary" Catholic Church

In the Soviet zone of Germany this took a special significance regarding the Protestant Church, since it was still formally linked with those in the Western zones. SED party leaders as well as Tiul'panov believed if they were able to influence prominent Protestant religious leaders in the Soviet zone, this could in turn allow them to influence the actions of religious leaders in the western zones of Germany. At the very least, these policies would drive a wedge between clerical "progressives" and "reactionaries" in the Soviet zone and limit the Protestant churches' capacity for independent action in opposing SVAG-SED policies.

During the Ulbricht era numerous historians affliatied with the SED derided Martin Luther, as "the gravedigger of German freedom", for his support of the German princes against the Peasant Rebellion in 1524–1526, especially his clear defense of divine-right monarchy by pointed to Paul's letter to the Romans.[1] Interestingly, the "religious freedom" propaganda campaign maintained a neutral to positive view of Martin Luther, and encouraged the Protestant Church to celebrate his accomplishments. Once again, a policy which later emerged during the *Kirche im Sozialismus* era had its origins during the Soviet occupation, paving the way for Erich Honecker's statement in 1983 that Luther represented a "progressive force" in German history.[2]

The SVAG and SED authorities also kept at a distance those Protestant clerics who desired to work with them in promoting a combination of Marxism-Leninism with Christianity. This is not to say they did not use groups in Berlin-Brandenburg such as the League of Religious Socialists, but were careful never to give too authority much to "red" clergy besides writing newspaper articles praising religious freedom in the Soviet Union, preferring to keep the propaganda offensive concerning religious freedom to remain largely a top-down process, controlled exclusively by SVAG and SED authorities. This, in turn, limited the effectiveness of the propaganda campaign, as it appeared as a top-down process dictated by the Soviet authorities rather than something sympathetic clergy took an active and independent role in.

The Catholic populations of Berlin-Brandenburg as well as its clergy were, by and large, not won over by the SVAG and later the SED propaganda offensive, especially since the Catholic leadership in Berlin, Konrad von Preysing, and in the Vatican, Pius XII, were deeply and outspokenly anticommunist. The SVAG and SED only experienced limited success with the Protestant Church in Berlin-Brandenburg, given the fact Otto Dibelius, was scarcely less hostile to the Communists than Preysing. Nevertheless, by 1949, the SVAG and SED could point to limited success to sowing internal divisions in senior Protestant leadership in Brandenburg between Dibelius and officials such as Kurt Krummacher and Heinrich Gruber, who were much more sympathetic to the idea of religious freedom continuing to exist under a German state led by the SED.

In addition, the SVAG and SED authorities recruited numerous "progressive" clerics at the lower levels of the Protestant hierarchy who active worked against attempts by clerical "reactionaries" to work against the goals of the

Soviet authorities. Like so many other aspects of the GDR's religious policies, the extensive infiltration of the Protestant Church in the GDR, which seriously weakened its senior leadership's ability to resist the SED-dictatorship, began under SVAG auspices during the Soviet occupation of Germany. It is important to note, however, this process was in its infancy during the late 1940s, and would not be expanded into a major Stasi operation until the late 1950s.

The question of collaboration with the SED regime in East Germany remains an unsettled question in the historiography of the Protestant Church under Communism. As Gerhard Besier argued, whatever claims can be made for the merits of the eventual cooperation between the church and the SED regime, the process morally compromised Protestant leaders and assisted the GDR's political police, the Stasi, in its attempt to infiltrate the administration of the Protestant Church with spies and informers from the late 1960s to late 1980s.[3] However, as Horst Dähn points out, the limited agreement between the church leaders and the SED authorities did provide an independent space for the churches to continue their charitable activities and to subtly support the emerging East German dissident movement in the 1970s by using the churches as "free spaces" for diverse groups to discuss their opposition to the regime.[4]

Works written after the fall of the GDR such as those by Robert Goeckel have built on the Dähn's argument discussing the benefits of the churches' independent role in the GDR's society, and the aid it provided at the grassroots level for the East German dissident movement in the 1980s, even with those elements which did not have a strong religious character. Goeckel also notes, however, the success of the Stasi infiltrating the administrative apparatus of the Protestant Church, a process which greatly accelerated once the staunchly anti-communist position of Otto Dibelius was discarded in the mid-1960s.[5]

While much of the historiography concerning the accommodation between religious and state leaders in the and the Soviet zone and the GDR discusses why the church ultimately embarked on such a policy, considerably less attention is made as to why the Communist authorities in East Germany, first the SVAG and later the SED, pursued these attempts to win over Christian laity and clergy with promises of "religious freedom." Answering the neglected question of what the Soviet and SED hoped to gain from obtaining the support of religious institutions rather than simply trying to suppress them will be the main contribution of this chapter to the existing historiography on church and state relations in East Germany as well as the history of the Soviet military occupation.[6]

THE CREATION OF THE "RELIGIOUS FREEDOM" CAMPAIGN IN SOVIET-OCCUPIED GERMANY JUNE 1935 TO OCTOBER 1946

The three key events for understanding the SVAG and SED attempt to integrate religious freedom into their broader propaganda campaign for the hearts and minds of the German people from 1945 to 1949 are the KPD's exile conferences in Brussels in June 1935 and Bern in April 1939 and Stalin's meeting with Metropolitan Sergei of Moscow in September 1943. At the KPD's first exile conference in Brussels, the party for the first time recognized freedom of religious belief as a fundamental right of the German people. Two years later the KPD's Central Committee issues a proclamation congratulating the Confessing Church and opposition Catholics for their resistance to the Nazi regime. At the Bern Conference in 1939, the KPD reaffirmed its commitment to religious freedom and promised in a future socialist Germany the Protestant and Catholic churches would be able to play an independent and vital role in society. The further cooperation of KPD members and dissident German clergy in the Soviet-sponsored National Committee for a Free Germany (NKFD) and shared imprisonment in Nazi concentration camps also contributed to hopes of a lasting cooperative relationship between the KPD and the German churches, especially since the KPD had presumably abandoned the militant atheism which characterized its policies regarding the religious question from 1918 to 1935.[7]

A similar "breakthrough" between religious and communist leaders occurred in September 4, 1943, when Stalin met with Metropolitans Sergei of Moscow, Aleksei of Leningrad, and Nikolai of Kiev. After twenty-six years of relentless persecution which came near to destroying the Russian Orthodox Church as an institution, the Soviet government made a few limited concessions to the Orthodox leaders. At the meeting Stalin praised the Orthodox Church's support for the Soviet war efforts and promised they would be allowed to elect a new Patriarch (left dormant since the death of Patriarch Tikhon in 1925), open a few seminaries which had been closed by Soviet authorities, and publish a church newspaper. In addition, Stalin created a branch of Sovnarkom to serve as link with Orthodox and Soviet leaders, the Council of Russian Orthodox Church affairs. The fact Stalin staffed the Council with NKVD veterans, including its leader Colonel Georgii Karpov, provided clear evidence as to his real intentions towards the churches, but this still marked a remarkably turnaround by the Soviet leadership.[8]

In reality, neither of these apparent reversals of anti-religious policies marked a genuine move by the KPD and the Soviet government away from the creation of an atheistic society as part of their long-term goals. Both were tactical considerations designed to temporarily win over religious allies in order to serve the broader plans of the KPD and the Soviet Union. In the case of the KPD, both Pieck and Ulbricht were simply interested in recruiting as broad a base as possible to support their reconstruction of a post-Hitler Germany; the commitment to religious freedom could be affirmed publically while the German communists built gradually built their power base, and then discarded once the KPD was strong enough to turn on religious institutions.[9]

In the case of Stalin, the moderate concessions to the Orthodox Church in 1943 were designed for future propagandistic purposes in claiming "religious freedom" existed in the Soviet Union, and, more importantly, to use the Russian Orthodox Church in suppressing independent Orthodox churches in Ukraine and Byelorussia, which were often centers for nationalist resistance to Soviet rule.[10] The KPD/SED and SVAG propaganda offensive in the Soviet zone in should be viewed in the same light. At no time was it a serious attempt to build a lasting and peaceful relationship with religious institutions, but rather it was intended to sow divisions within the church leadership and make them unable to resist anti-religious policies in the Soviet zone.

As with numerous other religious issues, the SVAG authorities took an active role in the religious propaganda campaign before the KPD/SED. The KPD leadership stalled initially in defining its position on religious issues after its reorganization in the Soviet zone in June 1945, which gave the CDU the opportunity to describe its ideology as aggressively atheist, much to the consternation of certain SVAG officials, especially in the Propaganda Administration. The KPD's newspaper, *Deutsche Volkszeitung*, rarely discussed religious issues, and when it did, it usually either denounced the Vatican or German Catholic clerical leaders, or strictly emphasized the need to secularize the education system in Germany.[11]

In comparison, the SVAG newspaper *Tägliche Rundschau* immediately began to stress the existence of religious freedom in the Soviet Union, and continued to do so throughout the first three years of the Soviet occupation. The Soviet publishers of newspaper were quick to recruit German clergy who would testify to the tolerant attitudes of the Soviet military authorities towards religious institutions. One of the first issues of the newspaper, published on June 9, 1945, contained an article entitled "Church Life in Brandenburg," written by a Catholic priest named Hermann Schubert. Schubert wrote the Red Army had allowed the Catholic Church to re-open the churches of Saint Gotthardt and Saint Katherinen in the city of Brandenburg, both of which had been closed since the end of the war.[12]

Another significant early article which developed this theme appeared three days later in the SVAG newspaper. Written by an Protestant pastor named Karl Fischer, it was entitled: "The Church-Yesterday and Today." Fischer began the article by emphasizing the Nazis' long-term plans included the elimination of religious belief and all religious confessions from Germany, and that this process had already begun during their last years in power. Fischer noted the Nazis claimed a victory of the atheistic communist Russians would mean the death of religious belief in Germany. He reminded Germans that the Nazis claimed the Communists would shoot every priest they found, destroy churches, ban religious belief, and generally treat religious believers with scorn and derision if they had won the war.[13]

Looking on from a month after the surrender of Germany and the beginning of the Russian occupation, Fischer claimed the only destroyed church buildings had been those by the effects of the war. The only priests and ministers removed from their positions had been those who were supporters of the Nazis, that church services have continued, and religious freedom has been restored in Germany following years of Nazi persecution. He concluded the Red Army clearly did not want a "Kirchenkampf" and both the Protestants and the Catholics should ally themselves with the new democratic order in Germany. Fischer concluded it would be a painful but necessary process to root out the remaining Fascist sympathizers in the Protestant and Catholic churches but it had be done, especially concerning the "German Christians." The churches could only endanger themselves through opposition to the Soviet occupation and therefore had to reform along democratic lines in cooperation with the Allied authorities.[14]

Another popular theme was the existence of peaceful relations between the Russian Orthodox Church and the Soviet authorities. Many of the initial articles stressed how the Soviet people were struggling to rebuild religious life in the USSR after the ferocious assaults on Russian Orthodoxy by the invading German armies. One notable example was an article by an Oleg Kurganov on August 3, 1945. Kurganov mentioned how the monastery of New Jerusalem in the town of Istra suffered the most, since the Germans stole most of its precious valuables, exploded the bell tower and used the medieval buildings as an ammunition supply depot. Kurganov concluded his article by writing the assault on the monastery was representative of Germany's assault on Russia's religious heritage.[15] A similar article on September 18 also mentioned the destruction of cathedrals and monasteries throughout the Soviet Union by the German army, noting the pillaging of religious valuables and artwork, noting in particular the desecration of the Uspensky Cathedral in Kiev.[16]

The clear intention of these and other articles was to depict the Nazis as the true enemies of religious belief as opposed to the Soviets. Articles testifying to peaceful cooperation between Orthodox leaders and Soviet authorities frequently appeared in *Tägliche Rundschau,* beginning with an article on November 15 entitled "Die Religionsfreiheit in der USSR" by E. Levin. Levin admitted it was true complete legal separation of church and state existed in the USSR, but complete religious freedom existed as well, and had contributed to peaceful relations between religious and secular authorities. Levin also noted the Soviet Union should serve as the model for states with diverse religious groups, since Orthodox, Catholic, Protestant, Jewish, and Islamic religious communities lived in complete peace with each other and with the secular government in Moscow.[17]

The SVAG newspaper made a visible attempt to recruit prominent Protestant leaders in its December 5 1945 article. The head of the Protestant Church Chancellery in Berlin-Brandenburg, Dr. Kurt Krummacher, wrote a lengthy article regarding his time in Soviet captivity from 1943 to 1945, noting the Soviet authorities at the POW camp allowed the German prisoners to celebrate Christmas, even going so far as to provide them with Christmas trees. Krummacher also revealed he had recently met with the head of the Council for Russian Orthodox Church Affairs Georgii Karpov, who assured him any remaining issues between the Russian Orthodox Church and the Soviet government were in the process of being rectified. Much like Levin, Krummacher concluded his article by claiming other churches, including those in Germany, should emulate the model established by the Orthodox Church in the Soviet Union.[18]

At the same time the SVAG authorities were concerned the relatively free environment in the Soviet zone during the early period of the occupation with regards to religious belief could possibly "infect" Red Army soldiers and officer stationed in Germany. A report sent on April 28 1946 from the head of the SVAG Propaganda Administration in Potsdam, V. M. Stroilov, to the head of the Propaganda Administration for Brandenburg I. I. Mil'khiker, illustrated this. Stroilov had attended a recent religious service at the Aleksandr Nevsky cathedral, a Russian Orthodox Church built in the nineteenth century. Stroilov noted he attended the service since he was aware some Orthodox priests who currently served in the Cathedral had, during the Nazi era, praised the German invasion as the only way to save Russia from atheistic Bolshevism. Stroilov informed Mil'khiker he saw seven Red Army officers attending the service, none above the rank of major. He also noted the priest mentioned during the service the suffering inflicted on Russian Orthodox believers by the Nazis during the Second World War. He concluded his report by claiming the small number of Red Army officers attending the service was a good sign, but the Propaganda Administration authorities had to remain vigilant against local Orthodox churches obtaining an "undue influence" over Red Army personnel.[19] Clearly, the SVAG's proclamation of Soviet support for religious belief had its limits when it applied to Soviet soldiers.

Despite the propaganda push during the first seven months of the occupation, SVAG authorities remained dissatisfied with their progress on the question of "religious freedom." In a report written by Arkadi Sobolev, a member of the Political Council of SVAG, and sent to SVAG Supreme Commander Georgii Zhukov on January 26 1946, Sobolev claimed the SVAG needed to redouble its efforts on the religious question. He wrote the SVAG still needed a clear and united religious policy which would prevent clerical reactionaries from making unfavorable comparisons between the Soviet authorities and the Nazis. Furthermore, the Soviet authorities had find progressive-minded clerics, especially in the Protestant Church, in order to use them to gain greater influence over the German population. If the SVAG, particularly its Propaganda Administration, failed to act in this manner, the churches in the Soviet zone would fall under the influence of the "Anglo-Americans" as had already been the case in the American and British zones.[20]

Sobolev's fears were rooted in the fact the KPD still had not clarified its position on the question of religious freedom, and, given the KPD's and the SVAG's aggressive push to secularize the education system in fall of 1945 and spring of 1946, this led to charges by Protestant and Catholic clerics as well as CDU leaders the SVAG and their German "friends" in the KPD were determined to create an atheistic society in Germany. The leadership of the KPD was also aware of this possibility. In a report sent a few months earlier to Wilhelm Pieck by Otto Winzer, the head of the Abteilung Volksbildung in the Soviet Sector of Berlin, Winzer noted numerous Protestant and Catholic clergy in the Soviet zone assumed the educational policies of the KPD and the SVAG gave proof to their suspicions both were avowedly atheistic.[21]

It would not be until the KPD merged with the SPD to form the Socialist Unity Party in April 1946 that the German Communists finally began to clarify their position on the question of religious freedom. The first hint of the SED's toleration of religious freedom occurred in April 1946, when the SED agreed to allow optional after-hours religious education in secondary schools in the Soviet zone, moving away slightly from their earlier determination to completely secularize the education system in the Soviet zone.[22]

This step was clearly not enough for the SED's executive leadership in countering charges made by the churches and CDU that SED was an avowedly atheist political party. A directive dated July 5, 1946, sent by Dr. Naas Weiman, the deputy head of the SED's Department for Culture and Education, to all provincial and district SED leaders in the Soviet zone, demonstrated this. The directive informed them they had to incorporate three central points regarding religious freedom in their efforts to win the support of the Soviet zone's inhabitants. The first was the socialist transformation of Germany must allow freedom of thought, including the free exercise of religious belief. The second was the possession of religious belief should not be a barrier against any German's participation in the building of Socialism. The third was to remain aware the churches themselves have a positive contribution to make to the reconstruction of Germany after the disastrous effects of Nazism and the Second World War. The directive concluded by emphasizing SED party members should also remind the population of the SED's open support of SVAG efforts to reconstruct church buildings and assist their material needs.[23]

By this point, the SED was also using the party newspaper, *Neues Deutschland*, in a manner similar to the SVAG newspaper *Tägliche Rundschau*, printing newspaper articles by Protestant clergy who argued there was common ground between Christianity and Marxism-Leninism. In an article in the July 26 issue of the SED newspaper, the SED and SVAG favorite Kurt Rackwtiz, claimed since Socialists and Christians shared beliefs on a number of key issues, genuine and lasting compromise between church and State in a future socialist Germany was entirely possible. Conversely, Rackwitz also noted the churches in Germany could no longer expect the same privileges from state authorities, who were rightly committed to building a secular political order.[24]

While this article was followed by several others in a similar vein, it would not be until August 30 1946 as elections neared in the Soviet zone, that the leadership of the SED finally issued its attempt at a definitive statement regarding its position on religious freedom in the pages of *Neues Deutschland*. In a statement signed by SED leaders Wilhelm Pieck and Otto Grotewohl, the party proclaimed all antifascist and progressive Christians could count themselves as an important part of all democratic forces in the Soviet zone. This was especially true since the goals of the SED's scientific socialism were the same as those of the churches, namely the pursuit of peace, an end to poverty, and recovery from the effects of the war. Pieck and Grotewohl promised full religious freedom would exist in a German state under SED leadership, but the party rejected the notion it would subject itself to religious concerns, just as the church should not expect to submit itself in any partisan sense.[25]

Weiman sent another directive dated September 30 1946 to all district and provincial SED leaders. Weiman ordered them to make immediate contact with "Socialist Priests" and use them to assist the SED in the next month's elections, especially in dispelling rumors concerning the hostility of the SED towards religious belief.[26] The next day at the Martin Luther celebrations in the city of Eisleben in Sachsen-Anhalt, SED leader Wihlem Pieck gave a speech in the presence of Otto Dibelius, Moritz Mitzenheim, Kurt Krummacher, and other Protestant Church leaders which praised its role in rebuilding democracy in the Soviet zone. Pieck specifically pointed out both the SED and the church were dedicated to "the democratic Renewal, the preservation of National Unity, and the securing of peace throughout Germany and Europe."[27]

The final propaganda push by the SED and their clerical allies was a front page article in *Neues Deutschland*, signed by a number of Protestant clergy in all five provinces of the Soviet zone, and likely written by Kurt Rackwitz. The article, entitled "Christianity and Socialism are not Opponents" (*Christentum und Sozialismus sind keine Gegensatze*) argued the socialist order which the SED and the SVAG would construct in the Soviet zone came very close to the central tenets of Christianity. The author made a specific comparison to the dictum of Matthew 22:37, that one should love God with all their soul and love their neighbor as themselves. It asked the readers to remind themselves of the shared imprisonment in concentration camps by socialists and Christians under the Nazi regime, to keep in mind the SED has worked with the Soviets to restore religious freedom to Germany, and has "given us back the task of religious education, which only we can accomplish successfully."[28]

The SVAG also continued their own propaganda offensive concerning the question of religious freedom during the run up to the zonal elections of October 1946. Officials in the SVAG's Propaganda Administration in Brandenburg noted the CDU's propagandizing concerning the SED's determination to enforce state atheism continued to have a damaging effect on the political fortunes of the SED in the upcoming elections. A report sent to Mil'khiker, from the head of Propaganda Administration for the city of Eberswald, N. M. Rosenzweig on August 31 1946 is an excellent example of this. Rosenzweig wrote to his superior the combined force of the CDU and their clerical allies had successfully portrayed the SED as intent on enforcing an atheist social order on Germany, a social order directly modeled on the Soviet Union. Rosenzweig argued the SVAG had to use its authority to prevent the continued collaboration of the churches and the CDU. One of the key tools it should use, according to Rosenzweig, was to continue to stress the existence of religious freedom in the Soviet Union.[29]

The SVAG had already implemented this policy in the pages of *Tägliche Rundschau* during the months leading up to the zonal elections of October 1946. On August 17, the newspaper printed out a front page article about the

status of the Orthodox Church in the Soviet Union. The author, a Soviet jour-
nalist named O. I. Tugan-Baranovskii, pointed out to readers of the Orthodox
Church's role in assisting the Soviet regime in defeating the Nazi invaders,
clear evidence of positive relations between the Orthodox Church and the
Soviet state. He also noted private religious education existed in the homes
of Soviet citizens, and the fact the Orthodox church operated its own newspapers, seminaries, and printing presses independently from state control.
The article concluded with the claim that the idea the Soviet authorities were
hostile to religious freedom was simply a myth spread by those who wished
to undermine the accomplishments of the USSR.[30]

Far more ambitious, however, was an article from the August 23 issue.
The issue contained a lengthy discussion by Metropolitan Alexander, head
of the Russia Orthodox church in Germany and Belgium, concerning his
recent visit to the Soviet Union in order to observe the status of the Orthodox
church under Communist rule. Alexander reported very positively on what he
observed in the Soviet Union, particularly his meetings with religious leaders
in Kiev and Moscow. He specifically noted in the article the Soviet government's attempts to assist the reconstruction of churches destroyed by the Nazi
invaders, as well as the full attendance at every religious service he attended.
Alexander noted in the article his visit had convinced him religious life was
thriving in the Soviet Union, and the Soviet model of church-State relations
could serve as an inspiration for the rest of Europe.[31]

The propaganda offensive concerning religious freedom in a future socialist Germany coincided with a general restraint on the part of SVAG and SED
authorities with regards to their relations with the Protestant and Catholic
churches during the early period of the occupation. While the determination
of both SVAG and SED education officials to secularize the German secondary education system led to some early conflicts with the church leadership
in Berlin-Brandenburg, religious charitable activity and religious youth and
women's work were generally not harassed by state authorities. The Soviet
authorities still hoped the SED's success in the upcoming zonal elections
in October would allow it to expand its influence in the Western zones of
Germany. This eventually would lead to an SED-dominated, united Germany
under Soviet control, which then could implement the same religious policies
which actually existed in the Soviet Union, policies which marginalized any
social or public role for any religious institutions.

The SVAG and the SED were careful to not implement Stalinist social,
economic, political, and religious policies during this early period, which
could jeopardize their chances of ruling a united Germany. Therefore, the
SVAG authorities were very careful not to create too great of dichotomy
between their propaganda supporting religious freedom and the reality of

religious life in the Soviet zone. Once the likelihood of the Western zones falling under Soviet influence became more distant as the occupation continued into 1947 and 1948, the SVAG and SED religious policies became more restrictive. This did not keep them from continuing their propaganda drive of religious freedom, just as they would never abandon their official commitment to a unified Germany despite the fact the Soviet policies of Stalinization in their zone made political and economic unification very unlikely.

THE PROPAGANDA CAMPAIGN IN THE AFTERMATH OF THE ZONAL ELECTIONS NOVEMBER 1946-DECEMBER 1947

As mentioned earlier, the zonal elections of October 1946 did not go well for the SED. While it was still the strongest political party in the Soviet Zone with fifty-three percent of the vote, its rivals the CDU, the LDP, and, in Berlin, the SPD, had done far better under the discriminatory tactics of the SVAG authorities than almost anyone in the SVAG or the SED thought possible.[32] In a report sent on November 18, 1946, to the head of the Central Committee's Foreign Department, Andrei Zhdanov, Colonel Sergei Tiul'panov admitted the "atheist" element played a substantial role in the SED's poor showing. Tiul'panov claimed despite the SVAG and the SED's attempts to portray themselves as supportive of religious freedom, the CDU and the churches were able to paint both as intent on creating an atheist social and political order in Germany. He argued the SVAG and SED would need to redouble their propaganda efforts against "reactionary" attacks by Christian clergy and their political allies, which was, by this time, the usual response.[33]

Ultimately the results of the zonal elections in October 1946 did little to alter the SVAG and SED's path to creating a German state on the Soviet model, especially once cooperation between the Soviets and the Western Allies regarding the administration of Germany began to break down. The elections made both the SED and the Soviet authorities more insecure of the degree of support they received from the population of the Soviet zone.

Just as Tiul'panov stated in his report to Zhdanov, the SVAG and the SED increased their propaganda efforts regarding the question of "religious freedom" in a future socialist Germany. Both *Tägliche Rundschau* and *Neues Deutschland* continued to emphasize the existence of religious freedom under the Soviet government, and how this would exist in a socialist Germany as well. The Christmas issue of *Tägliche Rundschau* combined this theme with another prominent topic in the SVAG newspaper, the benevolent treatment of German POWs who remained in Soviet hands. The article informed German families their husbands and sons were still allowed to celebrate Christmas with religious services with the support of Soviet military officials in the POW camps, just as SVAG officials allowed religious Germans to continue to observe Christmas.[34]

The Christmas 1946 issue of *Neues Deutschland* contained an article by Kurt Rackwitz. He emphasized religious Germans needed to rededicate themselves to the unified causes of Christian brotherhood and socialism in the coming year. Rackwitz concluded the article by claiming only if religious Germans understood the crucial linkage between Christianity and socialism could a peaceful and democratic government be created in Germany.[35]

In the aftermath of the disastrous October 1946 zonal elections, Rackwitz and other leftist Protestant clergy in Berlin-Brandenburg were eager to actively assist the SED in fending off additional attacks from the Protestant Church leadership and the CDU. Their organization, "The Working Group of Religious Socialists" had its founding conference in the Soviet sector of Berlin from November 9 to November 11, and reported on its activities to SED leader Wilhelm Pieck on November 26. Led by Rackwitz, the group had fairly extensive ambitions for its activities. In the report Pieck received, Rackwitz argued their first goal was first was make Christians aware that belief in Christ must also be followed by belief in Socialism. They would instruct all of their parishioners a true Christian must also be a socialist. They also promised to make all Christians in Germany aware atheism was not prerequisite for belief in Socialism.[36]

Rackwitz also informed Pieck they wanted to work with the other Evangelical clergy and laity to ensure religious institutions in Germany would support the creation of socialist democracy. It also would strive to create a community of socialist priests, ministers, theologians, and seminarians, as well as to win over sympathetic members of the church administration at all levels throughout Germany. Furthermore, Rackwitz and his followers promised to inform religious believers and in the religious press the SED's positive attitude towards religious freedom.[37]

Rackwitz and the other leaders of the Working Group of Religious Socialists sent another letter to Pieck and SED co-leader Otto Grotewohl on December 11, 1946. The letter thanked the SED for its declaration supporting religious freedom. They admitted often in Germany's past religious leaders and institutions have often served as an obstacle to the socialist parties, although this will no longer be the case. The letter concluded with a plea by the Working Group of Religious Socialists stating their hope the people of Germany were not so cynical after twelve years of Nazi lies that they would doubt the promises of the SED to support religious freedom.[38]

The importance of the Working Group of Religious Socialists for the leadership of the Protestant Church in Berlin-Brandenburg was minimal.

The office records of Bishop Otto Dibelius scarcely mention the activities of Rackwitz and the Working Group of Religious Socialists, besides the occasional warning to clergy to avoid following political groups which ascribed to a "materialist-atheistic worldview" and especially of attempting to link Christian theology with Marxism-Leninism. Even Protestant Church leaders such as Kurt Krummacher and the Bishop of Thuringia, Moritz Mitzenheim, who were inclined to a more cooperative relationship with the SVAG and SED, were still quite resistant to SED policies regarding Evangelical administration of schools and hospitals. Rackwitz and his followers lacked an appeal to these clerics, since neither Krummacher nor Mitzenheim were interested in attempting to merge Christianity with Marxism-Leninism.[39]

Rackwitz was disappointed in the progress made by members of the Working Group during its first year of existence in winning over more of the clergy and laity to their cause. On October 22, 1947, after his organization was renamed the Union of Socialist Priests, he wrote a letter to Pieck and Grotewohl about his concerns about the lack of progress made by the socialist clerics. Rackwitz blamed SED party members whose open hostility to religious belief aided reactionaries in the Protestant and Catholic churches. He specifically pointed to a meeting of cultural functionaries of the SED (which he referred to as "our party") in Berlin on at the beginning of October, during which a Dr. Stern and a Dr. Ruhiner made successive speeches arguing the fundamental tenets of Marxism-Leninism left no room for Christian beliefs.[40]

Rackwitz argued these statements only played into the hands of reactionary clergymen who completely opposed the SED. He suggested a rejection of the principle of atheism as a prerequisite for membership in the SED would go a long way to convincing religious Germans the Socialist Unity Party was not hostile to religious institutions. He argued many religious Germans could not abandon their belief in God. Therefore if the SED openly proclaimed atheism and dialectical materialism, this would only serve to drive Christians into the hands of the CDU. According to Rackwitz, anything less than neutrality on the religious question for party membership would put "our politicians" at a disadvantage, although he understood many of the party members of the SED would maintain an atheistic worldview. He concluded by arguing his appeal was based not his profession as a Protestant cleric, but as a dedicated member of the SED who wanted it to lead a democratic, antifascist Germany.[41]

Given the fact the SED was remaking itself as a Stalinist "Party of the New Type" during this period Rackwitz could hardly have expected a benevolent response. In fact, Rackwitz did not receive a response at all. Otto Grotewohl did reference Rackwitz's letter in a memorandum sent to Wilhelm Pieck on November 10, 1947. Grotewohl wrote while the SED could not abandon dialectical materialism as part of the foundations of Marxism, it could be more careful concerning how this was presented in party schools and for public consumption, and emphasized it was not in the SED's interests to appear hostile to religious institutions. He promised at the end of the memorandum he would discuss the issue fellow party leaders Ulbricht, Meier, Ackermann, and Oelssner.[42]

Pieck also responded to Rackwitz's concerns six days later on November 23 in a letter sent to Grotewohl, Ulbricht, Ackermann, Meier, and Oelssner. Pieck wrote all SED party members had to be well-versed in fundamentals of Marxism-Leninism. This meant teachers in party schools had to be knowledgeable of and be able to instruct the principles of dialectical materialism, since dialectical materialism was an essential element of the philosophical foundations of Marxism-Leninism. This did not mean religious Germans could not be members of the Socialist Unity Party, but neither could the SED abandon dialectical materialism as an essential part of their ideology.[43]

Pieck added the churches did not automatically place themselves in conflict with the SED merely because they were religious institutions, but did so when they opposed the policies of the SED. This in turn would cause the clergy, especially those who shared the views of the SED, to make a choice between the party and their clerical leadership. If the churches truly desired peace between it and the SED, it could continue its work among religious Germans but had to recognize the SED would make every effort to spread its influence through an ever-broader segment of the population. Ultimately the churches could not prevent this.[44]

Clearly the SED's public pronouncements of support for religious freedom had its limits when placed against its ideological commitment to dialectical materialism and atheism. This was also the case with the SVAG authorities. On May 22, 1947, Tiul'panov sent a letter to the heads of the Information Administration for the five provinces of the Soviet zone, entitled "Church Life in Contemporary Germany." Tiul'panov noted the active involvement of the Protestant and Catholic churches in political life in the Western zones of Germany, would soon emerge in the Soviet zone. Tiul'panov pointed to Otto Dibelius, as among the most active clerical collaborators with the CDU. Dibelius had been instrumental, according to Tiul'panov, in attempting to link the SVAG and the SED with militant atheism.[45]

Tiul'panov mentioned it was in the SVAG's direct interests to recruit "progressive" clerics against the "reactionaries" in both the Protestant and Catholic churches, a process which would be eased by the SVAG's and SED's constant emphasis of religious freedom under socialist rule. At the end of his report, he outlined SVAG's religious policies and its specific goals for the Protestant and Catholic churches in Germany. The first goals was to shift the church leadership organs from West to East Berlin, there it will be under their influence. The second was to decrease the influence of the church under young people and elimination the church-run youth organizations. The third, final, and most important goal was to reduce the influence of conservative clergymen in the churches and to neutralize religious institutions in the area of politics.[46]

As their private correspondence reveals, despite their propaganda concerning religious freedom, neither SVAG nor the SED believed in anything but a very limited institutional role for the churches in a future socialist Germany. This did not mean the propaganda offensive of "religious freedom" in the pages of *Neues Deutschland* and *Tägliche Rundschau* ended as the Soviet occupation entered 1947 and the process of Stalinization began to accelerate. An article in *Neues Deutschland* on February 2 1947 entitled "Our Position towards the Churches and Christianity" demonstrates a subtle shift in the SED's propaganda approach. Written by one of the SED's chief ideology experts, Otto Maier, the article started by claiming the SED was the last institution in Germany which desired any confrontation with the Catholic and Protestant churches. Maier rather surprisingly wrote the SED recognized the supreme authority of the churches in spiritual affairs. The churches must be prepared to accept the full and complete authority of the state in secular affairs. He claimed while Christians and socialists may have different views on metaphysical issues, their ultimate goal of peace and an alleviation of poverty was the same. The articled denounced the demagogues in the CDU and the churches who argued the SED was hostile to religious beliefs.[47]

Surprisingly, given the predominance of KPD members in the leadership of the SED, Maier pointed to the SPD's Gothaer Programm of 1875 and its Erfurter Programm of 1891, in which the SPD recognized freedom of religious belief as a fundamental human right, as evidence German socialists had always tolerated the *private* expression of religious belief. He concluded the article by stating the SED would continue to abide by this respect for religious freedom, but forcibly concluded the churches would never play a political role in the new Germany led by the SED, since "political religious movements are reactionary elements within reactionary states."[48]

Tägliche Rundschau continued to print articles which testified to the existence of religious freedom in the Soviet Union. A prominent leader of the FDJ in the Soviet zone, Robert Menzel, wrote an article in the August 30, 1947 concerning his examination of religious life in the Soviet Union. Menzel specifically mentioned his visit to the St. Nikolai-Kirche in Leningrad. He commented the Orthodox services he viewed during his week in Leningrad were consistently full of worshipers, both men and women. Menzel recounted how he asked the Orthodox priests he encountered at the church whether the Soviet claims for the existence of religious freedom in the Soviet Union was a mere façade, which the priests sharply denied. According to Menzel, the priests he encountered stated they were free to celebrate all religious holidays and the Orthodox churches were always full of parishioners. He concluded his article by recounting the claim of numerous Orthodox priests who assured him the Soviet government in the previous thirty years had never interfered with the internal affairs of the Orthodox Church or the freedom exercise of religious belief by Soviet citizens.[49]

The use of the Russian Orthodox Church's status in the Soviet Union for propaganda in the Soviet zone of Germany was approved of at the highest level of the Soviet government. The head of the Council for Orthodox Church Affairs, Georgii Karpov, in January 1947, reported to Politburo member Georgii Malenkov, head of the Central Committee of the Soviet Union's Communist Party Secretariat, concerning this policy. Karpov informed him Russian Orthodox clerics who met with foreign visitors in Moscow and Leningrad and testified to the existence of complete religious freedom in the USSR provided a valuable service for the Soviet state. Karpov noted this was especially important for SVAG propaganda in Germany, since the exiled Russian Orthodox clergy in the Western zones of Germany were actively collaborating with the American and British authorities in spreading "anti-Soviet" propaganda.[50]

The other main aspect of the "religious freedom" campaign, to split clerical "progressives" from "reactionaries" and create schisms in the Protestant and Catholic churches in the Soviet zone was also implemented on the orders of the Soviet government. The head of the Communist Party's Central Committee for Agitation and Propaganda (Agitprop), G. F. Aleksandrov, reported to Soviet ideology chief Andrei Zhdanov on October 1946 concerning SVAG attempts to demonstrate its tolerance for open expressions of religious faith. Aleksandrov specifically referred to the recent SVAG permission to allow the Protestant Church to publically commemorate the three hundredth anniversary of the death of Martin Luther in the cities of Eisleben and Berlin. He informed Zhdanov the leadership of the Catholic and Protestant churches in the Soviet and Western zones was entirely reactionary, and SVAG policies which supported "religious freedom" would make it easier to divide the "progressive" clergy from its "reactionary" leaders.[51]

Throughout 1947 and 1948, SVAG and to a lesser extent SED authorities in the German organs of self-government significantly altered the two parts of the "religious freedom" campaign. Gradually the themes of "religious freedom" in the Soviet Union were emphasized less and less, besides occasional references to freedom of belief in the SED-led *Volkscongress*-sponsored all-German constitution. Instead, atheistic-scientific propaganda explicitly attacking religious leaders and religious institutions gradually replaced it. In addition, another theme emerged regarding the religious question in the Soviet zone, namely the "progressive" role played by the Protestant Church as opposed to the "reactionary" politics of the Catholic Church.

This was reflected in the pages of *Tägliche Rundschau* and *Neues Deutschland,* as well as reports of the SVAG's Information Administration and correspondence between the leaders of the SED. The newspapers devoted much more of their time to attacking certain positions of the Protestant and Catholic churches with regards to political and educational issues. An example of this trend is an article in the October 17 1947 issue of *Neues Deutschland.* The unnamed author of the article denounced the CDU in the Soviet zone as well as the leadership of the Catholic and Protestant churches of Berlin-Brandenburg for opposing the wishes of the "progressive majority of parents in Berlin" who desired an entirely secular school system.[52]

The SED was not yet willing to cede the ground to the CDU on the religious freedom question. On November 16 1947, a few weeks before the SVAG's removal of Jakob Kaiser ended the political independence of the CDU, Kurt Rackwitz wrote a front page article entitled: "A New Path for the Churches." Rackwitz asked whether the church had abandoned the path that leads to "the torture of humanity, Capitalism, and Militarism." He suggested the positions taken by many Protestant and Catholic clergy in the Soviet and Western zones indicated the answer was no. Rackwitz emphasized the churches should allow the religious socialists who had clearly opposed Hitler to emerge to the forefront in the leadership of the Protestant Church, and not to be swayed by the nationalist and reactionary appeals of the CDU. Rackwitz concluded his article with a firm statement that the church must reconcile itself with the aims of the working classes, and accept that out of the ashes of war a new, dynamic, and just social order would be created.[53]

The SED newspaper also continued to publish articles highlighting the cooperative relationship between the SVAG authorities and certain leaders of the Protestant Church. On December 17, 1947, *Neues Deutschland* contained an article discussing a meeting between the Provost for Brandenburg, Heinrich Gruber, the head of the church Chancellery, Kurt Krummacher and Colonel Sergei Tiul'panov. Krummacher and Gruber made three requests to Tiul'panov. The first was a public promise by SVAG authorities to continue religious services in the Soviet internment camps. The second was to provide a "Christmas amnesty" to German youths who had been arrested by Soviet officials during the last four months. The third and final was for the SVAG to return church bells to Evangelical communities in the cities of Oranienburg and Apolda which had originally been seized by the Nazis. Tiul'panov was non-committal on the first two requests but promised the SVAG would eagerly acquiesce to the third request. The article concluded meetings such as this demonstrated the continued support of the SVAG authorities for the preservation of religious freedom in Germany.[54]

THE PROPAGANDA DRIVE DURING THE STALINIST TRANSFORMATION OF THE SOVIET ZONE, JANUARY 1948-OCTOBER 1949

Ironically, *Tägliche Rundschau* had, throughout 1948, largely abandoned the newspaper articles discussing religious freedom in the Soviet Union, although they continued to emphasize the policies of the SED which promoted religious freedom in the Soviet zone. An article in page three of the October 29 1948 issue of the newspaper discussed section five of the German Constitution proposed by the SED-dominated *Volkscongress* a few months before. The unnamed author of the article pointed out section five of the Constitution specifically preserved the SED's acceptance of religious freedom, and served as a refutation of charges of the CDU in the Western zones the SED was an "atheistic" political party. Section five specifically guaranteed religious freedom in Germany, and proclaimed there would be no "state church" in the future "German Democratic Republic." In addition, it expressly forbid the use of the churches for political purposes. The section also stated voluntary religious education would be allowed in the schools areas after regular school hours, to be provided by the Protestant and Catholic churches.[55]

In the Information Administration, Tiul'panov began to urge his subordinates in the Soviet zone to gradually scale back the "religious freedom" campaign and instead emphasize in SVAG propaganda material of a "scientific-atheistic character." In a report sent from Tiul'panov to K. V. Martem'ianov, the head of the Propaganda Administration in Brandenburg, on February 12, 1949, Tiul'panov discussed this theme in some detail. Tiul'panov informed Martem'ianov the Protestant and Catholic churches, in league with the CDU in the Western zones as well as British and American authorities, would continue to attack the accomplishments of the SVAG and the SED in the Soviet zone. In particular, "reactionary clergy" would demonize both the SED and the SVAG as determined to force atheism on the German population.[56]

Because of this situation, Tiul'panov argued Martem'ianov and those under his command were not allow "religious fanatics" to disseminate their own propaganda, and nor to allow the churches to publicly claim the SVAG and the SED were attacking religious institutions. Tiul'panov concluded his report by arguing "the heart of this work" had to be the dissemination of scientific-Marxist propaganda, through brochures, leaflets, speeches, presentations on the radio, and so on. It was also vital to disseminate material indicating the churches' were involved in activities of an anti-Soviet and antidemocratic character.[57]

Three days later, Martem'ianov sent a similar report to his subordinates in the SVAG's Information Administration in the province of Brandenburg. Martem'ianov instructed them, in addition to exercising greater control over the social and charitable activities of the churches, to work more aggressively in disseminating "scientific-atheistic" propaganda. He insisted they had to make absolutely sure the churches did not take political positions opposed to those of the SVAG and the SED. The goal of the SVAG authorities was to create in the German people a scientific-atheistic worldview, which meant removing the churches from a visible position in German society. At the conclusion of his report, Martem'ianov demanded his subordinates to be sure they used the most qualified people in their staffs to handle this assignment, and work in close coordination with the SED's anti-religious specialists. They also needed to gather more materials that provided evidence of the oppositional activities of both the Protestant and Catholic churches, as well as materials concerning personal information regarding clerics engaged in "antidemocratic" or "anti-Soviet" agitation.[58]

As Martem'ianov's instructions suggest, the SED had also largely abandoned much of the "religious freedom" propaganda campaign in favor of scientific-atheistic propaganda that attacked not only religious institutions but the very basis for religious belief. In a similar manner, *Neues Deutschland* blamed religious "reactionaries" for delaying necessary political and educational reforms in the Soviet zone. One notable example came from the November 14, 1948, issue of *Neues Deutschland*. An article on page five blamed the CDU in both the Western and Soviet sectors of Berlin for allowing the "religious motivations" of the Catholic and Protestant church to guide their attempts to hold up attempts to secularize the education system in Berlin.[59]

A more direct attack appeared in the February 13, 1949, issue of the SED newspaper. However, it also represented the more sophisticated tactics of the SED, which attempted to create a schism between the Protestant and Catholic churches in the Soviet zone of Germany. The article on page four, entitled "The Struggle against Clerical reaction in Hungary," discussed the trial in Budapest of Cardinal Joseph Mindszenty. It justified the trial of Mindszenty by arguing the Catholic churches throughout Eastern Europe, under direct orders from the Vatican, had waged a reactionary campaign against progressive political, social, and economic reforms in Eastern Europe

since the end of the Second World War. The article concluded with a statement which affirmed the Lutheran, Calvinist and many other European
Protestant churches had taken a "progressive" attitude towards the creation
of Soviet-style democracy following the end of the Second World War. In
comparison, the Catholic Church everywhere sided with counter-revolution,
and would continue to be used by the United States and "the other imperialist
powers."[60]

These tactics were not limited to the Soviet zone of Germany, as they
were replicated in all areas of Europe that fell under Soviet domination after
the Second World War. Indeed, it can be argued that Soviet tactics against
the Catholic Church in their zone were among the mildest during the time
period, certainly in comparison to the brutal repressions exercised in Ukraine,
Romania, and the Baltic States, which were designed to eliminate their influence entirely. It is not an exaggeration to state that Stalin viewed the church
in general and Pius XII in particular as dangerous enemies during the early
Cold War era, and was determined to destroy any influence they could play
over events in Central and Eastern Europe.[61]

The SED newspaper continued this tactic throughout 1949. The issue of
Neues Deutschland on April 3 1949 contained a front page article entitled
"The Church for the World Peace Movement." The article was written by
Bishop Beste of Mecklenburg, a prominent opponent in the Protestant hierarchy to Dibelius's harder line towards the Soviet and SED authorities. Beste
wrote the church would never again be used for propagandistic purposes or
help to create enemies between different states. The Protestant Church also
would try to prevent the violence of war from emerging in Europe again, with
the aid of democratic forces in the Soviet zone.[62]

Tägliche Rundschau eventually adopted this propaganda tactic as well,
attacking the Catholic Church and its leadership as leading the forces of international reaction, while noting the importance of "progressive" voices in the
Protestant Church in Germany. One notable article which attacked both Pius
XII and Cardinal Preysing came from the July 6, 1949, issue. The unnamed
author of the article stated Pius XII, along with his allies in Spain, Portugal,
and Berlin, in particular Cardinal Preysing, were the foremost allies of the
United States in its attempt to pursue the "Cold War" dividing the world into
democratic and imperialist spheres. The article also pointed to the Concordat
between the Vatican and Hitler in 1933 as evidence of Papal sympathy for
and collusion with Fascism.[63]

An article which appeared in August 27 in *Tägliche Rundschau,* emphasized the "reactionary" role played by Catholic Church in Europe. Entitled,
"Why has the Vatican played its last card?" and written by an anonymous
author who claimed to be a Protestant cleric, the article attacked Pius XII's

threat to excommunicate European Catholics who joined Communist parties in Europe, including the Socialist Unity Party in the Soviet zone. The author argued the Vatican saw Communism as a threat to its attempts to gain global spiritual influence, although this was not because Communism was anti-religious, since as the Orthodox Church functioned freely in the Soviet Union. Instead, the Catholic Church feared losing its "reactionary" influence over the newly constructed people's democracies in Eastern Europe. The author also claimed evidence of the Vatican's plans was its failure to condemn or excommunicate Hitler, because they viewed him as an ally in spreading their influence throughout Europe. The article did offer a minor concession to Catholics is the Soviet zone as it complemented individual Catholics for their bravery in joining Communist parties throughout Europe.[64]

Despite the attempts to separate the "progressive" Protestant Church from the "reactionary" Catholic Church, the SED and the SVAG leadership recognized attempts to split the churches in Berlin-Brandenburg would not bear immediate fruit. By 1949 Dibelius and Preysing had openly proclaimed their resistance to SVAG and SED policies, which they viewed as creating a new dictatorship in the Soviet zone of Germany. SED leader Wilhelm Pieck reported to the SED Secretariat in August 1949 Otto Dibelius continued to meet with members of the CDU in the Western sectors of Berlin, for the specific purpose of undermining SED policies in the Soviet zone. Pieck admitted Dibelius's belief the SVAG and SED created a new "red" German dictatorship left little doubt he would be an implacable enemy in the years to come.[65]

The SED leadership also had little doubt about the continued hostility of the Catholic Church in Berlin-Brandenburg to any German government led by the SED. A party resolution dated August 10, 1949, noted Preysing's support of Pius XII's recent declaration concerning the excommunication of Catholics for joining a Communist party. The SED leadership viewed this as an attempt to undermine the authority and legitimacy of Communist countries everywhere in Europe, but also as an opportunity for the SED to step up a recruitment drive of "progressive" Catholics in the Soviet zone.[66]

Likewise, the officials in the SVAG Information Administration in Brandenburg in 1949 had little doubt of the continued resistance of clerical "reactionaries" to the policies of the SVAG and SED would continue despite the three year "religious freedom" campaign and the more recent attempts to indoctrinate the population of the Soviet zone with scientific-atheistic propaganda. In a report sent by Martem'ianov to Tiul'panov on February 29, 1949, Martem'ianov wrote the Catholic and Protestant church leadership continued to undermine the CDU's attempts to align itself with the SED. He noted reactionary clerical leaders in Berlin-Brandenburg still had considerable success at convincing religious Germans the SED was determined to create an atheistic society in Germany. He concluded his report by assuring Tiul'panov he felt the change in Soviet propaganda from emphasizing religious freedom to emphasizing atheism and scientific materialism was the correct course, but it would take some time before it demonstrated any concrete results.[67]

With regards to the clergy of the Protestant Church in Berlin-Brandenburg, the SVAG-SED "religious freedom" propaganda campaign did have a limited but measurable effect. This was largely limited during the period of the Soviet occupation to lower-level clerics such as Kurt Rackwitz. In Brandenburg, many of the clerics in Evangelical Church concurred with Dibelius's openly hostile position to the communist authorities, such as their support of Dibelius's decision to publish his famous *Hirtenbrief* on June 1, 1949, which compared the communist order built by the SVAG and the SED to the Nazi regime. Two weeks after the letter was published, Dr. Hans Asmussen, the head of the EKD's press service, proclaimed in an open letter to the Protestant laity that the leadership of the church in Berlin-Brandenburg supported Dibelius's recent statement regarding political and religious life in the Soviet zone. Asmussen wrote the Protestant Church in the Soviet zone had been subject to continual intimidation and harassment. He also called upon clergy and laity in the West to support the embattled clergy within the Soviet zone of Germany and not to forget them in their struggles.[68]

Similarly, SED and SVAG propaganda efforts to split the "reactionary" Catholic Church from the "progressive" Protestant church in 1948 and 1949 had little effect on the church leadership in Brandenburg. Dibelius and von Preysing continued to make common cause on a number of issues central to both churches, such as their joint letter to the four military governments in Berlin protesting the School law of May 1949, which secularized the school system in the four sectors of the city.[69]

Fissures did emerge, however, between Dibelius and the rest of the leadership of the Protestant Church in the rest of the Soviet zone, as well as Heinrich Gruber and Kurt Krummacher. Also, Bishop Mitzenheim of Thuringia and Bishop Beste of Mecklenburg moved away from Dibelius's confrontational policy and searched for areas of cooperation with the SVAG and especially the SED authorities.[70] The emergence of this split in the Protestant leadership in Brandenburg was publicly obvious following Dibelius's and Gruber's visit to the now Soviet-run concentration camp at Sachsenhausen in March 1950. Gruber's stated opinion concerning relatively benign conditions at the camp in comparison to how it was administered under the Nazis was in sharp contrast with Dibelius's negative comparison between the two.[71]

It was also during this time that Karl Barth and his rejection of open conflict between the Protestant Church and the Communist State increased its influence over younger pastors and theologians. While Barth and his followers, such as Johannes Hamel, rejected the overtly propagandistic style of Kurt Rackwitz, they also argued against the confrontational anticommunist approach which denied any political legitimacy to the SED-regime, or eventually in the case of Dibelius, claimed East Germans owed no allegiance to their government. While this was limited to correspondence between Protestant pastors in the Soviet zone and Barth in Switzerland during the period of the Soviet occupation emerged as a full-fledged debate in the church in the 1950s.[72] This rupture would continue to fester throughout the 1960s until the temporary victory of the collaborationist "Kirche im Sozialismus" policy in the late 1960s.

CONCLUSION

The "religious freedom" propaganda campaign represented SVAG and SED religious policies at their most duplicitous. Neither the Soviet authorities nor their German allies seriously believed either the Protestant or the Catholic Church would have any long-term role in a Soviet-dominated Germany. The propaganda campaign roughly followed the general trend of SVAG and SED policies towards religious charitable work as well as youth and women's organizations. Just as a limited toleration for these activities existed on the part of the SVAG and the SED during the early period of the occupation, the "religious freedom" campaign was a temporary tactic while the SVAG and the SED established the foundations of the GDR.

Ultimately the propaganda campaign failed in its objective of winning over the majority of the Christian clergy in Berlin-Brandenburg, besides a handful of exceptions such as Kurt Rackwitz who were already inclined to cooperate with the Soviet authorities. The main reason for its failure was SVAG and SED claims of support for "religious freedom" contrasted too sharply with the reality of religious life in the Soviet zone. This resulted in the increasing estrangement of the Protestant and Catholic leadership from the Stalinist regime constructed in the Soviet zone, leading directly to the intense church-state conflicts during the beginning of the Ulbricht era in the 1950s.

Yet "religious freedom" propaganda campaign was more complicated than just an attempt to demonstrate to the inhabitants of the Soviet zone the existence of religious freedom in the Soviet Union. Towards the end of the occupation, as the Soviet offensive against the Vatican increased in its intensity, both *Tägliche Rundschau* and *Neues Deutschland* attempted to separate the "progressive" Protestant Church from the "reactionary" Catholic Church. While this would predate the "double isolation" of the Catholic Church noted in the historiography of church-state relations in the GDR, it had very little success with the Protestant Church leadership in Berlin-Brandenburg. The strongly anti-Communist Otto Dibelius and Konrad von Preysing found common cause on the number of issues, in particular SVAG and SED religious education policies. Nor do the conversations of the Protestant Church leadership in the Soviet zone indicate any deep hostility to the Catholic Church in the Soviet zone or even the Vatican.

The impact of the "religious freedom" campaign had on the Protestant and Catholic laity is difficult to exactly determine given the available sources. Officials in the SVAG's Propaganda/Information Administration often complained of the continued (and largely correct) belief among religious Germans in Brandenburg that the SVAG and SED were determined to create an atheist social and political order. The "Working Group of Religious Socialists," composed largely of clerics such as Kurt Rackwitz who were deeply supportive of the SVAG and SED policies, was a part of the "religious freedom" campaign insofar as they wrote articles in both *Tägliche Rundschau* and *Neues Deutschland* attesting to the common ground between Marxism-Leninism and Christianity. Their efforts to open SED membership to religious believers and to minimize the importance of dialectical materialism in the SED's ideology were almost completely ignored by the SED leaders Wilhelm Pieck, Otto Grotewohl, and Walter Ulbricht. Even Protestant leaders in Brandenburg such as Heinrich Gruber and Kurt Krummacher, who were not in league with Dibelius's openly anti-Communist stance, were not taken in by the "religious freedom" campaign in the manner of Rackwitz and his supporters.

The "religious freedom" propaganda campaign begun at first by the SVAG and then the SED reveals complexity of their religious policies during the history of the Soviet occupation. While their long term plans for religious institutions were not in doubt, in the first few years of the Soviet occupation they were more than willing to promise complete protection of religious freedom in an SED-led German state, and temporarily backed this promise up by toleration of religious charitable activities and the April 1946 compromise on religious education.[73]

The propaganda campaign from 1945 to early 1948 has to be seen in the light not only of the SVAG and SED efforts to win the support of the population of the Soviet zone, but also the inhabitants of the Western zones as well, since the SVAG as well as Stalin aspired for the SED to lead a Soviet-dominated, united Germany. As the Cold War between the Soviets and West emerged in occupied Germany and chances of a united Germany under Ulbricht's leadership became more remote, the "religious freedom" campaign was altered and partially abandoned by the SVAG and the SED due to the political situation in occupied Germany after 1948.

Notes

1. Dan Beck, "The Luther Revival:Aspects of National *Abgrenzung* and Confessional *Gemeinschaft* in the German Democratic Republic," *Religion and Nationalism in Soviet and East European Politics.* Sabrina Ramet, eds. Duke, NC: Duke University Press, 1988. 222–240. 222. Frequently cited by Marxist critics of Luther was his notorious pamphlet *Against the Murderous, Theiving Hordes of Peasants (Wider die räuberischen und mörderischen Rotten der Bauern)*, which justified the use of harsh measures against the rebellious peasants, and where Luther attempted to discard his own responsibility for the rebellion.

2. Beck, 222–223.

3. Besier, 722.

4. Dähn, 133.

5. Goeckel, 297.

6. The sources for this chapter include the records of the SVAG's Propaganda/Information Administration, both its headquarters in Karlshorst and its branch in the Brandenburg capital of Potsdam. Tiul'panov's subordinates in Brandenburg followed his lead in attempting to recruit clerical "progressives" to the cause of promoting the idea of religious freedom under Stalinist-style socialism. Also vital are the official papers of three leaders of Socialist Unity Party, Wilhelm Pieck, Otto Grotewohl, and Walter Ulbricht, which discuss how the SED dealt with Christian clergy who openly supported the ideology and policies of the SED. The materials from SED's Working Group for church Questions, a branch of the Central Committee's Secretariat founded in October 1949, also contain some valuable information concerning the SED's attempt to use guarantees of religious freedom as a propaganda tool during the Soviet occupation. The newspapers of the SVAG and SED, *Tägliche Rundschau* and *Neues Deutschland*, are of central importance, since these were the main mediums by which the SVAG and their German allies promoted the claim of complete religious freedom existing in the Soviet Union and that similar conditions would exist in a socialist Germany. Of additional importance are the records of the Evangelical and Catholic churches in the Soviet zone, as well as materials from the Christian Democratic Union in the Soviet zone.

7. Goeckel, 31.

8. Chumachenko, 15.

9. Goeckel, 45.

10. Miner, 315.

11. *Deutsche Volkszeitung*. 22 Jun 1945. 1. 13 Jul 1945. 2.

12. *Tägliche Rundschau*. "Kirchliches Leben in Brandenburg" 9 Jun 1945. 2.

13. *Tägliche Rundschau*. "Die Kirche-Gestern und Heute" 12 Jun 1945. 1. Perhaps not coincidentally, this was same day SVAG Supreme Commander Georgii Zhukov issued order number two which allowed for the creation of antifascist political parties

14. Ibid.

15. *Tägliche Rundschau.* 13 Aug 1945. 2. The New Jerusalem monastery was known in Russia as the Voskerensky Monastery, it finally re-opened as an Orthodox monastery in 1990.

16. *Tägliche Rundschau.* 18 Sept 1945. 2. Among the destroyed churches noted by the article were 1670 Orthodox, 237 Catholic and 69 Protestant churches, as well as 532 synagogues.

17. *Tägliche Rundschau.* 15 Nov 1945. 2.

18. *Tägliche Rundschau.* 5 Dec 1945. 1.

19. GARF, f. 7077 (SVAG Brandenburg), op. 1 (Upravlenie propagandy), d. 196 (Correspondence January–April 1946), ll.77–78.

20. *Die UdSSR und die Deutsche Frage 1941–1948: Dokumente aus dem Archiv für Aussenpolitik der Russischen Föderation Volume 2*: 9 Mai 1945 bis 3. October 1946. Eds, Jochen Laufer, Georgii Kynin and Viktor Knoll. Berlin: Duncker & Humbolt, 2004. 241–242.

21. SAPMO-DDR Abteilung, DY 30- SED Zentral Kommittee IV 2-ZK Secretariat, 12-Arbeitsgruppe für Kirchenfragen, 124-Juni-December 1945.

22. SAPMO-DDR Abteilung, DY 30-SED Zentral Committee, IV 2- ZK Secretariat. 9.05-Abteilung Volksbilding,78-Mai bis December 1946.

23. SAPMO-DDR Abteilung, DY 30- SED Zentral Kommittee IV 2-ZK Secretariat, 12-Arbeitsgruppe für Kirchenfragen, 1-Januar-October 1946.

24. *Neues Deutschland.* 26 Jul 1946. 1.

25. *Neues Deutschland.* 30 Aug 1946. 1.

26. SAPMO-DDR Abteilung, DY/30/IV 2/14/1.

27. *Neues Deutschland.* 1 Oct 1946. 2.

28. *Neues Deutschland.* 18 Oct 1946. 1. The impact of the article may have been limited by the fact that, while the article had a number of signatories form the entire Soviet zone, no high ranking Evangelical church officials in Berlin-Brandenburg had signed it.

29. GARF, f. 7077- (SVAG Brandenburg), op. 1 (Upravlenie propagandy), d. 201 (Correspondence August–October 1946), ll. 66–78.

30. *Tägliche Rundschau.* 17 Aug 1946. 1.

31. *Tägliche Rundschau.* 23 Aug 1946. 4. The article was part of the "Soviet Union Today" series which ran once a week in the newspaper which discussed various aspects of the political, economic, cultural, and social life in the USSR.

32. Norman Naimark, *The Russians in Germany: A History of the Soviet Zone of Occupation 1945–1949.* Cambridge, MA: The Belknap Press of Harvard University Press, 1995. 329.

33. *Die UdSSR und die Deutsche Frage 1941–1948: Dokumente aus dem Archiv für Aussenpolitik der Russischen Föderation Volume 3*: 6 Oktober 1946 bis 15 Juni 1948. Eds, Jochen Laufer, Georgii Kynin and Viktor Knoll. Berlin: Duncker & Humbolt 2004. 52–60.

34. *Tägliche Rundschau.* 25 Dec 1946. 3. The issue also contained an article by the pro-SED Protestant pastor Karl Kleinschmidt reminding German readers to keep

in mind the devastation brought about Germany's armies during the war, and not to become too enraptured in their own suffering.

35. *Neues Deutschland.* 25 Dec 1946. 4.

36. SAPMO-SED Abteilung NY 4036/756-Nachlässe Wilhelm Pieck.

37. Ibid.

38. Ibid.

39. ELAB, Bestand 603-Nachlässe Otto Dibelius A 17. 1.1. Despite their considerable disagreements on a number of issues pertaining to the relationship between the Protestant Church and the SVAG/SED authorities, Krummacher and Dibelius were in complete agreement regarding the preservation of religious education in the German schools.

40. SAPMO-SED Abteilung NY 4036/756.

41. Ibid.

42. Ibid.

43. Ibid.

44. Ibid. The implication Pieck made was the churches would have to accept this arrangement permanently.

45. GARF, f. 7077 (SVAG-Brandenburg), op. 1 (Upravlenie propagandy), d. 220 (Correspondence January–May 1947), ll. 55–59. Tiul'panov noted the Catholic Church, particularly Cardinal Von Preysing of Berlin, was little better in its support of reactionary politics.

46. Ibid.

47. *Tägliche Rundschau.* 2 Feb 1947. 2.

48. Ibid. "Das politische Kirchentum als reaktionares Element eines reaktionaren Staates hat."

49. *Tägliche Rundschau.* 30 Aug 1947. 2. This particular issue also condemned CDU leader in the Western zones Konrad Adenauer for trying to create a "political Christianity" to serve reactionary political ends.

50. RGASPI, f. 17 (Tsentralnyi Komitet Kommunisticheskoi partii Sovetskogo Soiuza), op.125 (Sovet po delam religii pri Sovete Ministrov SSSR), d. 407 (Correspondence January–April 1947), ll. 1–50. The Council of Orthodox Church Affairs was a branch of Sovnarkom, the supreme executive organ of the Soviet government.

51. RGASPI, f. 17, op. 125, d. 407, ll. 76–77.

52. *Neues Deutschland.* 17 Oct 1947. 4.

53. *Neues Deutschland.* 16 Nov 1947. 1.

54. *Neues Deutschland.* 17 Dec 1947. 2.

55. *Tägliche Rundschau.* 29 Oct 1948. 3. As chapter five demonstrated, this was a promise which was rarely honored.

56. GARF, f. 7077 (SVAG Brandenburg), op.1 (Upravlenie informatsii), d. 254 (Correspondence January–April 1949), ll. 39–43.

57. Ibid.

58. GARF, f. 7077, op.1, d. 254, ll. 42–43.

59. *Neues Deutschland.* 14 Nov 1948. 5.

60. *Neues Deutschland.* 13 Feb 1949. 4.

61. Christopher Zugger, *The Forgotten:Catholics of the Soviet Empire from Lenin to Stalin.* Syracuse, NY: Syracuse University Press, 2001. 385–398.

62. *Neues Deutschland.* 3 Apr 1949. 1. Beste did remark the Dibelius agreed with the views Beste expressed in the article, and that they expressed the views of the entire Protestant leadership in the Soviet zone.

63. *Tägliche Rundschau.* 6 Jul 1949. 3.

64. *Tägliche Rundschau.* 27 Aug 1949. 2. The SVAG newspaper even went so far as to allow Dibelius to publish an article in May of 1949 pleading for all four Allied powers and for the German people to work towards maintaining the unity of Germany.

65. SAPMO-DDR Abteilung, NY 4036/756.

66. SAPMO-DDR Abteilung, DY/30/IV 2/14/12.

67. GARF, f. 7077 (SVAG Brandenburg), op.1 (Upravlenie informatsii), d. 256 (Correspondence January-May 1949). ll. 19–30. Martem'ianov admitted efforts to divide clerical progressives from reactionaries in the Protestant Church was progressing faster than attempts to turn Protestant clerics against those in the Catholic Church.

68. EZA, Bestand 4-Kirchenkanzlei der EKD, Repositur 448, 157–158. This contrasted sharply with events a decade later, as the EKD leadership in Brandenburg and most of the GDR repudiated Dibelius's call for a massive civil disobedience campaign in his open letter to the Evangelical population, entitled *Obrigkeit* (Authority).

69. ELAB, Bestand 603, B 17.

70. EZA Bestand 4, Repositur 448. It would not be accurate to say those who opposed Dibelius's more hard-line stance had simply been completely duped by the "religious freedom" propaganda campaign of the SVAG and the SED. It is accurate to hypothesize the declarations by both the SVAG and the SED authorities supporting religious freedom as opposed to the destruction of religious institutions convinced them some type of compromise could be made between the Protestant church and an SED-led German state.

71. *Tägliche Rundschau.* 13 Mar 1950. 1.

72. Solberg, 278–282.

73. Ultimately, the use of the issue of religious freedom in SVAG and the SED propaganda supports the view of historians such as Vladislav Zubok, Dirk Spilker, Gary Bruce and Hubertus Knabe who argue Stalin and the SED leadership always desired a Soviet-controlled East Germany even if they failed to control the entire country. Yet it also lends credence to Norman Naimark's interpretation of SVAG policies as dictated primarily by events on the ground, in this case, the continued importance of the Catholic and Protestant churches as two of the few German institutions which survived Nazism.

Chapter Eight

The Allied Religious Affairs Committee and the Impossibility of a United Religious Policy for Germany

INTRODUCTION

While Lieutenant Colonel Vsevolod Ermolaev served as Tiul'panov's deputy for religious affairs in the Propaganda/Information Administration, the previous chapters have demonstrated it was Tiul'panov himself who took the most active role in the SVAG for devising and implementing religious policies. There was, however, one assignment where Ermolaev had a relatively free hand, and this was on the Allied Religious Affairs Committee.

The Allied Religious Affairs Committee (ARAC) was a subsidiary branch of the Directorate of Internal Affairs and Communications (DIAC), which in turn was a subsidiary branch of the Allied Control Authority Coordinating Committee (ACACC), which served directly under the Allied Control Council for Germany, the governing body for the four-power administration of Germany after May 1945. The ARAC was composed of representatives from each of the four occupation powers and met from August 1945 until March 1948, when the Soviet withdrawal from the Allied Control Council led to dissolution of all bodies designed to forge a unified four-power policy for all the zones of Germany.

The ARAC was designed to ensure that Germany would be governed as a unified country, like so many other inter-allied bodies created by the four powers in the summer of 1945. As the spirit of wartime cooperation began to dissipate and the Soviet and Western zones began to move in starkly different directions over the next three years, the possibility that the Soviet Union and the Western allies could govern Germany as a unified country became more unlikely. The Soviet withdrawal from the Control Council in March 1948 effectively ended even the pretense of Allied cooperation in jointly governing

Germany, although it would not be until 1949 that the division became a political reality.

This chapter discusses how and why the Allied Religious Affairs Committee failed in its task of providing recommendations for the creation of a unified religious policy for all of Germany, and what role its Soviet representative, Lieutenant Colonel Vsevolod Ermolaev, played in this process. The ARAC, like the other committees at the lowest levels of the four-power administration, received only the most general directives from middle and high-level authorities on how to perform its task of providing recommendations for the creation of a joint religious policy and what the goals of Allied religious policy should be. Consequently, the members of the ARAC were forced to provide policy recommendations based on realities at the ground level of the four zones, which proved to be a difficult and divisive process.

By and large, the actions of Vsevolod Ermolaev, the Soviet representative on the ARAC, complement his role as the director of Religious Affairs for Sergei Tiul'panov's Propaganda/Information Administration, in that he operated from a number of set priorities that were designed to gradually limit the role the Protestant and Catholic churches could play in public life in occupied Germany. However, he occasionally demonstrated a willingness to show a certain flexibility when circumstances dictated it.[1]

THE ROLE AND FUNCTION OF THE ARAC IN THE FOUR-POWER ALLIED CONTROL AUTHORITY

The ARAC was formed by the Directorate of Internal Affairs and Communications to advise the DIAC on how to implement a coordinated religious policy in the four zones of Germany, when the UK, the US, France, and the Soviet Union still planned on governing Germany as a unified country. The four powers agreed to the need to restore religious freedom in Germany and the status of the Protestant and Catholic churches as two of the few institutions that could demonstrate resistance to Hitler's regime. This was rather erroneous as overt resistance to Hitler's regime was the exception rather than the rule in the Protestant and Catholic churches in Germany. Nevertheless, the general consensus amongst military and political authorities was that because of the spiritual and moral authority of the German churches, they could be used in each zone to help create a united antifascist Germany.[2]

The ARAC did not have a decisive impact on religious policy-making by zonal authorities, as it was unable to accomplish its primary task of providing recommendations to the DIAC for creating a unified religious policy for

Germany. The main reason for its failure lied in its inability to reach a consensus on major and minor questions concerning religious affairs from 1945–1948. The secondary reason was the fact that numerous decisions concerning religious policy were not even addressed to the ARAC. The DIAC failed numerous times to ask the ARAC for recommendations concerning certain religious issues, preferring to instead direct their questions to other directorates, and then informing the ARAC about the decisions after the fact.

The DIAC and the Coordinating Committee never spelled out the central long-term purpose of the Allied religious policy in occupied Germany for the ARAC, except for the issues such as the need to purge Nazi influence from the churches and to return church property seized by the Nazi regime. Instead of focusing directly on a certain group of vital religious issues, such as the question of religious education in any future German state or how the German churches, as supposedly antifascist organizations, could help construct a democratic German state, the ARAC tended to deal with a huge variety of different religious concerns brought to their attention, which varied greatly in their importance.[3]

The representatives from the four nations on the ARAC brought different understandings of how religious affairs in occupied Germany should be dealt with, but this was a less important issue than the fact that the Soviet representatives on the ARAC, from the fall of 1945 onwards, demonstrated a tendency to avoid seeking a unified religious policy when matters of disagreement arose between themselves and the representatives. Instead, Ermolaev would usually request that each zone follow its own religious policy when conflicts emerged as opposed to seeking a consensus and then recommending this to the DIAC, although there were exceptions when the Soviet representative specifically objected to a religious policy enacted in the Western zones and insisted that they be abandoned. The American, British, and French representatives often did not press the Soviet representative for the creation of a unified religious policy for all of Germany but instead attempted to forge a unified religious policy for the three western zones. Occasionally, the French representative took the same positions on religious questions as his Soviet colleague, although this occurred less and less after 1946.[4]

The result of this process was that the DIAC received very few unified recommendations, although the ARAC fairly regularly did send pairs of recommendations, one supported by the Western representatives, and one by the Soviet representative. Disagreements on religious issues in the DIAC nearly always broke down along the same lines as the ARAC, paralleling cold war tensions with the Soviets on one side and the Americans, British, and French on the other, although at the times the Soviets were successful in playing the

French off of the British and Americans. When the DIAC was unable to make a decision, the Allied Coordinating Committee usually turned over the matter to zonal religious authorities to make their own decisions on what type of policies should be enacted.

Problems that existed among the top levels of the administrative organs designed to govern Germany as a single unit, namely the fact that the Soviets went one direction in their zone and the Western powers went another in theirs, also existed at its lowest levels, and the "solutions" for these problems that the four powers devised from the summer of 1945 to the spring of 1948 at the top and bottom had the same result, in that they furthered the division of Germany into two states, as opposed to helping to create a united Germany.

THE CREATION OF THE ARAC:
NOVEMBER 1944 TO AUGUST 1945

On November 7, 1944, the first clear statement on the direction of Allied religious policy in Germany emerged when the Allied Joint Planning Committee prepared a draft directive that was intended to be sent to the future supreme commanders of the British, American, and Soviet zones of Germany. The existence of a French zone was not agreed to until the Yalta conference in January 1945.

The directive stated throughout Germany, the Allied Control Council would coordinate religious policy jointly throughout all the occupation zones of Germany, and that its primary goals were to restore freedom of religion, revoke Nazi religious laws, return seized church property, allow public religious ceremonies, and permit German clergymen of both the Evangelical and Catholic faiths to reform the churches on their own, but also to ensure that any remaining Nazi influence in the churches be swiftly stamped out. In August 1945, the same directive was sent by the DIAC to the ARAC's first meeting for consideration in helping them to formulate a unified religious policy for Germany.[5]

The decision to create the ARAC was made at the first meeting of the Directorate of Internal Affairs and Communications on August 14, 1945 at the Allied Control Authority building in Berlin (where all future ARAC meetings would be held as well). Formed by the Coordinating Committee along with the Legal, Political, Finance, and Military Affairs directorates, the DIAC was designed to provide recommendations to the Coordinating Committee on various internal aspects of life in the four zones.

At its first meeting the DIAC decided to establish committees for the Civil Administration, Public Health and Welfare, Public Safety, and Religious Affairs. The DIAC's members decided all of these committees would contain representatives from each zone, who would all be appointed from branches of the military governments in each zone. In the case of the ARAC, this supposedly meant members from the religious affairs branch of the military governments, where the American and Soviet representatives to the ARAC were drawn. Major Marshall Knappen, the American representative on the ARAC during most of this three-year period, was the head of the Religious Affairs Section of the Office of Military Government for Germany, United States (OMGUS) and a former Rhodes Scholar in Reformation Studies and a professor at the University of Michigan.

Lieutenant Colonel Vsevolod Ermolaev, the Soviet representative on the ARAC, also served as the liaison officer between the German churches in the Soviet zone and the Propaganda/Information administration of the Soviet Military Administration of Germany. Before the war he had been a professor at Leningrad State University, sharing a similar academic background to Tiul'panov. Neither Lt. Colonel Lloyd Percival, the British representative, nor Minister Eduard Carteron, the French representative, worked with the religious affairs branches of their countries' zones, but each man had served extensively in British and French colonies in the pre-war era.[6] This new committee would provide policy recommendations designed to ensure a unified religious policy for all four zones of Germany.[7]

It was not until the second meeting of the DIAC on August 24, 1945 that the ARAC was given its actual name by DIAC members and its representatives were appointed by the heads of the DIAC. On its third meeting on August 28 the DIAC decided that the ARAC's recommendations would not be moved immediately towards the Coordinating Committee for implementation unless the ARAC made unanimous recommendations. If ARAC members disagreed on certain issues, the disagreements would be noted in their reports to the DIAC, which would then decide on what appropriate actions to take, such as attempting to reach an agreement on the issue or sending it back to the ARAC for further evaluation. The ARAC could either address questions brought up from German civilians or zonal authorities or issues the representatives themselves had noticed, or, less often, the DIAC or other directorates would suggest to the ARAC to examine certain religious issues that emerged in one or more of the zones. From the available evidence, it appears there was no indication that DIAC planned to refer religious questions to any other committees or directorates besides the ARAC.[8]

THE INITIAL PERIOD OF COOPERATION:
AUGUST 1945 TO JUNE 1946

The first meeting of the ARAC was held on August 31, 1945. There was no discussion of religious issues, but all four representatives did agree on the establishment of secretaries for every representative at each meeting, and to meet twice a month. All members would be given seventy-two hours to examine issues that other members desired to bring to the attention of the committee.[9]

During the second meeting on September 10, 1945, no recommendations were made by the ARAC to the DIAC, but all of the members of the committee agreed the Allied authorities should interfere as little as possible in the internal affairs of the Protestant and Catholic churches, as they did not want to give the impression that the Allied authorities were simply dictating religious reforms to the German clergymen, as they believed that whatever reforms the German clergy supported would suffer as a result. This did not mean, however, that the ARAC members believed that the Allied authorities should not have the final word when it came to purging Nazi influences from the German churches, especially given the prominence of certain members of the German Christian movement in leadership positions in the Protestants Church. The German Christians were a movement that, during the years of the Hitler dictatorship, attempted to merge the doctrines of Lutheran Christianity and National Socialism and to gain control of the Protestant Church leadership in order to propagate this ideology.[10]

At the next meeting of the ARAC on September 25, 1945, the first discussion of religious issues occurred, as well as the first major disagreement between committee members. Numerous Protestant churches in the Western zones had requested the zonal authorities give permission for the revival of religious youth organizations that could promote charitable work amongst German youths in destitute regions as well as sponsoring outdoor sporting events.[11] While Percival, Knappen, and Carteron agreed to this, and hoped to recommend this to the DIAC, Ermolaev objected, stating youth activities and sporting events, regardless of whoever was sponsoring them, needed to be strictly regulated by zonal authorities. If British, French, and American authorities allowed this in their zones, that was fine, but Ermolaev stated the Soviet zone was not ready for such a development. The recommendation the ARAC supplied to the DIAC broke down on these lines, with the British, American, and French delegates promoting one approach and the Soviet delegate promoting another. When the recommendations were discussed at the DIAC's seventh meeting on October 4, 1945, its members disagreed along exactly the same lines, and failed to make a decision on the matter.[12]

Disagreements occurred at the early meetings of the ARAC because not every representative felt qualified to make a decision on certain matters. At the fourth meeting of the ARAC, the representatives discussed whether the Salvation Army should be allowed to renew its charitable work in Germany. No decision was reached on this matter, but this was due to the fact that Ermolaev admitted the Salvation Army did not exist in the Soviet Union, and so he did not feel qualified in making a recommendation.[13]

Records suggest there were more agreements than disagreements among members of the ARAC during the first year of the occupation. For example, the committee members in the fourth meeting made a broad agreement that zonal authorities in the zones would assist in meeting the material needs of the Evangelical and Catholic churches. Carteron promised his zone would help provide the wine for church services in all of the zones, while Ermolaev reassured his colleagues that the Soviet zone would provide candles for use in religious services in the western zones.[14] The ARAC representatives accepted the appointment of Bishop Theophil Wurm of Stuttgart as president of the provisional council of the Protestant Church in Germany, and with the dissident pastor Martin Niemöller of Berlin-Dahlem as vice-president.[15] Finally, the four representatives came to a preliminary agreement on the major and eventually divisive issue of religious education, recommending to the DIAC that: "Zonal authorities, working with the local population, should determine which religious schools can be opened or allowed to continue their work if conforming to general rules guiding education. In any case, no school drawing on public funds should refuse to children the possibility of receiving religious instruction, and no school drawing on public funds should make it compulsory for a child to attend classes for religious instruction."[16] Ermolaev's agreement appears rather incredible given his later actions, although this could have been due to the fact that since the school reform law passed in 1946 in the Soviet zone had already prohibited religious education in schools with the exception of voluntary religious instruction after school hours, the matter of religious education did not appear to be an issue worth fighting over with the Western representatives.[17]

But two months later the consensus broke apart when Knappen and Percival at the ARAC meeting on December 31, 1945, attempted to issue a recommendation that all German schools would allow two hours or less of religious education to their students if the students' parents desired it. While Carteron agreed to this, Ermolaev stated that the school reforms enacted in the Soviet zone mandated that any religious education in schools occur specifically *after,* not *during,* school hours. He recommended discussion of the matter be tabled for an indeterminate time, and while the American, British, and French delegates agreed to this, they also stated that they would provide their recommendation to the education authorities in their respective zones. Although the issue of a unified policy for religious education in schools was raised again, the deadlock on the issue between the Western and Soviet representatives continued into the spring of 1948. Ermolaev's proposal was exactly what the education authorities in the Soviet zone agreed upon four months later in April 1946.[18]

Ultimately, a compromise was reached in the Soviet zone in April 1946 regarding religious education, as the SVAG, SED, and the CDU agreed to allow two hours of optional religious education after school hours in school buildings.[19] However, on August 26, 1946, Ermolaev informed the General Secretary of the Protestant Church, Dr. Kurt Krummacher, the Soviet authorities in their sector of Berlin as well as in the Soviet zone, were determined to bring about a clean break between the church and state in the educational system.[20]

At other points in 1945 and early 1946, the four representatives of the committee agreed on certain important issues, such as the need to work with both the DIAC and the Legal Directorate in abolishing the Reich Law of July 14, 1934, which recognized the constitution of the German Protestant Church of July 11, 1934. Each representative also agreed that while the Allied Control Authority was purely within the limits of its power in acting to abrogate religious laws established by Hitler's regime, it should not try to change the constitution of the church itself. Instead of drafting a new constitution on their own and then demand that the Protestant Church leaders accept it, the ARAC representatives decided to let the issue of forging a new constitution for the Protestant Church be handled by its leaders internally. The unanimous recommendation was passed on to the DIAC after the December 31 meeting, which then forwarded it to the Coordinating Committee. The Reich Law of July 14 was duly abolished in October of 1946, when the Council of the EKD developed a new church constitution to take its place.[21]

One month later, the ARAC continued to articulate its support of the internal reform efforts of the Protestant Church leadership. This issue marked the highpoint of cooperation between the four representatives of the ARAC. The representatives expressed their approval of the Stuttgart declaration of October 18, 1945, by the Council of the EKD, where the EKD's leaders admitted the failure of the Protestant Church leadership to speak out more decisively against the Nazi regime had contributed to the regime's horrible crimes against humanity. The ARAC also supported the role of the Council as acting as a provisional authority for the Evangelical churches in Germany.[22] Knapp later wrote that these recommendations were agreed upon by all four representatives in order to encourage, but not control, the emergence of a solidly antifascist Protestant Church in Germany.[23]

Support for internal church reforms had its limits within the ARAC. In May 1945, the ACA received a letter from the EKD Council authored by Bishop Wurm asking that church authorities alone be allowed to remove clergymen who had supported the Nazis from positions of authority, in essence asking that the German Protestant Churches carry out the policy of denazification internally.[24] Since the surrender of Germany in May 1945, the position of the leaders of the German Protestant Church, including such active leaders of the Confessing Church movement such as Niemöller and Wurm had been that the issue of removing Nazi influences from the Protestant Church, especially high-ranking members of the German Christian movement, was an issue to be decided solely by church leaders, and *not* by Allied authorities. The leaders of the Confessing church, a movement of Protestant clergymen who during the Third Reich attempted to keep the Protestant churches free of the influence of the Nazi ideology, believed that they knew best which tainted clergy needed to be removed from church offices.[25]

While all four representatives expressed an agreement that the policy of allowing internal church reforms should continue at their fourth meeting on June 25, 1945, denazification remained one of the issues in occupied Germany where zonal authorities had to have the final say, although there remained a slight disagreement as to whether a new criteria would have to be established for German clergymen. The ARAC unanimously recommended that zonal commanders should continue to apply the denazification policy to German clergy as it did with other groups within German society.[26] The ARAC informed the EKD of this decision, which did not raise the issue again, possibly because both the high and low levels of the German churches' hierarchy were barely affected by the official Allied denazification policies. Allied religious authorities in all of the zones had largely turned over the removal of unsuitable clergy to the churches themselves.

In the American zone, for example, no Catholic and only a few Protestant clergy were denazified by the Allied authorities (and consequently removed from church office), while numbers in the British zone were even lower, although they were considerably higher in the French zones.[27] Within the Soviet zone during the initial period of the occupation from the summer of 1945 and to the fall of 1946, the occupation authorities largely allowed the churches to conduct their own internal process of denazification, in all likelihood because the Soviet occupation authorities did not want to alienate the churches at a time when they were dependent upon both Evangelical and Catholic charitable organizations to meet basic needs of residents in the Soviet zone, especially with those individuals who had been expelled from former German territories in Czechoslovakia and Poland.[28]

THE EMERGENCE OF MAJOR DIVISIONS AND THE DEBATE ON THE GERMAN CHRISTIANS: JUNE 1946 TO JUNE 1947

The period in the early summer of 1946 proved to be the highpoint of cooperation between the representatives to formulating what passed for a consistent unified policy for the four zones, namely by allowing the Protestant Church leadership to pursue its own course of internal reform that would purge Nazi and German Christian influence from its ranks. Afterwards, despite the occasional consensus on various issues, the representatives on the ARAC failed to agree on most issues and were unable to provide many unified religious policy recommendations. Among the most divisive issues from the summer of 1946 to the spring of 1948 were those of the German Christians, the relationship between the EKD and the World Council of Churches, the distribution of religious literature, the movement of the clergy between the four zones, and the issue of the Concordat between Hitler's government and the Vatican in 1933.

This state of affairs was partially due to the fact that the purpose of the religious policy in the four zones as stated by the Allied Control Authority was rather vague once the denazification of the churches had been accomplished and "religious freedom" had been reestablished. The four representatives on the ARAC reported to the DIAC this had for all intents and purposes occurred by April of 1946.[29] According to Knappen, both he and Percival began to view the process of working with Ermolaev in implementing a unified religious policy as hopeless, due to the fact that the Soviets were pursuing a religious policy at odds with what the western powers desired.[30]

Another consequence of the vague definition of the Allied religious policy's ultimate goal, as well as the haphazard manner by which issues came to the attention of the ARAC, was that at certain meetings the committee representatives had relatively little to discuss, as was the case during the meetings of the ARAC in the late summer of 1946, as they reviewed exactly how much church wine was sent to which regions of Germany.[31] At other times meetings could be extremely important and would involve discussion of central religious issues. This was the case at the seventeenth meeting on September 25, 1946, when a number of dominant major religious issues were discussed and the representatives failed to reach a consensus on any of them, and consequently sent no recommendations to DIAC for an adoption of an all-zone approach to these issues. The first issue concerned that of the German Christians.

Having been expelled from the clerical ranks of the Protestant Church after the war, a group of German Christians had asked the authorities in the British zone to form a denomination separate from the EKD called the

Freie Volkskirche.[32] Percival suggested that while the German Christians had been expelled by the EKD, zonal religious authorities should not recognize them as a separate group, although he left open the possibility that this might occur at a later date. Knappen claimed as long as the German Christians were kept under close surveillance by zonal religious authorities, they should be allowed to form a separate denomination. Since the beginning of the occupation, British religious authorities in particular had shown a general leniency towards the activities of members of the German Christian movement in their zone, even allowing them to make public (non-political) speeches. The American authorities had also allowed the German Christians to continue to meet as an organization as long as they did not express their ideology publicly.[33] Carteron and Ermolaev resolutely refused to consider this, stating that, because of their close relationship with National Socialism, the German Christians could not be allowed to ever function again in Germany. Consequently, the German Christians ceased to exist as any type of movement in their zones.[34]

A month later, on October 22 at the nineteenth meeting of the ARAC, the issue of the German Christians emerged again. Percival stated a uniform policy throughout the four zones was absolutely necessary in dealing with the issue due to its controversial nature. Between the end of the September and the end of October, all four representatives had consulted with religious authorities in their respective zones as to the activity of the German Christians. Knappen and Percival stated that there were a number of German Christians in their zone who were attempting to form their own independent churches, although not under the name of "the German Christians". Both recommended the German Christians should be allowed to assemble for religious purposes and should eventually be allowed to form their own church, but they would also have to be kept under close observation and could not pursue "undesirable political activity," especially the propagation of anti-Semitism or the anti-Allied propaganda. Changing his position, Carteron stated although no individuals involved in the German Christian movement were active in the French zone, if any did emerge he agreed with the British and American policy towards them.

Ermolaev stated the German Christians did not exist in the Soviet zone, and that the zonal authorities would never allow them to pursue religious activity, because of the Nazi background of their movement. He pointedly suggested that, due to the Nazi influences within the German Christians, the Western zones should also not allow them to conduct any sort of religious activity. Two different recommendations were again sent to the DIAC, which also failed to come to a consensus on the issue along the exact same lines as the ARAC.[35]

The decision by Carteron to side with his American and British colleagues on this matter marked the beginning of an increasing unanimity on the part of the Western representatives against Ermolaev that would continue until the dissolution of the ARAC in March of 1948. Before this point the Soviet representatives had been somewhat successful in dislodging Carteron from the other Western representatives on a few of the disputed issues, such as the earlier debates concerning the status of the German Christians.

The next major issue discussed was whether to allow the World Council of Churches to establish a liaison between themselves and the Protestant churches in Germany. This issue would bedevil both the ARAC and the DIAC until the fall of 1947. Knappen and Percival enthusiastically supported the idea at the meeting on September 25, 1946, Carteron less so, while Ermolaev rejected it, claiming that the time was still too early for the Protestant Church to have any liaisons outside of the Allied Control Authority. It would not be until the four powers gave up even the pretense of governing Germany as a single unit that the EKD was allowed to form liaisons with international bodies.[36]

During the first few months of 1947, it appeared for the first time since the summer and fall of 1945 that the Western powers and the Soviets were moving towards governing Germany as a single unit. The most divisive issue was over industrial reparations from Germany's Western and Soviet zones, as the Soviet policy of dismantling factories and railways in the Soviet zone and shipping them back to the USSR prevented the governing of Germany as one economic unit. During the spring of the 1947, the head of the US military government in Germany, General Lucius Clay, attempted to work out an agreement with the Soviet zonal authorities over which economic reparations could be taken from industrial production in the Western zone.[37]

Perhaps in the spirit of this new mood of cooperation between the four powers, on May 28, 1947, at the twenty-eighth meeting, the representatives of the ARAC agreed to a joint recommendation supporting the creation of a liaison officer between the World Council of churches and the German Protestant Church. It forwarded this proposal to the DIAC immediately after the meeting.[38] The issue would be debated by the DIAC representatives in three different meetings over the next four months, who finally concluded in July of 1947 that it was still too early for the Protestant churches in Germany to have a direct liaison with any group outside of Germany, no matter how well-intentioned the international organization was.[39] This decision by the DIAC reflects poorly on the value they placed on the ARAC, as even on the rare occasions when the ARAC provided united recommendations to the DIAC, it tended to ignore them or reverse them.

At the end of the 1946, another dispute broke out between the representatives at their meeting on December 17, 1946, when the American, French and British representatives protested the refusal of the Soviet authorities to allow the distribution of religious literature from the Western zones in the Soviet zone. Knappen, Carteron and Percival tried to send a unified recommendation insisting on the open distribution of all forms of religious literature in all four zones. Ermolaev refused to agree, claiming authorities in the Western zones did not allow the distribution of political journals from the Soviet zone (the three Western representatives disputed this) and therefore the Soviets were within their rights in suppressing the distribution of religious literature in their zone. No recommendations were made to the DIAC concerning a uniform policy on the distribution of religious literature.[40]

THE FIGHT OVER THE CONCORDAT: JUNE 1947 TO NOVEMBER 1947

The next important meeting for the ARAC was its twenty-ninth on June 29, 1947, when Ermolaev raised the issue as to whether the 1933 Concordat could be considered a "Nazi document," and which religious laws the ARAC could recommend abolishing due to any Nazi influence prevalent in them. The representatives failed to come to an agreement on the issue and agreed to discuss it again on a later date. The issue of the Concordat had been referred to the ARAC by the DIAC, which had first referred it to the Legal Directorate in April, which had then failed to come to any consensus on the issue. It became such a divisive and dominant issue that it prevented the ARAC from performing its duties of providing recommendations for a unified religious policy for much of 1947.

The breakdown of cooperation over this issue in the summer of 1947 paralleled the failure of the Allied Control Commission to reach an agreement on the reparations issue, as both U.S. Secretary of State George Marshall and UK Foreign Secretary Ernest Bevin refused to consider reparations payments from the Western zones of Germany to the Soviet Union until they could manage their industrial economies without British or American assistance, a development which was theoretically years away.[41] The final breakdown over the reparations issue in the summer of 1947 was probably the last realistic chance for the four powers to govern Germany as a single unit. The bitter disagreements in meetings and growing insignificance of the ARAC during this final year reflected the gradual breakdown of the four-power institutions from 1947 to 1948.

Ermolaev raised the matter of whether the 1933 Concordat should be banned in the next two meetings in August and September of 1947. On both occasions Ermolaev insisted that, because of the use of the Concordat by Hitler's government to further the goals of National Socialism, such as requiring personal loyalty oaths by Catholic clergy to Hitler, it had to be banned immediately. At each meeting the French, British, and American representatives insisted that the Concordat was a *treaty*, as opposed to a law, and hence the ARAC should not provide a recommendation to abolish it, as this would be a matter between a future sovereign German government and the Vatican. The Western representatives held the Soviet representative had misunderstood the Concordat's significance, disputing the claim concerning loyalty oaths.[42] The meeting ended inconclusively with an unsuccessful attempt by the Western representatives to reach a compromise on the issue.[43]

On October 28, the representatives avoided discussing the Concordat and deadlocking over the issue again. Knappen and Percival accused the Soviet authorities of furthering the religious division of the country by refusing to allow either the Protestant or Catholic clergy from the Soviet zone to travel to the Western zones, and by consistently failing to come to a joint agreement concerning the movement of clergy within the four zones, a charge the Soviet representative strongly denied.[44]

Carteron raised the issue of the Concordat again at the next meeting on November 21. The French representative stated no recommendation on the abolishment of the Concordat should be made as long as the German Catholic Church had not yet composed any alternatives for it, in order to avoid "undesirable repercussions."[45] The British and American representatives agreed to this, and while the Soviet representative insisted on the need to ban the Concordat, he agreed to postpone the matter. The ARAC decided to inform the DIAC that no agreement on the issue existed.[46]

This proved to be the last time the ARAC would debate on the issue of the Concordat, as the DIAC decided not to refer the matter to them again, but rather turn it over to the Legal and Political Directorates. When these two groups also failed to reach a consensus, the DIAC attempted to work out the issue at their ninety-fifth meeting on January 29, 1948, but failed. This proved to be a particularly bitter and acrimonious meeting, as the Americans, British, and French representatives argued since no agreement could be made, the issue should be referred immediately to the Allied Control Authority's Coordinating Committee, which served directly under the Control Council.

The Soviet representative strongly disagreed with this position, stating that the Concordat was the first foreign policy arrangement made by Hitler and that it was designed both to support the Nazi regime in Germany and to extend its influence to other countries. This prompted an inquiry by the

British representative as to whether the Nazi-Soviet pact of August 1939 was still considered to be valid by the Soviet government, a remark which caused the Soviet representative to temporarily walk out of the meeting. Of course, the Soviet government certainly considered certain provisions of the treaty to be valid, such as the provisions regarding the reincorporating of Western Byelorussia and Western Ukraine into the Soviet Union, but the Soviet representative was probably not willing to admit that to his Western counterparts. Neither the DIAC nor the Coordinating Committee was able to make a decision on the matter before their dissolution in March 1948.[47]

In its last three meetings, the ARAC avoided discussing any major religious issues, and Ermolaev made a number of proposals to facilitate the revival of a unified religious policy. At the thirty-fifth and thirty-sixth meetings on December 14, 1947, and January 13, 1948, Ermolaev informed his Western counterparts of a meeting between officers from the Soviet Military Administration of Germany (SMAG) and leaders of the Protestant Church. Ermolaev stated that at the meeting the Soviet authorities allowed for the wider distribution of religious literature in the Soviet zone and to allow for religious services in internment camps, which the Soviet representative assumed already occurred within the Western zones. He then revealed to the Western representatives evidence in the form of letters from clergy in the Soviet zone that testified to this. While the Western representatives expressed surprise at Ermolaev's proposal, they noted that it did open up the potential of a revived unified religious policy in the four zones.[48]

While the committee representatives set the date for their next meeting, March 22, 1948, events at the top of the ACA's Control Council ended any possibility for renewed cooperation between the members of the ARAC. At the Allied Control Council's eighty-second meeting on March 20, the Soviet representative, Marshal Vasilii Sokolovskii, walked out of the meeting with his assistants and advisers over the issue of decisions made at the recent London Conference that paved the way for the introduction of a joint currency for the three Western zones. The Soviet withdrawal from the ACA was soon followed by the other powers, and the structures of the Allied Control Authority were dissolved.[49]

CONCLUSION: THE FAILURE OF THE ARAC AND ITS SIGNIFICANCE

The ARAC's record in providing recommendations to the DIAC for the creation and implementation of a unified religious policy for Germany was a failure, despite some early successes from 1945 to 1946. The ARAC representatives could point to some accomplishments, as they had consistently reached agreement on cooperation between the zones to providing for certain church needs such as the supply of wine and candles, and during the first year of the occupation, provided numerous unified recommendations for pursuing the denazification of the clergy as well as for the restoration of religious freedom and church property. During the first sixteen months of the Allied occupation of Germany, the ARAC followed a consistent policy of letting the EKD reform itself to as great extent possible and came to a general agreement on the abolishment of certain religious laws passed in the Nazi era. This fits with broader pattern of SVAG religious policies as illustrated in the dissertation, as the initial broad freedom of action gave way to increasingly stricter policies on both the Evangelical and Catholic churches from 1947 onward.

From late autumn of 1945 onward, however, a pattern of deadlock between the Western and Soviet representatives on the ARAC emerged, one which would always result in the emergence of divided recommendations to DIAC. Over the next three years, this pattern would continue over the issues of religious education, the German Christian movement, the distribution of religious literature, the necessity of establishing liaison officers between the German churches and the World Council of churches, and the status of the 1933 Concordat between the Vatican and Germany. On all these major issues the ARAC failed to provide joint recommendations to the DIAC for a unified approach in the four zones. In the words of Marshall Knappen, speaking both of his work on the ARAC and his opinion of the Control Council's decisions in general:

> There existed a tendency to consent to admittedly vague and unsatisfactory quadripartite acts in the effort to prevent the complete breakdown of the system from the failure to accomplish anything at all. This practice was justified only on the assumption that some appearance of agreement was better than none.[50]

The cause of much of this failure lies with the ARAC members. The Soviet representatives on the ARAC demonstrated the same tendency as their superiors on the Control Council that they would direct affairs in their zone as they saw fit with little interference from the Western representatives. Many times the Soviet representatives on the ARAC failed to work with their Western counterparts on making unified recommendations on religious policy and insisted on following their own path in their zone. Also, like their superiors on the Control Council, the Soviet representatives on the ARAC did not seem concerned that a unified policy was not being formed between themselves and the Western representatives and instead were generally content to let the

Western representatives on the ARAC make recommendations for the three western zones of Germany.

The exceptions to this pattern of Soviet behavior were the issues surrounding the German Christians and the 1933 Concordat, where Soviet representatives on the ARAC (and the DIAC) appeared convinced that the differing religious policies in the zones would harm Soviet interests in their zone. This also reflects Soviet behavior on the Allied Control Council, as they too were concerned about certain decisions made in the Western zones, such as how industrial reparations to the Soviet Union would be handled, and the attempt by the Western powers to introduce a new currency for their zones in March 1948.[51] Given the fact that, as previous chapters have indicated, the Soviet authorities in Germany deeply feared the penetration of the Soviet zone with "reactionary" clergy in the service of the Anglo-Americans, Ermolaev's lack of cooperation with the other Committee members can hardly be considered surprising, especially given the emerging Cold War in Germany between the Soviets and the Western Allies.

The American and British members of the committee very early on consigned themselves to two differing religious policies for Germany, a conclusion that the French representatives would eventually adopt. Consequently, the Western ARAC members put very little pressure on the Soviet representatives to form unified recommendations to the DIAC during their meetings, and when disagreements did emerge over major issues they usually took the approach of providing two recommendations to the DIAC rather than attempting to reach any type of compromise.

The DIAC did not provide the ARAC with any clear goals for Allied religious policy after the initial steps had been accomplished (denazification, return of church property, etc), nor did it provide them with consistently important issues to discuss. Nor did it put any pressure on the ARAC to send it one unified recommendation instead of the usual two along Western and Soviet lines, but quickly accepted this as the order of business and usually failed to send ARAC recommendations on to the Coordinating Committee because they disagreed with them along the same East/West divide. Major decisions were turned over to zonal authorities, and any hope of a unified religious policy for Germany was dashed.

Given the differing Western and Soviet approaches to the religious question it is unlikely that a uniform religious policy in the four zones of Germany could ever have been created. The frequent disagreements between the representatives on low-level bodies such as the Allied Religious Affairs Committee meant that since the Control Council's Coordinating Committee rarely received recommendations on constructing a unified policy for all of Germany, decisions on matters such as religion, but also numerous other aspects of the occupation that were supposed to be decided between the four allies in Berlin were instead turned over to the discretion of local, regional, and zonal commanders in the different zones. The reality of divergent religious policies between the Soviet zone and the Western zones was no threat to the increasingly hostile direction of the Soviet authorities and their German allies towards religious institutions in Germany, policies often spearheaded by Ermolaev's immediate superior, Colonel Sergei Tiul'panov, the head of the SVAG's Propaganda/Information Administration.

Notes

1. The primary source base for this chapter consists largely of the files from Record Group 260 in the National Archives II in College Park, Maryland, covering both the American Military Government for Germany as well as American records from the Allied Control Authority (ACA). The files I have utilized for this essay consist of the minutes for each of the meetings of the ARAC and its immediate supervisory body, the Directorate of Internal Affairs and Communications, as well as reports and memoranda sent between the ARAC and DIAC to different committees and directorates within the Allied Control Authority. Both the minutes of the first meeting and the American representative to the ARAC Marshall Mason Knappen's memoir *And Call It Peace* mention that the committee secretaries serving under the representatives of the four Allied powers strove to ensure that, the language differences aside, minutes, memos and reports used by each representative would be as similar as possible. These records were declassified in the 1970s and have been available at the National Archives II since its creation in 1995.

   While I have been unable to access similar material from British, French, and Russian archives concerning the ARAC and the DIAC, both the minutes themselves and Knappen's text state that, according to the Allied Control Authority's wishes, the secretaries and interpreters of each of the representatives worked together after the meetings to ensure that the minutes of the meetings, as well as records and memoranda distributed to committee members, be as uniform as possible. This process was eased by the fact that at times meetings were conducted in German, the language that each of the representatives was familiar with. Therefore, it is safe to assume that materials from the American archives concerning the Allied Religious Affairs Committee were largely, if not entirely, similar to records kept by the British, French, and Soviet authorities.

2. Maria Mitchell, "*Stunde Null* in German Politics? Confessional Culture, *Realpolitik*, and the Organization of Christian Democracy." *Stunde Nuell: The End and the Beginning Fifty Years Ago*. Geoffrey Giles, eds. Washington D.C.: German Historical Insititute, 1997. 25–38. 27.

3. Marshall Knappen, *And Call it Peace*. The University of Chicago Press, Chicago: The University of Chicago Press, 1947. 134. Knappen's memoirs promised an

insider's view of the four-power occupation of Germany, which Knappen was quite critical of, as he believed it would not allow Germany to emerge as a peaceful liberal democracy.

4. Knappen, 135.

5. Directorate of Internal Affairs and Communications/Allied Religious Affairs Committee/Memorandum (45) 1. Modern Military Branch, Record Group 260: Department of Defense: OMGUS, Directorate of Internal Affairs and Communications, 1945–1948. From this point on, all records from the DIAC and the ARAC will be identified by their document notation, as all came from the same record group in the National Archives II, located at College Park, Maryland.

6. Knappen, 133.

7. DIAC/Minutes/(45)1.

8. DIAC/Minutes(45) 2–3. In practice, the DIAC would often forward the recommendations to the Coordinating Committee even if disagreements existed, although they frequently sent reports back to the ARAC requesting that the Committee examine the issues in more detail, such as the issues of the denazification of the clergy, the abrogation of the Lutheran Church's 1933 constitution, and the status of the 1933 Concordat between the Vatican and Hitler's government.

9. DIAC/ARAC/Minutes(45) 1.

10. DIAC/ARAC/Minutes (45) 2. This was probably the one issue that the ARAC maintained a general consensus on throughout 1945 and 1946, and the unified position on the issue by the ARAC would lead directly to the only open controversy between the DIAC and the ARAC in the spring of 1946. The unity of the four representatives was considerably important, given the resistance on the part of the Protestant Church to allow the Allied authorities *any* role in the denazification of the clergy.

11. DIAC/ARAC/Minutes(45) 3. As historian Mark Ruff notes in his recent work *The Wayward Flock* (Chapel Hill: The University of North Carolina Press, 2005), the Catholic churches within the Western zones lost little time in reviving religious organizations that had been suppressed under the Nazis, which for a brief period after 1945 experienced an impressive revival in terms of members and influence in the Western zones of Germany.

12. DIAC/ARAC/Minutes (45) 3, DIAC/Minutes (45) 7. What usually occurred during such disagreements such was that zonal commanders ultimately made decisions concerning religious issues in the absence of recommendations from the Coordinating Committee, which then often followed the original lines of the original respective recommendations of the ARAC.

13. DIAC/ARAC/Minutes (45) 4. Two meetings later in November the ARAC did recommend allowing the Salvation Army to renew its charitable work in Germany, which was later implemented by the Coordinating Committee. The Western representatives were usually willing to allow certain religious groups to operate in Germany as well as allow outdoor religious events if they found out that this existed before 1933.

14. Ibid.

15. DIAC/ARAC/Memo (45) 3. Eventually, the Protestant churches in the Western zones formed their own federation in late 1945, as did the Lutheran churches in the Soviet zone as well. In 1948, most of the united Lutheran-Reformed German churches in the Soviet zone joined the church federation in the Western zone, the *Evangelische Kirche Deutschlands*(EKD), or the Evangelical Church of Germany. This union would last between East and West Germany until 1968, when the members of the EKD in East Germany broke with those in the West under considerable pressure from the East German government. Interestingly, the Soviets did not attempt to stop this merger, possibly because they believed they could influence religious or political developments in the western zones through exerting pressure on EKD churches in the Soviet zones.

16. DIAC/ARAC/Minutes (45) 4. The actual compromise was not submitted to the DIAC until the next ARAC meeting, however, although it was adopted by the DIAC at its tenth meeting on October 15 1945.

17. Naimark, 453. Naimark remarks in his work that the Soviet authorities and the East German communists were still discussing the issue of education, specifically regarding personnel, at this point.

18. DIAC/ARAC/Minutes (45) 8. Later, in October of 1946, numerous Catholic bishops sent a letter to the Allied Control Authority Coordinating Committee complaining that the Soviets were not respecting laws providing for religious education in the Soviet zone, which was then sent to the ARAC and discussed at its nineteenth meeting on October 22, where the Soviet representative refused to discuss the matter with his Western colleagues. This foreshadowed later developments, as joint agreements between the Western and Soviet representatives on a united religious policy were not always implemented at the ground level.

19. Naimark, 454.

20. EZA (Evangelisches Zentral Arkhiv, Central Archive of the Evangelical church in Berlin), Bestand 4- Central Evangelical church Chancellery, #313. It is important to emphasize that even when religious education was offered in schools in the Soviet zone, the churches did not press their luck by asking that it should be made an official part of the curriculum.

21. Ibid.

22. DIAC/ARAC/Minutes (45) 10. The mood of humility and remorse of the German Protestant leadership appeared to have a considerable effect on the ARAC representatives, although the promises to remove German Christians and others who actively supported the Nazi government from any positions of authority in the church may have impressed them even more.

23. Knappen, 50.

24. DIAC/ARAC/Papers (46) 9. While not especially belligerent, the letter from Bishop Wurm did state that the EKD was more qualified to make decisions on this matter than could Allied authorities. As Matthew Hockenos points out his book *A Church Divided: German Protestants Confront the Nazi Past* (Bloomington, IN: Indiana University Press, 2004) Bishop Wurm was one of the most vocal among Protestant leaders in the Western zones in proclaiming the need for the German

Protestant churches to reform themselves internally, and for propagating the idea of the widespread victimization of the German Protestants by the Nazis during the years of the Third Reich.

25. Doris Bergen, *Twisted Cross: The German Christian Movement in the Third Reich*. Chapel Hill, NC: The University of North Carolina Press, 1995. 208. The leaders of the EKD, especially those in the Western zones, had forcefully stated this position numerous times to Allied authorities and were determined that the removal of the German Christians from the Protestant church hierarchy by the EKD leadership would serve as an effective substitute for the process of denazification of the Protestant clergy conducted by Allied authorities. This eventually led to complaints on the part of members of the ARAC that the leadership of the Protestant Church was dragging its feet on the denazification issue.

26. ARAC/DIAC/Minutes (45) 4.

27. Mitchell, 28.

28. Patricia Meehan, *A Strange Enemy People: Germans under the British, 1945–1950*. London: Peter Owen Publishers, 2001. 106. Maria Mitchell, 25–38. 27.

29. DIAC/ARAC/P(46) 4. Of course, what "the restoration of religious freedom" meant from a Western and a Soviet context was considerably different in practice, but wording of the document implied that it meant the ability of all religious groups to worship freely within the four zones.

30. Knappen, 151. In Knappen's words: "Where a routine matter was obviously not related to their major objective, they were only too happy to agree with the proposals of the Western representatives. On the other hand, they neither could nor would approve of anything that ran counter to their predetermined policy. In the Soviet zone, church and state were to be separated as far as possible, and the powers of the churches minimized if they could not be eliminated entirely."

31. DIAC/ARAC/Miuntes (46) 7 and DIAC/ARAC/Minutes (46) 8. One notable incident from both meetings occurred when Ermolaev accused his Western colleagues of failing to do enough to suppress criticisms by East Prussian and Silesian exiles in the Western zones of Soviet religious policy in their zone. Most of which concerned a failure to provide for adequate religious education and the censorship of religious literature from the Western zones). All three representatives promised to look into the matter, although at the next meeting they all informed the Soviet representative that they could not discover any incidents that merited suppression by Western authorities.

32. DIAC/ARAC/Papers (46) 27.

33. Bergen, 208.

34. DIAC/ARAC/Minutes (46) 9. Since no real consensus was reached on this point, the matter was tabled instead of promoting two separate recommendations to the DIAC, and would emerge again two meetings later at the end of October.

35. DIAC/ARAC/Minutes (46) 11. Religious authorities in the British and American zones did allow for open religious expression by the German Christians the next year, but by then the movement had lost whatever little strength it had left.

36. Ibid. Two differing recommendations were sent to the DIAC after the meeting in memo DIAC/ARAC/Memo (46) 27, although the DIAC would not discuss either until their forty-seventh meeting on November 14 1946, and did not make any sort of decision on the matter until January of 1947, when the American and British members of the DIAC agreed with the recommendations of the Soviet representative on the ARAC, namely that, while a liaison between the World Council of Churches and the German Evangelical churches would be desirable in the future, it was still too early to grant it.

37. Trachtenberg, 57.

38. DIAC/ARAC/Minutes (47) 15. The WCC had directly requested to the Allied Control Authority for the second time March 1947 that it be allowed to establish a liaison officer. The Coordinating Committee of the ACA immediately forwarded the request to the DIAC, who one month later referred the matter to the ARAC after failing to reach an agreement on the issue.

39. DIAC/Minutes (47) 27. This was more observed in theory than in reality, given the aid sent to the Protestant churches in Germany by Lutheran churches in the United States and Scandinavia.

40. DIAC/ARAC/Minutes (46) 13. Exactly what type of religious literature under dispute was never explicitly mentioned in the minutes of the meeting. In addition, for the first time, the Soviet representative mentioned the need to examine the 1933 Concordat between the Vatican and Hitler's government in see if it had to be replaced, an issue that would be bitterly debated in ARAC and DIAC meetings throughout 1947 and early 1948.

41. Trachtenberg, 59.

42. DIAC/ARAC/Minutes(47)10, DIAC/ARAC/Minutes(47)11. The Concordat actually did not require German clergymen to take personal loyalty oaths to Hitler, unlike officers of the Wehrmacht, although German bishops did have to take oaths of loyalty to the German government. Ermolaev may have confused the provisions of the Concordat with that of the Civil Constitution for the clergy during the French Rev-olutionary era. In addition to the debate on the 1933 Concordat, the issue of establishing a liaison between the WCC and the German Protestant churches emerged due to another request by the WCC headquarters in Switzerland. This time all the ARAC representatives agreed not provide a recommendation supporting its creation, given the DIAC's decision in July that the time was still too early for such an action.

43. DIAC/ARAC/Minutes (47) 11. The Western representatives on the ARAC decided to inform the DIAC that, since no agreement on the Concordat could be reached within the ARAC, they would attempt to find an agreement on which parts of the Concordat it could keep and which ones that they could discard. However, the Soviet representative refused to agree to even this approach and insisted that the Concordat be abolished immediately.

44. DIAC/ARAC/Minutes (47) 12. Ultimately, no agreement was ever made between the four representatives concerning the movement of the clergy between the four zones, although clergy in the western zones were allowed to travel freely between the three zones after 1946.

45. DIAC/ARAC/Minutes (47) 13.

46. Ibid. The British representative also reiterated the argument that the Allied Control Authority had no ability to ban treaties, although it could abolish laws made by the Nazi government. The Western representatives all agreed that while the Soviet representative's argument that the Concordat had Nazi influences may have been somewhat accurate, this did not validate the Soviet claim that the Concordat was a Nazi document and had to be immediately banned.

47. DIAC/Minutes(48) 1. The Concordat continued to govern relations between the German Catholic Church in the Western zones and after 1949, in the Federal Republic of Germany. In 1957, the West German government finally decided that the Concordat was still valid for church-state relations in the Federal Republic. It is impossible to discern from the ARAC and DIAC documents exactly why the Soviets were so unbending on this issue, although it may have been connected to Stalin's propaganda campaign against the Catholic Church in the immediate post–WWII era, as well as his attempt to eliminate the Greek Catholic Church in Ukraine and to minimize contact between East European churches and the Vatican.

48. DIAC/ARAC/Minutes (47)14, DIAC/ARAC/Minutes(48)1. The Soviet representative also informed the other members of the committee that the Soviet military authorities had allowed for the revival of religious journals in the zone.

49. ACC/Minutes (48) 5. Foreign Relations of the United States, Diplomatic Papers, 1948. Germany and Austria, Volume II. Washington DC: U.S. Government Printing Office, 1973. 882.

50. Knappen, 148.

51. Trachtenberg, 83.

Conclusion

Following the creation of the German Democratic Republic in October 1949, President Wilhelm Pieck and General Secretary of the SED Walter Ulbricht moved in next decade to complete the Stalinization process which had begun during the Soviet occupation of Germany. As historian Robert Goeckel wrote: "Stalinization entailed heightened ideological struggle against the churches and religion. The church saw its traditional privileges attacked in what can aptly be called a *Kirchenkampf.*"[1]

In fact, the *Kirchenkampf* had already begun in the Soviet zone by the SVAG and their German allies, as a vital part of the transformation of the zone into a German state based on the Stalinist model. While its charitable activities had not come under sustained harassment, the churches' ability to provide religious education and conduct youth and women's work had been sharply reduced. The independence of the CDU, which supposedly represented the interests of religious Germans, had been effectively repressed. Under the leadership of Otto Nuschke, it was a shadow of the party which had under Jakob Kaiser's leadership.

Nor did most clergy believe the promises of the SVAG and SED propaganda organs that "religious freedom" was possible in an SED-led German state. This was partially due to the deep distrust of Communism shared by most Protestant and Catholic clergy in Germany, but also because the "religious freedom" campaign contrasted so sharply with the reality of religious life in the zone, especially as the Stalinization process accelerated in 1948. By 1949, the leadership of the churches in Berlin-Brandenburg openly and repeatedly expressed their opposition to the atheistic authorities, who in turn viewed the creation of the GDR as an opportunity to neutralize the social role played by the churches.

Neither the SVAG authorities nor their allies in the SED, especially principal creators of religious policies in the Soviet zone such as Sergei Tiul'panov,
believed religious institutions had any place in a future socialist Germany.
Attempts by the Protestant and Catholic church leadership to demonstrate
resistance to Nazism or a sincere desire to work with the antifascist political parties in rebuilding German democracy after the war were essentially
useless. The SVAG and SED authorities viewed the churches as hopelessly
reactionary institutions, which would have little public role to play in a Stalinist German state.

This did not mean that authorities in the Soviet zone wished to destroy the
churches entirely, as their charitable work and to a greater extent their connections with the Western zones of Germany made them potentially if temporarily valuable in the eyes of the Soviet and German authorities, just as the
churches would be for the government of the GDR during the Honecker era.
The efforts by the SVAG to force the churches to incorporate their charitable
work with the SED-led *Volkssolidaritat* reveals how much independence the
Soviets and SED leaders were willing to tolerate. It would not be until much
later when the Protestant Church adopted the collaborationist *Kirche im Sozialismus* policy that the SED reconciled itself to the permanence of religious
institutions in German society.

Another major reason for the church-state conflict during the Soviet occupation was the fact every major institutional actor in the zone had radically
different notions for the future of Germany after the end of Nazism. The
church leadership and the CDU hoped to bring about a revival of Christian
humanism in German culture. In addition, both Andreas Hermes and especially Jakob Kaiser desired that Germany's economic and political foundations be rebuilt along the lines of Christian Socialism, a program which could
create a just social order in Germany while avoiding the violence and social
upheaval inherent in the Marxism-Leninism of the SVAG and the SED.

The plans of the Soviets and their German allies to remake the Soviet zone
in the image of the Soviet Union meant conflict with the churches and the
CDU under Hermes's and Kaiser's leadership was inevitable. The relative
restraint shown by the SVAG and the SED in their religious policies demonstrated their preference to wait until the SED had firm enough control of
the antifascist bloc and of the German organs of self-government before the
definite turn to the Stalinization of the Soviet zone began. Even during the
relatively free early period of the Soviet occupation when both the Soviets
and their German allies could realistically envision SED dominance of all of
Germany, neither ever considered abandoning their eventual plans to suppress religious institutions in German society.

The question then, is not whether conflict between church and state in postwar Berlin-Brandenburg could have been avoided and some type of *modus vivendi* between the churches and the Communist authorities could have been reached. Instead, I have argued that the conflict between the church and CDU leadership and the SVAG and SED reveals how power realities in postwar Germany shaped the political and religious history the Soviet occupation, and how the churches' response to the rebuilding of dictatorial authority in East Germany after the fall of Nazism foreshadowed their later actions in the GDR.

An analysis of the SVAG's and the SED's religious policies in Berlin-Brandenburg show they did not differ greatly from other economic, social, and political decisions made by the SVAG authorities and their SED allies. The foundations for the Stalinist transformation of religious life in the Soviet zone were established in 1945 and 1946, and then implemented from 1947 to 1949. By the end of the Soviet occupation, the independent role the churches could play in the social life of the Soviet zone had been sharply limited, although the Ulbricht government tried to eliminate it entirely in the 1950s.

There were certain religious policies of the SVAG were unique in the Soviet Union's "outer empire" in Central and Eastern Europe. The charitable activities of the Protestant and Catholic churches were allowed to continue largely without interference as they performed a vital economic and social function the state authorities were not able to provide. The potentially useful role of the German churches with their connections to West Germany contributed directly to the "religious freedom" propaganda campaign as well as the fact neither Dibelius nor Preysing became a symbol of religious martyrdom under Communism such as Cardinal Joszef Mindszenty of Hungary. In addition, the brutal attacks on Greek Catholic churches in western Ukraine and Romania were not replicated in the Soviet zone of Germany, despite the targeting of certain clerical and lay leaders for arrest by the Soviet authorities. While the plans of Soviet authorities in Karlshorst and Moscow for religious life in the Soviet zone were the same as the rest of Eastern Europe, the unique circumstances of the Soviet zone dictated different solutions to the religious question than those implemented in Hungary or Ukraine.

The CDU rejected any remaining support for Jakob Kaiser's Christian Socialism during its Sixth Party Congress in October in 1952, when it formally announced its support for the Marxism-Leninism of the SED. Otto Nuschke and his two successors as chairmen of the CDU in the GDR, August Bach and Gerald Götting, continued a policy of unhesitatingly supporting the SED in its foreign and domestic policies, the one exception being the decision by a handful of CDU deputies to vote against the legalization of abortion in the Volkskammer in August 1972. This did not mean Kaiser's influence in the GDR was entirely dead, as he served as Minister for All-German Affairs in Konrad Adenauer's first government in West Germany from 1949 to 1957. His attempts to make the CDU's ideology into a genuine alternative to that of the SED were not forgotten by East German dissidents, especially those who advocated the adoption of a mixed economy that rejected both free market capitalism of the West and the centrally planned economy of the GDR and the USSR.

The response of the Catholic Church in Berlin-Brandenburg to the Stalinization of the Soviet zone under Preysing was not surprising, given the Catholic bishop's staunch anticommunism, his previous willingness to confront the Nazi regime over its euthanasia policies and the fact he was the largely unchallenged voice for the Catholic Church in the province. Preysing was also assisted by the fact that nearly all high-ranking Catholic clergy in the Western zones as well as Pope Pius XII concurred with his opposition to the Soviet authorities. Much like his Protestant counterpart in Berlin-Brandenburg Otto Dibelius, Preysing waited until the later stages of the occupation before openly speaking out against SVAG and SED rule in general as opposed to just specific policies such as those involving religious education.

Interestingly in Berlin-Brandenburg under Soviet occupation, there were few hints of the "double isolation" of the Catholic Church in the GDR, cut off from both the atheistic SED government and the majority Protestant Church. Preysing and Dibelius found common ground on a number of issues, especially in preserving the churches' central role in providing religious education for youths in the Soviet zone and continuing religious charitable activity independently from *Volkssolidaritat*. This cooperative relationship between the two was grounded in their shared anticommunism and desire to preserve their respective churches' autonomy from state interference. Preysing's death in 1950 and Dibelius's gradual isolation in the leadership of the Protestant Church by the early 1960s contributed to the isolation of the Catholic Church in Berlin-Brandenburg by the late 1950s just as it was in every other province of the GDR, a status that continued until the fall of the Berlin Wall in 1989.

The situation regarding the Protestant Church was more complicated as Otto Dibelius did not have the same authority to speak for his church in Berlin-Brandenburg as Preysing. Dibelius found his staunch opposition to the SVAG and SED authorities challenged in East Germany by Bishop Moritz Mitzenheim of Thuringia, and Heinrich Gruber and Kurt Krummacher in Brandenburg. This set the stage for the internal struggle in the Protestant church leadership during the 1950s and 1960s regarding how to respond to the Communist authorities. During much of this period the approach by Dibelius and his supporters, which rejected the fundamental legitimacy of the East German regime, had the upper hand. By the early 1960s, with the construction of the Berlin Wall having established the seeming permanence of the SED state, the accommodating approach of Mitzenheim and Gruber won out. Dibelius's retirement from office in 1963 and his death in 1967 marked the temporary defeat of the anticommunist stance. The policy of *Kirche im Sozialismus*, announced in 1969, had its roots in writings of clergy such as Kurt Rackwitz and in the internal struggles among the Protestant leadership on how it should deal with the Communist authorities during the Soviet occupation.

The SED under the leadership of Erich Honecker from 1971 onward reconciled itself to the continued existence of religious institutions in the land of "real existing socialism." The Protestant Church was allowed to continue its charitable activities relatively unhindered by the government, which, much like as they had for the Soviet authorities in the late 1940s, served as a valuable resource for the atheistic East German state. Most Protestant clergy no longer had to fear the constant threat of arrest and imprisonment by the Stasi. This came at a considerable cost, as the church in the GDR was forced to sever its formal administrative links with the churches in West Germany, and the Stasi succeeded in penetrating it at all of its administrative levels with its spies and informers, greatly weakening the institutional independence of the church during the 1970s and 1980s.

Ironically, Dibelius's approach of peacefully but forcefully rejecting the legitimacy of the East German regime, or at least many of its policies, was adopted by many lower-level Protestant clergy and laity during the 1970s, as they proved to be a vital element of the dissident movement in the GDR. Nowhere was this more apparent than the policy of Protestant clerics in the late history of the GDR to use their churches as meeting places for a broad variety of dissident groups, some of whom had no religious character at all. The vital role played by the church in the events of October and November 1989 which brought down the GDR has its antecedents in the efforts of clergy such as Dibelius and Hans von Arnim who worked with Preysing and political leaders such as Jakob Kaiser in resisting the creation of a Communist East German dictatorship in the late 1940s. Ultimately, however, it would be lower-ranking clergy in the late 1980s who followed the lead of Dibelius's and rejected the ideology of *Kirche im Sozialismus*, as opposed to most of the Evangelical bishops in the time period. The accommodation of the churches to dictatorial regime in East Berlin ultimately proved to be a one way street.

Dibelius, Preysing, Hermes, and Kaiser had the force of moral righteousness behind their attempt to resist the Stalinization of Berlin-Brandenburg, but they lacked the political power to halt the efforts of SVAG and SED officials such as Tiul'panov, Ermolaev, or Ulbricht who were equally determined to bring about the "socialist transformation" of the Soviet zone. By 1949, the Soviet and German authorities had succeeded in reducing the independence of churches in the public life of the Soviet zone. However, just as they failed to completely suppress religious institutions and erase religious belief in the Soviet Union, the Soviet authorities failed to do so in their outer empire in Eastern Europe, including East Germany.

The history of the Soviet occupation of Germany was that of the transformation of the zone into a German state on the Stalinist model. Yet it is also during this period that the seeds of the GDR's downfall in 1989 were sown. This proved true with religious life in the Soviet zone as both the Catholic and Protestant churches exploited to the greatest extent the limits of the SVAG and SED's authority in Berlin-Brandenburg to partially preserve the institutional independence of the churches. This independence would be critical for the churches contribution to the East German dissident movement, a movement which provided a major contribution to the end of Communist rule in the Soviet Union's most vital satellite in Eastern Europe.

Note

1. Goeckel, 45.

Bibliography

PRIMARY SOURCES

Russia

GARF-State Archive of the Russian Federation
f.7317-SVAG
       op. 17-SVAG Vynutrennii del I
       op. 18- SVAG Vynutrennii del II
       op. 54- SVAG Otdel narodnogo obrazovaniia
f.7077-SVAG-Brandenburg
       op. 1-Upravlenie propagandy
       op. 2-Otdel narodnogo obrazovaniia
f. 7133-SVAG Sachsen-Anhalt
       op. 1-Upravlenie propagandy
       op. 2-Otdel narodnogo obrazovaniia
f. 7212-SVAG Sachsen
       op. 1-Upravlenie propagandy
       op. 2-Otdel narodnogo obrazovaniia
f. 7103-SVAG Mecklenburg
       op. 1-Upravlenie propagandy
       op. 2-Otdel narodnogo obrazovaniia
f. 7184-SVAG Thuringia
       op. 1-Upravlenie propagandy
       op. 2-Otdel narodnogo obrazovaniia
RGASPI- Russian State Archive for Social and Political History
f. 17- Tsentralnyi Komitet Kommunisticheskoi partii Sovetskogo Soiuza
       op. 125-Agitprop I
       op. 132-Agitprop II

Germany

State Archives

Bundesarchiv-Federal Archive of Germany
  SAPMO- Stiftung archiv der partaken und massenorganizationen der DDR
DDR Abteilung
        DY 30/IV 2/14-Arbeitsgruppe für Kirchenfragen
        DY 30/IV 2/9.05-Abteilung Volksbildung
DY 30/IV 2/17-Abteilung Frauen
        DY 31-Abteilung Jugend
        NY 4182/931-Nachlässe Walter Ulbricht
        NY 4090/451-Nachlässe Otto Grotewohl
        NY 4036/756-Nachlässe Wilhelm Pieck
Archiv für Christlich-Demokratische Politik, St. Augustin
        Signatur 07–010-CDU Ost
        Signatur 07–011-CDU Ost
Landesarchiv Berlin
  Bestand C 101–104: Rat für Kirchliche Angelegenheiten
Brandenburgisches Landeshauptarchiv Potsdam
  Rep. 202A- Büro des Ministerpräsidents, Provinzial Verwaltung

Church Archives

Evangelisches Zentralarchiv Berlin
  Bestand 4-EKD Kirchenkanzlei
Evangelisches Landeskirchliches Archiv Berlin
  Bestand 603-Nachlässe Otto Dibelius
  Bestand 38- Nachlässe Kurt Scharf
Diosezän Archiv Berlin
  Abteilung I- Bischöfliches Ordinariat Berlin
  Abteilung V- Nachlässe Konrad von Preysing

United States

Archives of the Davis Center for Russian Studies, Harvard University
        Records of the Harvard Interview Project
National Archives II, University of Maryland
Record Group 260:
Department of Defense: OMGUS, Directorate of Internal Affairs and Communications, 1945–1948
Department of Defense: OMGUS, Allied Religious Affairs Committee, 1945–1948.
Archives of the University of Notre Dame
        UDIS 115/65-Cardinal Konrad von Preysing

PUBLISHED SOURCES

Foreign Relations of the United States, Diplomatic Papers, 1947. Germany and Austria, Volume III. Washington, DC: U.S. Government Printing Office, 1968.

Foreign Relations of the United States, Diplomatic Papers, 1948. Germany and Austria, Volume II. Washington, DC: U.S. Government Printing Office, 1973.

The Third Reich and the Christian Churches. Ed, Peter Matheson. Edinburgh, UK: T&T Clark, 1981.

SVAG: Upravlenie propagandy i S.I. Tiul'panov: Sbornik dokumentov. Moscow, RU: Rossiia Molodaia, 1994.

SVAG i religioznye konfessii Sovetskoi zony okkupatsii Germanii 1945–1949: Sbornik dokumentov. Eds, V. V. Zakharov, O. V. Lavinskaia, D. N. Nokhotovich, and E. V. Poltoratskoi. Moscow, RU: Rosspen 2006.

Politika SVAG v oblasti kul'tury, nauki, i obrazovaniia: tseli, metody, resul'taty, 1945–1949: Sbornik dokumentov. Eds, K. Mueller and A.O. Chubar'ian. Moscow, RU: Rosspen 2006.

Die UdSSR und die Deutsche Frage 1941–1948: Dokumente aus dem Archiv für Aussenpolitik der Russischen Föderation Volume 2: 9 Mai 1945 bis 3. October 1946. Eds, Jochen Laufer, Georgii Kynin and Viktor Knoll. Berlin, DEU: Duncker & Humbolt, 2004.

Die UdSSR und die Deutsche Frage 1941–1948: Dokumente aus dem Archiv für Aussenpolitik der Russischen Föderation Volume 3: 6 Oktober 1946 bis 15 Juni 1948. Eds, Jochen Laufer, Georgii Kynin and Viktor Knoll. Berlin, DEU: Duncker & Humbolt 2004.

Die Protokolle der Kirchlichen Ostkonferenz 1945–1949. Eds, Michael Kuhne, Gottingen, DEU: Vandenhoeck & Ruprecht, 2005.

Newspapers

Deutsche Volkszeitung 1945–1946
Der Taggesspiegel 1945–1949
Frankfurter Allgemeine Zeitung 1945–1950
Neues Deutschland 1946–1950
Tägliche Rundschau 1945–1950
Neue Zeit 1945–1949

Dissertations

Schroeder, Steven. Reconciliation in Occupied Germany, 1944–1954. (Ph.D diss) University of Notre Dame 2008

Memoirs

Adenauer, Konrad. *Memoirs*. London, UK: Weidenfeld and Nicolson, 1966.

Clay, Lucius. *Decision in Germany*. Garden City, NY: Doubleday & Company, 1950.

Dibelius, Otto. *In the Service of the Lord*. New York, NY: Holt, Rinehart, and Winston, 1964.

Klimov, Grigorii. The *Terror Machine: The Inside Story of the Soviet Administration in Germany*. New York, NY: Praeger, 1953.

Knappen, Marshall Mason. *And Call it Peace*. Chicago, IL: The University of Chicago Press, 1948.

Leonhard, Wolfgang. *Child of the Revolution*. Trans., C. M. Woodhouse, Chicago, IL: Henry Regnery Company.

SECONDARY SOURCES

Baranowski, Shelley. "Consent and Dissdent: The Confessinf Church and Conservative Opposition to National Socialism" *The Journal of Modern History*. Volume 59, Number 1, Mar 1987. 53–78.

Beck, Dan. "The Luther Revival:Aspects of National *Abgrenzung* and Confessional *Gemeinschaft* in the German Democratic Republic" *Religion and Nationalism in Soviet and East European Politics*. Sabrina Ramet, eds. 222–240.

Besier, Gerhard. *Der SED-Staat und die Kirche: Der Weg in die Anpassung*. Munich, DEU: C. Bertelsmann, 1993.

Bergen, Doris. *Twisted Cross: The German Christian Movement in the Third Reich*. Chapel Hill, NC: The University of North Carolina Press, 1996.

Blessing, Benita. *The Antifascist Classroom: Denazification in Soviet-Occupied Germany 1945–1949*. New York, NY: Palgrave, 2006.

Bruce, Gary. *Resistance with the People: Repression and Resistance in Eastern Germany 1945–1955*. New York, NY: Rowman & Littlefield Publishers, 2006.

Burleigh, Michael. *Sacred Causes: The Clash of Religion and Politics from the Great War to the War on Terror*. New York, NY: Harper Collins Publishers, 2007.

Chumachenko, Tatiana. *Church and State in Soviet Russia: Russian Orthodoxy from World War II to the Khrushchev Years*. London, UK: M. E. Sharpe Publishers, 2002.

Conway, J. S. *The Nazi Persecution of the Churches 1933–1945*. New York, NY: Basic Books, 1968.

Creuzberger, Stefan. *Die Sowjetische Besatzungsmacht und das politische System der SBZ*. Weimar, DEU: Böhlau Verlag, 1996.

Dähn, Horst. *Konfrontation oder Kooperation? Das Vehältnis von Staat und Kirche in der SBZ/DDR 1945–1980*. Düsseldorf, DEU: Westdeutscher Verlag, 1982.

Eisenberg, Carolyn. *Drawing the Line: The American Decision to Divide Germany*. Oxford, UK: Cambridge University Press, 1996.

Filitov, A. M. *Germanskii vopros: ot raskola k ob'edineniiu*. Moscow, RU: Mezhdunarodnye otnosheniia, 1993.

Gaddis, John Lewis. *We Now Know: Rethinking Cold War History*. New York, NY: Oxford University Press, 1997.

Gimbel, John. *The American Occupation of Germany: Politics and the Military, 1945–1949*. Stanford, CA: Stanford University Press, 1968.

Goeckel, Robert. *The Lutheran Church and the East German State: Political Conflict and Change under Ulbricht and Honecker*. Ithaca, NY: Cornell University Press, 1990.

Goerner, Martin Georg. *Die Kirche als Problem der SED: Strukturen kommunistischer Herrschaftsausübung gegenüber der evangelischen Kirche 1945 bis 1958*. Berlin, DEU: Akademie Verlag, 1997.

Griech-Polle, Beth. "Image of a Churchman-Resister: Bishop von Galen, the Euthanasia Project, and the Sermons of Summr 1941" *Journal of Contemporary History*. Volume 36, Number 1, Jan 2001. 41–57.

Hamel, Johannes, and Karl Barth. *How to Serve God in a Marxist Land*. New York, NY; Association Press, 1959.

Helmreich, Ernst. *The German Churches under Hitler: Background, Struggle, and Epilogue*. Detroit, MI: Wayne State University Press, 1979.

Heschel, Susannah. *The Aryan Jesus: Christian Theologians and the Bible in Nazi Germany*. Princeton, NJ: Princeton University Press, 2008.

Hockenos, Michael. *A Church Divided: German Protestants Confront the Nazi Past*. Bloomington, IN: Indiana University Press, 2004.

Jantzen, Kyle. "Propaganda. Perseverance, and Protest" Strategies for Clerical Survival Amid the German Church Struggle" *Church History*. Volume 70, Number 2, Jun 2001. 295–327.

Jeanrond, Werner. "From Resistance to Liberation Theology: German Theologians and the Non-resistance to the National Socialist Regime" *The Journal of Modern History*. Volume 64, Dec 1992. 187–203.

Kissinger, Henry. *Diplomacy*. New York, NY: Simon & Schuster, 1994.

Knabe, Hubertus. *Tag Der Befreiung?: Das Kreigsende in Ostdeutschland*. Berlin, DEU: Propyläen. 2006.

Knappen, Marshall. *An Introduction to American Foreign Policy*. New York, NY: Harper & Brother Publishers, 1956. (229–272).

Krisch, Henry. *German Politics under Soviet Occupation*. New York, NY: Columbia University Press, 1974.

Loth, Wilfried. *Stalin's Unwanted Child: The Soviet Union, the German Question, and the Founding of the GDR*. New York, NY: St. Martin's Press, 2000.

Meehan, Particia. *A Strange Enemy People: Germans under the British, 1945–1950*. London, UK: Peter Owen Publishers, 2001.

Miner, Steven. *Stalin's Holy War: Religion, Nationalism, and Alliance Politics, 1941–1945*. Chapel Hill, NC: University of North Carolina Press, 2003.

Mitchell, Maria. "*Stunde Null* in German Politics? Confessional Culture, *Realpolitik*, and the Organization of Christian Democracy." *Stunde Nuell: The End and the Be-*

ginning Fifty Years Ago. Geoffrey Giles, eds. Washington DC: German Historical Insititute, 1997. 25–38.

Naimark, Norman. *The Russians in Germany: A History of the Soviet Zone of Occupation, 1945–1949*. Cambridge, MA: Harvard University Press, 1995.

Nettl, J. P. *The Eastern Zone and Soviet Policy in Germany in 1945–1950*. New York, NY: Oxford University Press, 1951.

Peterson, Edward. *The American Occupation of Germany: Retreat to Victory*. Detroit, MI: Wayne State University Press, 1978.

Peterson, Edward. *Russian Commands and German Resistance: The Soviet Occupation 1945–1949*. New York, NY: Peter Lang, 1999.

Pike, David. *The Politics of Culture in Soviet-Occupied Germany 1945–1949*. Stanford, CA: Stanford University Press, 1992.

Plischke, Elmer. "Denazification in Germany: A Policy Analysis" *Americans as Proconsuls: United States Military Government in Germany and Japan, 1944–1952*. Robert Wolfe, eds. Carbondale, IL: Southern Illinois University Press, 1984.

Pritchard, Gareth. *The Making of the GDR 1945–1953: From Antifascism to Stalinism*. Manchester, UK: Manchester University Press, 2000.

Roberts, Geoffrey. *Stalin's Wars: From World War to Cold War 1939–1953*. New Haven, CT: Yale University Press, 2006.

Rodden, John. *Painting the Little Red Schoolhouse: A History of East German Education, 1945–1995*. Oxford, UK: Oxford University Press, 2002.

Rodden, John. *Textbook Reds: Schoolbooks, Ideology, and Eastern German Identity*. University Park, PA: The Pennsylvania State University Press, 2007.

Ruff, Mark. *The Wayward Flock: Catholic Youth in Postwar West Germany 1945–1965*. Chapel Hill, NC: The University of North Carolina Press, 2005.

Sandford, Gregory. *From Hitler to Ulbricht: The Communist Reconstruction of East Germany 1945–1946*. Princeton, NJ: Princeton University Press, 1983.

Schaefer, Bernd. *Staat und katholische Kirche in der GDR, 1945–1989*. Berlin, DEU: Berghahn, 1999.

Schaefer, Bernd. *The East German State and the Catholic Church, 1945–1989*. Jonathan Skolnik and Patricia Sutcliffe, trans. New York, NY: Berghahn Books, 2010.

Scholder, Klaus. *The Churches and the Third Reich: Volume I: Preliminary History and the Time of Illusions*. Philadelphia, PA: Fortress Press, 1988.

Seidel, J. Jurgen. *"Neubeginn" in der Kirche? Die evangelischen Landes-und Provinzialkirchen in der SBZ/DDR im gesellschaftspolitischen Kontext der Nachkriegszeit 1945–1953*. Göttingen, DEU: Vandenhoeck & Ruprecht, 1989.

Solberg, Richard. *God and Caesar in East Germany: The Conflicts of Church and State in East Germany since 1945*. New York, NY: The Macmillan Company 1971.

Spilker, Dirk. *The East German Leadership and the Division of Germany: Patriotism and Propaganda*. Oxford, UK: Oxford University Press, 2006.

Spotts, Frederic. *The Churches and Politics in Germany*. Middletown, CT: Wesleyan University Press, 1973.

Stanke, Volker. *Die Gestaltung der Beziehungen zwischen dem Land Sachsen und der Evangelisch-Lutherischen Landeskirche Sachsens von 1945 bis 1949*. Frankfurt am Main, DEU: Peter Lang, 1993.

Steege, Paul. *Black Market, Cold War: Everyday Life in Berlin 1946–1949*. Cambridge, UK: Cambridge University Press, 2007.

Tischner, Wolfgang. "Die Kirchenpolitik unter Konrad Kardinal von Preysing 1945– 1950." *Katholische Kirche in SBZ und DDR*. Wolfgang Tischner and Christoph Kösters, eds. Munich, DEU: Ferdinand Schönigh, 2005.

Trachtenberg, Marc. *A Constructed Peace: The Making of the European Settlement, 1945–1963*. Princeton, NJ: Princeton University Press, 1999.

Wagner, James. *Day is Dawning: The Story of Bishop Otto Dibelius*. Philadelphia, PA: The Christian Education Press, 1956.

Zubok, Vladislav. *A Failed Empire: The Soviet Union in the Cold War From Stalin to Gorbachev*. Chapel Hill, NC: University of North Carolina Press, 2007.

Zugger, Christopher. *The Forgotten: Catholics of the Soviet Empire from Lenin through Stalin*. Syracuse, NY: Syracuse University Press, 2001.

Index

CPSIA information can be obtained at www.ICGtesting.com
Printed in the USA
BVOW010902211111

276207BV00004BB/1/P

9 780739 151259